ENVIRONMENTAL GORE

A CONSTRUCTIVE RESPONSE TO
EARTH IN THE BALANCE

Edited by

JOHN A. BADEN

PACIFIC RESEARCH INSTITUTE FOR PUBLIC POLICY
SAN FRANCISCO, CA

ISBN 0-936488-78-6

Printed in the United States of America
10 9   8   7   6   5   4   3   2   1

PACIFIC RESEARCH INSTITUTE FOR PUBLIC POLICY
755 Sansome Street, Suite 450
San Francisco, CA 94111
(415) 989-0833

Distributed to the trade by National Book Network, Lanham, MD.

Chapter 2 is reprinted by permission of The Yale Law Journal Company and Fred. B. Rothman & Company from *The Yale Law Journal,* Vol. 102, pp. 1719–1761. Chapter 6 is reprinted by permission of the Cato Institute from *Regulation,* Spring 1992, Vol. 15, No. 2.

Library of Congress Cataloging-in-Publication Data
Environmental Gore : a constructive response to Earth in the
balance / edited by John A. Baden.
p.   cm.
Includes index.
ISBN 0-936488-78-6
1. Environmental policy. 2. Environmental protection. 3. Human
ecology. 4. Gore, Albert, 1948–   Earth in the balance. I. Baden,
John. II. Pacific Research Institute for Public Policy. III. Gore,
Albert, 1948– Earth in the balance.
GE170.E575   1994
363.7—dc20   94-6362
                                                                  CIP

Director of Publications: *Kay Mikel*
Cover Design: *Arrowgraphics Inc.*
Interior Graphics: *Reider Publishing Services*
Index: *Shirley Kessel, Primary Sources Research*
Printing and Binding: *Edwards Brothers, Inc.*

FOREWORD

AN OPEN LETTER TO AL GORE

Dear Mr. Vice President:

On behalf of the Foundation for Research on Economics and the Environment, I am pleased to transmit this analytical examination of your book, *Earth in the Balance*. In this volume, scientists in a variety of specialized fields, policy and legal analysts, and even a philosopher have taken your work very seriously, taking time from their own work to respond. I hope you will repay them in kind by reading this book and by engaging them in more of the constructive dialogue that you have begun.

I read your book with awe, admiration, and at times aggravation. The breadth and depth of your knowledge about various aspects of ecology was impressive and, frankly, surprising; few, if any, politicians have mastered so much material of a technical and scientific nature as a result of their interest in policy issues. Any reader would have to admire (and any writer envy) the way in which you kept your theses fresh and interesting with metaphors, anecdotes, and extraordinarily frank personal reflections.

At the same time, I was dismayed by your conclusion that the only appropriate long-term solution to our environmental problems requires that we "dramatically change our civilization and our way of thinking about the relationship between humankind and the earth" (p. 163). There is a large gap between acknowledging the existence of a serious problem—as any sensible observer must do—and calling for a dramatic change in our civilization and our thoughtways.

As a generalist reading your book, I could not always fill that gap from my own resources. Even so, I was acutely conscious of the possibility—indeed, the probability—that considerably less than dramatic change in our civilization and our "relationship [to] the earth" would accomplish our common objectives more readily and at less expense. Some of the essays in the current volume develop that theme.

In particular, the essays in Part IV, Toward Real Reform, emphasize the importance of property rights and sound economic analysis in addressing the problems of the environment. As you illustrate time and again in your book with examples of the environmental outrages committed by the communist governments of Eastern Europe and the former Soviet Union, the absence of clear and enforceable private property rights is itself a great threat to the environment. It is the common experience of humankind that people take better care of their own property than they do of property owned by others or by the "public," that is, by no one. Hence, we see depletion of ocean fisheries and pollution of air and water for want of enforceable property rights in those resources.

Thus far it has been public policy to address the problems created by the absence of property rights primarily through governmental regulation, which is supposed to restrain would-be polluters from responding to the incentive that exists when they can use a common resource free of charge. A more direct solution, of course, would be to create the missing property rights so the incentive problem does not arise in the first place. (The most recent amendments to the Clean Air Act include modest steps in this direction.) It is a move in the opposite direction—dealing even more indirectly with the incentive problem—to think in terms of changing human nature, but that seems to be the thrust of your long-run proposals.

Before joining issue with you on matters of policy, however, a wealth of facts must be settled. You have consistently portrayed the scientific community as being in essential agreement on the facts relevant to such matters as global warming, ozone depletion, and the significance of deforestation and desertification. As shown, however, in the essays in Parts II and III, Climate Issues and Resource Issues, there is a good deal more disagreement than you may have thought. In part, it appears that the available scientific data have simply changed, even in the few years since you conducted Senate hearings into these issues. In part, too, the data are subject to conflicting interpretations within the scientific community. Your impatience with those who would defer acting with respect to global warming, for example, will seem less prudent when you have read these essays.

As a lawyer you know the virtues of the adversary system. The point and counterpoint of conflicting presentations, marshaling facts and policy arguments based upon those facts, sharpens and narrows the issues over which people divide—whether in court, in the Congress, or in the public debate over matters of policy. In *Earth in the Balance* you laid out the facts as you understood them, made arguments based upon both science and common sense, and in conclusion urged specific proposals under the heading "A Global Marshall Plan." And I might add that your brief was polished and compelling and, when read in isolation, is as persuasive as the briefs I read as a judge on the federal court of appeals. Now, however, there is an answering brief from "the other side." (I place that phrase in quotation marks because the contributors to this volume are not your opponents in the way that opposing parties and lawyers are in court. On the contrary, they are concerned and learned members of the environmental movement and of the scholarly community concerned with environmental issues; not one represents an industry or special interest with an ax to grind.) As you will see, their brief is unsettling. Your facts are not uncontroverted in the scientific community, and your policy arguments are persuasively met by theirs.

Can the differences brought out in this volume be bridged? To some extent, I think they can. The analyses in this book will give you pause and reason to rethink some of the proposals you have made. Of course, you too may have new information, new insights, or rejoinders that would meet some of the objections published here. Can we talk?

I am confident that we would find some common ground between the new resource economics, as reflected in part in this book, and your own thinking. For example, we agree with the Administration that the current system of setting fees for grazing on lands owned by the federal government should be changed. Economic analysis suggests that the problem of overgrazing is one of poorly aligned property rights: Ranchers have no long-term stake in the proper management of the public lands they use. More micro-regulation—such as Secretary Babbitt's recent proposal to raise fees and then give a discount to ranchers who follow certain environmental practices—does not respond to the underlying problem. A system of long-term use permits that ranchers could buy and sell, on the other hand, might solve the problem. It would at least give ranchers a market incentive to avoid overgrazing. Surely there is much more, however, and more of global significance, on which we could all reason together.

I invite you not only to read this book but, having read it, to convene a forum in which we can continue in person the dialogue now begun in print. Drawing upon your experience chairing the hearings of the Senate Subcommittee on Science, Technology and Space, I suggest a similar format in which to hear not from the people whose work you already know and rely upon in your book but rather from those who, like the contributors to this volume, bring a different perspective to bear. It is our earnest hope that as the most influential environmentalist in the United States you will also be one of the best informed.

Sincerely,

Douglas H. Ginsburg

Judge, United States Court of Appeals

Washington, D. C.

April 1994

CONTENTS

ACKNOWLEDGMENTS

One of the treats of my position is the opportunity to work with business leaders who understand and care about public policy. While many busy people claim an interest in public affairs, budgets are excellent tests of sincerity. With these thoughts, I acknowledge Furman Moseley, Thomas O'Leary, and John Creighton for providing the stimulus and the means to undertake this project.

Several foundation officers provided support for seminars and conferences that led to inclusion of these chapters. Although these people work outside the glare of publicity, they know who they are and I would like to recognize their contribution to this project.

Several of the contributors are friends and so I thank them for their personal as well as intellectual contributions. It was a pleasure to work with Steve Hayward who played a key role in developing this book for Pacific Research Institute. I would also like to thank three people who played an especially important role in bringing this project to a timely conclusion. Karen Humphrey, a graduate student at the University of Washington, was my most diligent, competent, and highly responsible assistant on this project. She has demonstrated the capacity to go very far indeed. Tracy Fenne, my friend and associate at FREE, had the Herculean task of keeping me on track and on schedule. Those who know me realize how much credit she deserves. I most warmly thank my wife, Professor Ramona Marotz-Baden, for her dedication, good cheer, and contributions to the several seminars that helped formulate this book.

Finally, I would like to recognize the genius of America's Founding Fathers. They who designed a set of institutions that permit a mere academic, farmer, and think tank director to produce a strong and fundamental criticism of the "central organizing principle" offered to the world by the Vice President of that world's greatest power. How lucky we are to be here. I hope this book helps keep it so.

PREFACE

BALANCING THE EARTH'S ECONOMY AND ECOLOGY

John Baden
with Gus diZerega

When Europeans first settled North America, many were awestruck by the abundance and beauty of the land. This abundance was quickly turned into goods for human comfort and wealth. Alexis de Tocqueville observed during his travels in America that "living in the wilds, [the pioneer] only prizes the works of man." By contrast, "in Europe people talk a great deal of the wilds of America, but the Americans themselves never think about them; they are insensible to the wonders of inanimate nature and they may be said not to perceive the mighty forests that surround them till they fall beneath the hatchet."[1]

Today, nature is increasingly subdued and turned to human purposes. But our very success in increasing our society's material well-being is now teaching us, as it once taught the elite of Europe, that there is also value in the natural world. This value extends beyond board feet of timber, important as that also is. Both de Tocqueville's observations and the contemporary rise of environmental concerns in the U.S. and Europe indicate a paradox. Appreciation for nature is connected with prosperity.

As more and more of the natural world is turned to human purposes, an important question arises. Natural relationships are enormously complex and, on balance, symbiotic. As our power to use the natural world increases, will we inadvertently upset the balance of these relationships, impoverishing the future world for our children as well as for the rest of life on earth?

Vice President Gore is concerned with this question. *Earth in the Balance* makes his case for a radical change in our way of life. He sees this as necessary if our world is to remain a hospitable and beautiful place.

Many of us are impressed that a contemporary American politician can actually write an important book that is taken seriously. Vice President Gore has done so, and we give him credit for his achievement. Yet , we have found his book to be severely flawed on both scientific and political economy grounds. If Gore's recommendations are acted on, *they* will inadvertently impoverish the future world for our children as well as for the rest of life.

Our arguments come from people who are also concerned with environmental well-being. We are the loyal opposition. And a loyal opposition should offer an alternative program.

Many of the writers in this volume endorse an approach identified as *adaptive economics*. *Adaptive* sensitizes us to the similarities between economics and ecological processes. *Economics* reminds us that all living things, from microbes to mice, from pines to people, must use resources to sustain and enhance their lives, and must do so in a way that also complements other life. We call this *ecology* in nature and *economics* in the purely human world, but the fundamental principles are the same. Adaptive economics captures these insights.

A Primer on Adaptive Economics

As Aldo Leopold explained in *The Land Ethic*, the judgment of appropriate environmental behavior depends on values. Although values do change over time and with changing economic circumstances, in general it is far easier to change institutions than to change values. Adaptive economics can guide the design of new institutions to make them more sensitive to evolving environmental values.

Adaptive economics stresses liberty, the mischief of concentrated power, and the importance of building in counterweights to special interests. Its principles help us keep our hopes from being confused with reasonable expectations. It helps us explore the ecologist's first question when contemplating change: "And then what follows from the change?"

Liberty and individual responsibility are fundamental to a constructive and harmonious social order, which in turn fosters prosperity. When pushed by economic circumstances, most people will trade off environmental quality for economic security. Therefore, individuals who care about the environment have a stake in promoting environmental laws and policies that protect our resources without needlessly damaging the economy. The very idea of economic progress and of our materialistic culture is repulsive to many. However, the reality is that economic security and prosperity contribute greatly to our environmental concern.

Adaptive economics is a part of market liberalism, a belief that free people and free markets are essential to a healthy and open society. Our approach emphasizes the constructive potential private property rights can play in preserving what is valued. What is not owned is often lost. While buffalo and elk were threatened with extinction, horses and cows thrived.

When property rights are clearly and successfully defended, prices provide information and incentives to act responsibly upon that information. We do not say that market prices adequately measure all values, for they neglect some of the most important. But we do say that ignoring prices threatens even those values least amenable to being captured by prices. Here's why.

Together, incentives and the information generated by prices foster the voluntary cooperation that integrates our economy. Higher prices signal greater scarcity. When prices go up, people face incentives to conserve and to seek substitutes for the scarce resource. When energy prices rise, we discover that brains are excellent substitutes for BTUs.

This perspective helps us understand how economic progress can be harmonized with environmental quality. Principles of adaptive economics can be applied to the private preservation of wildlife habitat, sometimes even within commercial timberlands. Private landowners can be given incentives to consider public goods such as water quality or ecological integrity. Commercial land need not equal ecological wasteland.

A person using the adaptive economics approach sees economics, politics, and natural resources as intertwined aspects of ecosystems that must be approached as an integrated whole. With adaptive economics we can often see how environmental values can be honored and some resources developed in a responsible and sensitive way.

New directions and goals for public policy normally involve new institutions and new sets of rights and obligations. We must be highly sensitive to the incentives that will be created under these systems or great mischief is likely to be the major fruit of reform. Good intentions will not suffice. Alone, they seldom yield good results. Insight and wisdom applied to the design of institutions are also necessary to transform good intentions into good results.

In the U.S. Forest Service we see a legacy of environmental degradation and insensitivity to the competing values of our national forests. Yet the Forest Service was established with the same emphasis on scientific expertise and a long-term view that Vice President Gore advocates in his book. He does not explain why his approach will outperform a similar strategy that failed.

The trick is to design institutions that produce information and incentives to create the desired outcomes—but without relying on experts and politics to continually monitor information, incentives, and outcomes. Secure property rights and undistorted prices are important components of institutions able to accomplish these goals.

Adaptive economics looks at the incentives that public laws and policies give to citizens, special interests, and bureaucrats. What are the implications of below cost timber sales or government agents killing predators such as mountain lions, lynx, bobcat, and bear? Who gains from cheap, subsidized and nontransferable irrigation water? Existing mechanisms for controlling publicly held resources usually benefit a few at the expense of many. This is not an accident. Adaptive economics suggests how these perversities evolved. It also shows us how to create incentives that promote shared values and positive outcomes—not results hostage to special interests with rules rigged for inequitable control.

When individuals are held responsible for the full economic and environmental costs of their actions, they face incentives not to harm the environment and to provide public goods such as privately protected habitat. Resources are more likely to be allocated to their most desired use by the decentralized and innovative forces of a market undistorted by the politics of special interests. Pressure groups use the political process to rig the game to their advantage. Acrimony and despair naturally follow. Perhaps the greatest weakness of Vice President Gore's program is his failure to confront this problem.

Even if the public lands were allocated *only* by market demand— surely not the best idea—there would be far less resource extraction than we see today because subsidized development would cease. We could create clear rights to nonmarket values like clean air and water, constraining pollution and degradation. Developers would necessarily be more sensitive to environmental concerns because they would have to take the cost of these previously free public goods into account.

While private nonprofit and for-profit organizations have advantages, there is no one perfect system for economic and social coordination. Markets, government, and nonprofits have different but predictable benefits and flaws. For example, markets work only when we can establish easily enforceable, clear and transferable property rights. Further, not every value is adequately reflected in the market. Nonprofits face problems of motivation and monitoring. Government agencies often turn into engines of plunder. Each has advantages and flaws. Adaptive economics helps us evaluate them as we consider alternative models for reform.

Economy as Ecosystem

Economies are like ecosystems. The most basic law of ecology states that everything is interrelated. It is impossible to do just one thing.

This law also operates in economic systems. In the economy as in an ecosystem, actions have effects beyond those intended. Calls for restrictions on old growth cutting in the Pacific Northwest can lead to increased cutting in the short term as landowners anticipate future bans. Most tragically, by failing to consider the well-being of private owners on whose land endangered species are found, the Endangered Species Act has encouraged landowners to destroy habitat to preclude endangered species encroachment.

A rancher on BLM lands, faced with the capriciousness of the Bureau of Land Management, may decide that investments in erosion control and water reserves, while beneficial to the land and his own long-term well-being, are too risky. The fact that this investment may be denied him in the near future reduces his interest in producing a public good.[2] While we may hope that altruism alone will guide people to seek the health of the land, we should create incentives that encourage good land management by all.

When decision makers are insulated from the costs of their actions or denied access to the benefits, problems follow. For example, when individuals are not rewarded for preserving habitat, habitat is underproduced; when pollution is "free," it is overproduced. Those who approve public support of large-scale irrigation projects respond to a small group of beneficiaries who individually stand to gain a lot. The diffuse groups of individuals who are hurt have far less incentive to organize and object than do the more concentrated and homogeneous group of irrigators. Hence, people often unwittingly subsidize the destruction of the free flowing rivers they value.

Legal and economic institutions differ greatly in the quality of information and types of incentives they generate. When the institutions are arranged properly, so that the incentive structure ensures that individuals are held accountable for the consequences of their actions, economic progress and environmental quality are often complementary. If mining companies were certain that they would be held responsible for damaging trout or salmon spawning beds, they would work harder to avoid such injuries, not just meet minimum technical standards. If national forest managers knew their timber sales would be evaluated in light of true market prices, billions of board feet of subsidized lumber would still be standing.

The adaptive economics approach fosters mutually beneficial compromise and accomodation to the interests of others. And compromise is not always a dirty word. Carefully limited oil and gas drilling allowed on an Audubon-owned migratory bird sanctuary in Louisiana is a good example of a compromise beneficial to all. The oil companies compete to get energy in environmentally sensitive ways, and Audubon gets money to expand sanctuaries. In a few years, the wells will be played out and plugged, but the sanctuaries will remain. Birds, consumers, stockholders, and Audubon all win. But, of course, Audubon fights such development on BLM or Forest Service lands. Adaptive economics enables us to see why. On the one hand, Audubon receives the benefits of protecting wild land but pays none of the opportunity costs of not exploiting that land. On the other hand, oil companies are less likely to be as environmentally sensitive on public lands as on lands owned by environmental groups. Audubon can and does enforce expensive and innovative requirements as a condition of private exploration and production. Government is unlikely to be so innovative or to monitor so carefully.

Good intentions are not enough. Incentives significantly influence decisions, even among the well-intended. While altruism is important and valuable, the forces of self-interest are relentless. Adaptive economics applies the forces of self-interest to environmental quality. It takes advantage of but does not rely upon the often overridden forces of altruism and selfless action. The recent revelations of political pressures on the U.S. Forest Service and the Park Service offer compelling testimonies to the importance of this focus. With improper incentives, merely changing personnel to those *more committed* will not solve the problem. Only changing the institutions will.

Private property rights, market incentives, voluntary action, and entrepreneurial creativity foster the economic progress that encourages environmental concern. These insights are central to understanding adaptive economics. Further, they are powerful tools for achieving the goals of environmentally concerned citizens.

Adaptive economics looks beyond specific issues or causes to their unifying themes. As the failures of the command-and-control approach become more obvious, the value of market processes becomes increasingly evident. For example, innovative ideas such as nonprofit biodiversity trust funds can help to narrow the gulf between loggers, who want jobs, and spotted owls, which are important indicators of habitat quality.[3]

Some people will ask, "Why should I adopt such an impersonal, market-oriented system that may not reflect my values?" We respond that adaptive economics is as personal as the countless human transactions and interactions it promotes. By minimizing the distortions of the political process, adaptive economics makes personal values more, not less, clear. More important, it helps us design institutions in which those interested in environmental quality can have a voice, and those who are not so motivated must face the environmental consequences of their actions.

Not All Good Things Go Together, But Many Do

In our view, the most important components of a good society are liberty and ecology, and a community of people who value both. But only certain institutional arrangements are consistent with these ends. These include individual freedom and responsibility, the rule of law not of men, and strong constraints on bureaucratic independence and its exercise of arbitrary power. Gore's proposals fail these tests.

A roadside billboard proclaims, "The U.S. Constitution is divinely inspired." This claim has no empirical test. It must be taken on faith. While we don't all have that faith, it is certain that if any secular document is divinely inspired it surely is the U.S. Constitution. The men who wrote it, and those who defended it in *The Federalist Papers*, understood the appeal of power and the potential for pressure groups to capture the machinery of government and use government to plunder the less well-organized and less powerful. That is what has happened to much of the American West. Our Founders would understand, for they understood the dangers of political power.

Much of the worst damage in the West was done for noble motives: To make the deserts bloom. To promote prosperity. To provide homes for people. These laudable motives, when combined with inappropriate institutions, have led to enormous destruction. Sometimes they even destroyed the values they were supposed to serve. Always they ignored the wide framework of multiple values, focusing on one or a few ideas conceptually isolated from their surroundings.

Vice President Gore's proposals suffer from the same problem. Many of his goals are noble, but his specific analysis and proposals to achieve them are flawed. Gore's Global Marshall Plan is doomed to fail, and in failing will injure the very values he most praises. Adaptive economics will better serve our efforts to reach the goals we all share.

A Note about the Contributors

Like Gore's new elite, the contributors to this book share several characteristics. All have elite educations and have earned strong national and international reputations as specialists in their areas. All share with Thomas Jefferson, James Madison, and other founders of our republic a profound skepticism of concentrated political power. All understand that power and crisis are ingredients for oppression and opportunism. The authors recognize that political economies are like ecosystems; they are highly interdependent. This means that we cannot do only one thing. Actions are sure to have large and wholly unanticipated consequences. The proposals Gore advocates in his Global Marshall Plan—establishing a CO_2 tax, a virgin materials fee, higher mileage requirements for cars, and setting efficiency standards—presuppose that we already know what we should do and that we can anticipate the consequences of these actions. The contributors to this volume suggest otherwise.

In his conclusion, Gore makes the following observation: "Both in our personal lives and our political decisions, we have an ethical duty to pay attention, resist distraction, be honest with one another and accept responsibility for what we do" (p. 360). The contributors to this book share this view and employ a skeptical ethic. Every empirical assertion may be held up for review, and no one has legitimate claim to terminate the discussion. As Jonathan Rauch observed in *Kindly Inquisitors: A New Attack on Free Thought* (1993), "In most human societies for most of history, the search for knowledge has always been anchored by some propositions or some authorities . . . which were believed to be reliable and beyond error, and therefore not open to serious questioning" (p. 47).

The contributors to this book have worked as academics and analysts in the environmental arena and have been tested through peer review. In reading their work, you will note sincerity, competence, and skepticism regarding both Gore's claims and his proposals for reform. We urge you to listen to their reasoned arguments, consider the evidence, and examine the implications of the policies Gore recommends to us all.

Notes

1. Quoted by Roderick Nash, *Wilderness and the American Mind*, 3rd ed., (New Haven: Yale University Press, 1982), p. 23.
2. For a full treatment of this problem, see Karl Hess, *Visions Upon the Land*, (Washington, DC: Island Press, 1992.)
3. See, for example, John Baden and Tim O'Brien, "Toward A True ESA: An Ecological Stewardship Act," in *Building Economic Incentives Into the Endangered Species Act: A Special Report from Defenders of Wildlife*, Hank Fischer, Project Director and Wendy E. Hudson (eds.), (Washington, DC: Defenders of Wildlife, 1993) pp. 95–100. See also Randal O'Toole, "Building Incentives Into the Endangered Species Act," in the same publication, pp. 101–108.

ABOUT THE AUTHORS

JOHN A. BADEN is president of the Foundation for Research on Economics and the Environment (FREE) and teaches environmental economics and policy at the University of Washington. He also writes an environmental issues column for the *Seattle Times*.

ROBERT C. BALLING, JR., is director of the Office of Climatology, Arizona State University. A prolific writer, his most recent book is *The Heated Debate: Greenhouse Predictions versus Climate Reality* (San Francisco: Pacific Research Institute, 1992).

EVARISTO E. DE MIRANDA is professor of ecology at São Paulo State University, Brazil, research coordinator at the Remote Sensing and Environmental Monitoring Center, a branch of the Brazilian Agriculture Ministry, and chairman of the nongovernmental research and development organization ECOFORCE.

GUS DI ZEREGA is senior research associate at the Foundation for Research on Economics and the Environment, Seattle, Washington.

HUGH W. ELLSAESSER retired from the U.S. Air Force after 20 years as an Air Weather Officer and from the Lawrence Livermore National Laboratory after 23 years of atmospheric and climate research.

ROBERT W. HAHN is a resident scholar at the American Enterprise Institute and adjunct research fellow at the John F. Kennedy School of Government, Harvard University.

JAMES L. HUFFMAN is professor of law at the Lewis and Clark College of Law.

JAMES G. LENNOX is professor of history and philosophy of science at the University of Pittsburgh.

RICHARD S. LINDZEN is the Alfred P. Sloan professor of meteorology at the Massachusetts Institute of Technology.

JOHN R. LOTT, JR., is the Carl D. Covitz assistant professor at the Wharton School, University of Pennsylvania, and is the John M. Olin visiting assistant professor, Graduate School of Business, University of Chicago.

NANCIE G. MARZULLA is president and chief legal counsel of Defenders of Property Rights, a nonprofit legal foundation based in Washington, D.C.

DIXY LEE RAY was a former governor of Washington, chairman of the Atomic Energy Commission, assistant secretary of state in the U.S. Bureau of Oceans, and a long-time member of the zoology faculty of the University of Washington.

LYNN SCARLETT is vice president for research at the Reason Foundation and a senior fellow of the Foundation for Research on Economics and the Environment.

BARRETT P. WALKER is junior trustee of the Alex C. Walker Foundation in Atlanta, Georgia.

PART I

CIVILIZATION

IN THE BALANCE

CHAPTER 1

Comments on *Earth in the Balance*

James L. Huffman

INTRODUCTION

Apocalyptic Realism

Earth in the Balance, by Vice President Albert Gore, is an uneasy mixture of apocalyptic environmentalism and political realism. Its apocalyptics are firmly rooted in the tradition of Thomas Malthus, Barry Commoner, Paul and Anne Ehrlich, and Donella Meadows. Its realism is founded on a career in the United States Congress. While moving effortlessly from describing a "dysfunctional civilization" destined for an "increasingly violent collision . . . [with] the natural world" (p. 223) to defending the central values upon which Western civilization is founded, Vice President Gore is at once pessimist and optimist, pragmatist and mystic, harbinger of fear and herald of hope.

The book is impressive in its reach, but worrisome in its grasp. It is an impassioned call to arms by a converted true believer. Like most converts, Vice President Gore is fervent in his newborn environmentalism. His proselytizing will no doubt increase the ranks of the soldiers in the war to save the planet. Unfortunately, the book contributes little to our understanding of the environmental risks we face, and even less to our comprehension of either causes or solutions. Vice President Gore offers very little in terms of concrete institutional proposals. However, notwithstanding his occasional flattery of free marketeers and localists, Gore's

3

vague prescription seems to be for the globalization of command-and-control environmental regulation. His explanation of causes and his proposals for solutions evidence the ironic narrowing of vision that comes with thinking globally. Those who value a healthy environment in which free people can pursue their lives will be disappointed in Gore's book. He demonstrates little understanding of the powerful force of basic incentives in the lives of individual human beings, and little appreciation for the historic consequences of centralized political power.

Earth in the Balance is probably more extreme than its author. Extremism on both sides of many issues is a long and honored tradition in American politics. Environmental politics is no different. By describing a crisis as almost beyond resolution, advocates hope to arrive at a middle ground. It is in the nature of the logrolling [Gore defends it as "mutuality" (p. 340)] inherent to the democratic process. Although Gore the politician appears to be extremist in the interest of political compromise, Gore the environmentalist appears to be extremist in fact. Former Vice President Quayle was accused of distorting Gore's arguments when he suggested that Gore analogized the environmental crisis to Nazism, but Gore does say that "the evidence of an ecological Kristallnacht is as clear as the sound of glass shattering in Berlin" (p. 177). And Gore does say that "[i]t is not merely in the service of analogy that I have referred so often to the struggles against Nazi and communist totalitarianism, because I believe that the emerging effort to save the environment is a continuation of these struggles, a crucial new phase of the long battle for true freedom and human dignity" (p. 275).

Metaphorical Madness

The extremism of Earth in the Balance is no doubt magnified by Gore's persistent reliance on misplaced metaphors and absurd analogies. As Gore writes, "[t]he metaphor is irresistible" (p. 213), but as employed by Gore, the metaphor undercuts the persuasiveness of many of his central arguments. Nazis and communists are everywhere as Gore repeatedly tries to persuade the reader that the environmental crisis is somehow cut from the same cloth as the struggle against tyranny. Gore's forays into science and his travels around the globe lead him to arguments that challenge credulity. Readers in the environmentalist choir will say amen to much of this, but readers in search of understanding of environmental problems and solutions will surely puzzle at Mr. Gore's eclectic musings. He seems to be a man knowledgeable about much and understanding of

4

little. Like many of his fellow politicians, he is clearly a victim of analysis by sound bite.

Ecumenical Politics

There is much to criticize in the substance of Gore's arguments and analysis, but as a political document the book is first rate. It is ecumenical in every sense of the word. The only people who are not welcome in Gore's political tent are Nazis, Stalinists, and a few deep ecologists. Gore takes some time to explain his own religious beliefs and to set the record straight on the Judeo-Christian environmentalist traditions, but he is quick to acknowledge that "virtually all current world religions have much to say about the relationship between humankind and the earth" (p. 260). Primitive religion, Native American religion, feminism, ecofeminism, Aristotle, the Gaia hypothesis, the rule of law, liberty, freedom, social justice, democracy, community, free markets, and even something of deep ecology all contribute to Gore's ecumenical thinking on the environmental crisis. No one will be offended, and many will agree with Gore's predictable plea that this is an issue that rises above politics. This ludicrous notion that public decisions can be apolitical is one of many "knock down" arguments Gore relies on to make his case.

But the problems with this book are deeper than its poorly formulated arguments and its author's need to pay lip service to all interests on the political spectrum. Vice President Gore does take a very firm position on the condition of the environment—it is in desperate crisis caused by human actions. Although he offers abundant anecdotal evidence of this crisis, the dominant manifestation of the crisis (for the first eight chapters of the book) is global warming. Gore does not waffle on that claim. Some may want to challenge his confident reliance on scientific hypotheses about global ecological effects of human actions, particularly in light of his harsh criticism of the impacts of science on our civilization. I will leave that project to those who are better qualified. My purpose is to examine the implications of Vice President Gore's analysis and proposals on the assumption that we do face an environmental crisis.

This approach is appropriate because Gore is scarcely alone in his belief in environmental crisis. He and others in positions of political power around the globe are going to proceed as if the crisis exists. Indeed, they will use the claim of crisis to fuel their political efforts as Gore does. To the extent that their proposals will fail or even exacerbate the crisis, or to the extent that their proposals ignore or magnify other threats to human welfare, they must be challenged on those terms as well as on the science

5

upon which the perception of crisis is based. It is my belief that Vice President Gore's vague proposals have limited prospect for improving the global environment but pose serious risks to human welfare and freedom.

The remainder of this commentary will examine specific themes of Vice President Gore's argument. The first section examines his conception of the nature and causes of the "environmental crisis," including his discussions of economics, politics, and dysfunctional civilization. The second section considers Vice President Gore's solutions to the environmental crisis. The paper concludes with an examination of Vice President Gore's limited ideas about appropriate institutional arrangements.

ENVIRONMENTAL CRISIS

As they say in Tennessee, "[t]he global environmental crisis is as real as rain," (p. 16) and Vice President Gore inundates the reader with reminders of this grim fact. "[O]ur willingness to ignore the consequences of our actions has combined with our belief that we are separate from nature to produce a genuine crisis in the way we relate to the world around us" (p. 2). We are in a "grave crisis" (p.12) that "threatens absolute disaster" (p. 14). Vice President Gore says he has traveled around the world searching "for the underlying causes of the environmental crisis" (p. 21). His travels have revealed the prospect of an "increasingly violent collision between human civilization and the natural world" (p. 223) caused by "[m]odern industrial civilization [which], as presently organized, is colliding violently with our planet's ecological system" (p. 269). "[I]ndustrial civilization's terrible onslaught against the natural world" (p. 282) is leading to "horrific consequences" (p. 269). "[A] choice to 'do nothing' in response to the mounting evidence is actually a choice to continue and even accelerate the reckless environmental destruction that is creating the catastrophe at hand" (p. 37, emphasis in original). If we do not embrace the solutions he proposes, "the very survival of our civilization will be in doubt" (p.294). We are, warns Vice President Gore, "at the edge of history" (p. 50).

Gore finds evidence of environmental crisis everywhere, but many of his illustrations are suspect or misunderstood. Examples are Love Canal and the Aral Sea. Gore says that Love Canal, which is discussed at least three times, is "synonymous with the problem of hazardous chemical waste" (p.210). Indeed he analogizes Love Canal to "the way our society has allowed the inner city to become a toxic dumping ground for crime, drug abuse, poverty, ignorance, and desperation" (p. 210), but no mention is made of subsequent studies suggesting that there was little if any risk

6

to those who were evacuated at great human and government expense. The Aral Sea gets even more attention, as it should, but Gore fails to recognize that the tragedy is entirely a result of central economic planning.

But these and many other examples are "minor compared to the global threat we now face" —the threat of global warming (p. 4). Gore discounts the views of "a tiny group within the scientific community who argue that the threats don't exist" (p. 38), notwithstanding that the climate models upon which all the forecasts are based are so far unable to predict past climate changes not to mention future climates. He questions the reputability of scientists who challenge the global warming juggernaut, and suggests that to do nothing is to repeat the errors of those who failed to challenge Nazism when its dangers were first apparent. Gore's interesting but rambling chapter on the history of climate and civilization often seems to undercut the case for drastic measures. By his account, societies have managed quite well in the face of historic climate changes, and civilization seems to have prospered during the "unusually warm millennium in Europe" (p. 63).

Causes

Whether Vice President Gore's examples of environmental crises are persuasive, there can be no doubt that environmental problems do exist. Gore suggests many causes, some of which are convincing, others plausible, and still others rather imaginative. Few will doubt that population growth is an important factor. Gore says it "is certain to be ecologically and socially catastrophic" (p. 310). Of course this sounds a lot like Malthus, who Gore says was correct in his population projections but failed to anticipate changes in technology. Malthus also failed to anticipate the restraining effect of economic development and wealth generation on both population growth and environmental destruction. Vice President Gore is right to emphasize population growth, but like Malthus he sees the relationship between population and environment as far simpler than it is.

Technological innovation has been the fly in the ointment of many a future forecast, and it remains a critical variable in the future envisioned by Gore. He contends that technological optimism, "a kind of technological hubris" (p. 206), is another cause of the crisis, and he proposes an international agency—a Strategic Environment Initiative (SEI)—to promote "appropriate technology" (p. 319–320). Thus the problem is not just that we are technological optimists but also that we have selected technologies particularly detrimental to the environment. Gore is surely correct in asserting that "success [in environmental protection] will require careful attention to the way we relate through technology to the environment, and a much greater awareness of the profound effect any powerful technology can have on that relationship" (p. 206). Unfortunately, he gives scant attention to the institutions that will lead ordinary people to adopt the environmentally friendly technologies promoted by his SEI.

Like technology before it, information has exploded with various consequences for the environment. According to Vice President Gore, the problem with information is that we have both too much and too little. "Rarely do we examine," says Gore, "the negative impact of information on our lives" (p. 197). "The more information we consumed, the more our mental lives were dominated by direct experience with information representing the world rather than direct experience of the world itself" (p. 199). Information becomes a substitute for knowledge and wisdom, creating a "crisis in education" (p. 201). We face a situation of information "pollution," some of it "toxic," and "the problem is growing rapidly worse" (p. 201). The problem, it seems, is that in an effort to cope with all this information many people have come to "view the natural world merely as a collection of resources; . . . a giant data bank that they can manipulate at will" (p. 203). "[W]e have encouraged our best thinkers to concentrate their talents not on understanding the whole but on analyzing smaller and smaller parts" (p. 204). Gore might just as well have blamed Aristotle for this dividing and subdividing of our natural world, but it turns out that he rather likes Aristotle and would prefer to blame Plato. In any event, Gore's solution to the information pollution problem is Jefferson's "catholic understanding of the whole of knowledge" (p. 204).

Jefferson would have been the last to imagine the possibility of too much information and, notwithstanding his case against information, Gore goes on later in the book to call for more and better information. "The impetus for . . . change [in the politics of atmospheric pollution] will come from the forefront of science" (p. 291). He offers the example of a couple of scientists whose mid-1970s theories on change in the atmosphere led to "a form of scientific persecution" (p. 291). Perhaps Vice President Gore is less concerned about too much information than he is about the nature of the information. Gore comes to the defense of early proponents of the atmospheric change thesis but does not hesitate to question the reputability of those who think differently today. Vice President Gore's ambivalence on the information question is further underscored by his proposal for a global system of citizen monitoring.

Another aspect of the information problem, according to Gore, is the phenomenon of denial about the state of the environment. "Out of sight,

8

out of mind" is our approach to the waste problem, says Gore (p. 145). But there are reasons for denial that relate less to the availability of information than to the incentives individual actors have to acquire and make use of information. The not-in-my-back-yard (NIMBY) phenomenon, which Gore describes as "knee jerk" (p. 289), clearly underscores the relationship between incentives and information. It is not just a question of too much or too little but of whether decision makers have reasons to be interested.

Vice President Gore also attributes our environmental failings to a culture of purposeful wasting of resources in which people have no sense of responsibility for their environment and no concern for the future. "The powerful forces working against stewardship are . . . greed, self-involvement, and a focus on short-term exploitation at the expense of the long term health of the system itself" (p. 180). He talks about "unrestrained exploitation" (p. 31), production "in excess" (p. 146), and "rituals of production and consumption" (p. 221). He asserts that "the unrestrained burning of cheap fossil fuels has many ferocious defenders" (p. 6). He asks, "how did we make so many poor choices along the way?" (p. 167).

I wonder who these ferocious defenders of waste are. It is as if waste can be defined in the abstract, but waste is a function of circumstances. What is waste today may be a valuable resource tomorrow. What is a poor choice today may have been a wise choice yesterday. There is not and never has been a culture of waste. Rather, there have been cultures of people allocating scarce resources on the basis of what they know and within the constraints of the social institutions that govern their lives. The fix is in knowledge and institutions, not in the reformation of culture. Blaming it on culture is blaming it on no one.

Vice President Gore pleads for a sense of responsibility for ourselves and for the future. "The future whispers while the present shouts" (p. 170). Those people "who have no qualms about maximizing short-term gains at the expense of long-term sustainable use" (p. 125) engage in "future abuse" (p. 235). "We do this not because we don't care but because we don't really live in our lives" (p. 241). And where, might I ask, do we live? The Vice President has a lot of complicated and esoteric ideas about that, but he does identify two concrete reasons for our shortsightedness—economics and politics. Economists have convinced us to discount future costs and benefits to present value, the effect of which, asserts Gore, "is to magnify the power of one generation to compromise all future generations" (p. 191). But the point of discounting is to equalize the generations, as those who promoted laws against speculation in public land and water well understand. Increasing scarcity makes it more and more likely that a resource will be saved for future users rather than consumed by present users. To his credit, Vice President Gore recognizes the shortsightedness of the political system, but his remedy is more enlightened politics, not a search for better institutions.

All these factors contribute to what Gore considers to be the fundamental problem. "[O]ur willingness to ignore the consequences of our actions has combined with our belief that we are separate from nature to produce a genuine crisis in the way we relate to the world around us" (p. 2). "The problem is not our effect *on* the environment so much as our relationship *with* the environment" (p. 34). Gore argues that "we have become so successful at controlling nature that we have lost our connection to it" (p. 225). Plato, Descartes, Bacon, and Darwin, along with technology and information, are blamed for this separation from nature. It is evidenced, says Gore, in our factories, in our "waste disposal crisis" (p. 159), in our disintegrating communities, and in the fact that our philosophers ask whether there is sound when a tree falls in the forest and no person is present. This separateness from nature permits us to secure adherence to rules (presumably bad ones), leads us to separate ourselves from our communities, creates in us "an addiction to the consumption of the earth itself" (p. 220), all the while "obscur[ing] our understanding of our common destiny and render[ing] us vulnerable to an ecological catastrophe" (p. 276).

Economics

That Vice President Gore is a politician and not an economist is underscored in his chapter on economics. He sings the praises of capitalism, as every American politician must, while explaining the many failures of the free market that require government regulation. Gore's argument is less disconcerting for its insistence on the need for centralized planning than for its misunderstanding of basic economic theory. A few important insights are buried in a confusion of disconnected argument and misunderstood theory.

Gore begins the chapter with a recognition of the powerful forces of "free market capitalist economics," the laws of which he analogizes to the laws of motion and gravity. He then states that "[r]ival systems, like communism, have been unable to compete in the marketplace of ideas" (p. 182). This conclusion comports with his claim that communism fell in the face of concerted and unified pressure by the free world, but it does not describe a system the laws of which are like those of the physical universe. Is economic theory about immutable laws or about human values and choice? Gore is clearly not certain.

Gore confuses economic systems with economic theory. He confuses economists with central economic planners. He confuses macroeconomic theory with microeconomic theory. He confuses assumptions made for purposes of theoretical analysis with assertions of fact. He confuses economics with politics. He confuses government action with private action. And he even confuses economic theory about market failure with racism and anti-Semitism. It is a confusing chapter.

The free market capitalist economic system, according to Gore, is "the most powerful tool ever used by civilization" (p. 182) and has within it "the single most powerful force behind what seem to be irrational decisions about the global environment" (p. 183). Absent some evidence of other more positive effects, this surely condemns this economic system. But it has nevertheless prevailed, concludes Gore, because of "the perception on both sides of the Iron Curtain" that capitalism is superior to communism because "it better incorporates classical economic theory" (p. 182). No doubt ideas matter, but it is absurd to suggest that capitalism has prevailed because it incorporates classical economic theory. Few people have a clue about classical economic theory. What people do understand is that the freedom and autonomy of capitalism make their lives better. The economic system is one thing. Economic theory, which seeks to explain that system, is another. Classical economic theory is an explanation of, not a reason for, the success of capitalism.

Equating human social institutions with theoretical explanations of how those institutions function leads Gore to much of the rest of his confusion about economics. He assumes that economic theory necessarily translates into centralized economic management, even when he is talking about the free market economy. He writes about "impressive new powers" conferred by economics and about economists who "measure the good things" while ignoring the bad things in "their calculations" (p. 188). Good classical economists are no doubt measuring things, but not for the purpose of advising a supreme resource allocator of the social optimum. The point of classical economic theory is that the free market permits individuals to choose what they will, and net social good is maximized as a result. Classical economists have done much to explain the impact of various institutional arrangements and thus to recommend different institutions. But Vice President Gore can conceive of economics only as centralized economic management and of economists only as centralized economic managers.

Gore's presumption that economics is about centralized planning leads him to view all economics as macro. He makes important observations about the failure of national income accounting methods to include

11

resource depletion as an expense but then assumes that this is somehow related to the actions of private decision makers. He concludes that it is (almost) "intellectual arrogance" for economists to assert perfect information and perfect market clearing, "especially in light of the inability of classical economics to deal with the idea of accounting for lost nature resources" (p. 186). Classical economics does deal with lost or depleted resources at the micro level, and purports to say nothing about such losses at the macro level of national income accounting. Unless private market participants are affected by subsidies or regulations contingent on national income accounts, they are indifferent to such calculations. This does not deny that national income accounting methods are important, particularly in an international economy influenced by central economic planners like the World Bank, but it is simply incorrect to relate this problem in any way to classical economic theory. In the world that classical economic theory recommends, national income accounts would be of little interest except to those keeping score in some sort of economic olympics.

Gore nevertheless insists on linking an admittedly flawed system of national income accounting to classical economics and the free market system. After citing the names of some economists who agree with him on the income accounting point, he notes the "striking contrast between the awesome power and efficiency our economic system displayed in its philosophical rout of Marxism–Leninism and the abject failure of the very same system to even take note of the poisoning of our water, the fouling of our air, the destruction of tens of thousands of living species every year" (p. 185). What the latter contrast has to do with national income accounting is not explained, nor is the remarkable assertion that we are losing "tens of thousands" of species each year (p. 185). If it is true that "billions of economic choices every day" are leading us to the "brink of ecological catastrophe" (p. 185), we had better understand why before we start propounding remedies. Central economic managers may be interested in national income accounts, but the choices of individual economic actors will remain largely unaffected.

Vice President Gore must surely find some truth in the old joke about the economist who, when faced with hunger, a can of beans, and no can opener, proposes to assume that he has a can opener. It always gets a good laugh, but it badly distorts an essential and useful tool of economic theory. Like laboratory scientists who conduct experiments in a vacuum to answer questions about the real world (which is not a vacuum), economists make assumptions about some variables in an effort to better understand the effects of those and other variables. For example, an economist might assume zero transactions costs and thus improve our understanding of

12

the effects of transactions costs on market exchanges. The economist never means to assert that transactions are costless, nor does the economist mean to assert that information is perfect or that the market clearing function works perfectly. Yet Gore writes that "[c]lassical economists like to argue that all participants in the struggle between supply and demand have 'perfect information'" (p. 185). He further asserts that our economic system, by which he means classical economic theory, "insists upon the equally absurd assumptions that natural resources are limitless 'free goods'" (p. 186). Classical economic theory makes no such claims. Far from intellectual arrogance, the classical economists' claim is only that by making certain assumptions, which we know not to be true, we may be able to learn more about the truth.

Gore's discussion of externalities is even more revealing of his ignorance of economic theory. It is a "hard truth," writes Gore, but "our economic system is partially blind" (p. 182). So far, so good. Classical economic theory does recognize the existence of costs (and benefits) external to some market transactions. The notion is that individuals not party to market transactions may nonetheless bear costs and experience benefits resulting from those transactions. These are real costs and real benefits and are therefore relevant to the efficiency of the resultant allocation of resources. The existence of externalities, in other words, is evidence of market failure. Much environmental regulation is designed to correct for this market failure. Classical economists may disagree about whether or not externalities exist under particular circumstances, but they will not disagree about the reality of these costs and benefits where they do exist.

Classical economic externalities theory is a far cry from the "large waste-basket of economic theory" described by Gore (p. 347). Gore contends that "the Holy Grail of progress" leads economists to overlook and ignore the "bad side effects that often accompany improvements." This is accomplished, says Gore, by "resorting to an intellectual device labeled 'externalities'" (p. 188). "[B]ad things are simply defined away as external to the process and classed as externalities" (p. 189). They are, asserts Gore, "conveniently forgotten by classical economists" (p. 187). In all of this, Vice President Gore sees not only "intellectual arrogance" but also "a form of dishonesty" that is philosophically "similar in some ways to the moral blindness implicit in racism and anti-Semitism" (p. 189).

Either Gore is hopelessly ill-informed about economic theory or he is guilty of the very dishonesty he attributes to economists. Rather than assuming away the external costs of economic activity, externalities theory is an explicit recognition that they exist and that they matter. It is a

13

theoretical construct designed precisely to assure that "what is out of sight is [not] out of mind" (p. 183).

Many of the environmental problems Gore attributes to our economic system are more properly viewed as political failures. National income accounting is far more about politics than it is about economics, and there are powerful political incentives for maintenance of the existing methods. The destruction of tropical rain forests is far more the result of government subsidy than it is of a shortsighted pursuit of cheap hamburger. The ongoing debate over spotted owls and old growth trees is very little about economics and almost entirely about politics, as demonstrated by the universal dissatisfaction with the Clinton administration's recent attempt to resolve the dispute. This list goes on and on. What Gore fails to recognize is that the free market of classical economics with which he finds so many failings has never really existed. The market has always been buffeted by government regulations and subsidies, not to mention the influence of government resource management on public lands. If we want to understand our institutional failures, we need to sort out the effects of the market and the effects of government intervention.

Because Vice President Gore badly misunderstands classical economic theory, and because he attributes to the market many of the failures of the political system, his critique of classical economic theory is almost meaningless. The problem is not that he fails to comprehend the failures of our political system but rather that he seems to share the pervasive environmentalist bias against reliance on private institutions. It is an unfortunate bias most of all because it disserves the very interests Gore and his fellow travelers seek to achieve.

Politics

Vice President Gore is better at politics than economics, but his political theory could use some work. Although he is rare among politicians in his recognition of the short-term perspective of the political system, and he recognizes the "subtle and pervasive temptation . . . to attain and hold onto power, even when doing so means avoiding hard choices and ignoring the truth" (p. 181), he gets off on the wrong foot by suggesting that the ecosystem provides a useful analogy to our political system. The ecosystem analogy suggests there is a way things are supposed to be and that our task is to restore that natural equilibrium to allow the systems to work the way they are supposed to. It is an invisible hand argument no less so than the case for social optimization through the free market, but history provides little reason to be optimistic about the invisible hand of

14

politics. It has long been a central tenet of popular, if not professional, political culture in this country that the only invisible hand guiding government is that of the potential tyrant.

Vice President Gore has a lot of confidence in government, notwithstanding its failures. Gore defines politics as "the means by which we make collective decisions and choices" (p. 270). The assumption that there are no alternative institutions for making such decisions is reflected in the proposals Gore ultimately offers. The problem with modern politics, with its 30-second sound bites, is its distraction of "even the best politician from the real work at hand" (p. 168), which is apparently writing laws. "A keen sense for visual rhetoric is almost totally irrelevant to the task of writing laws" (p. 169). Gore takes pride in the laws he has written and condemns the Bush administration for the laws it did not write. The possibility of leaving matters to private decision makers on occasion does not occur to Gore as an example of good government.

Gore is critical of the influence of special interests in overriding the pursuit of the public interest. These special interests have led even democratic governments to contribute to environmental destruction. Making democracy serve the environment "will depend on our ability to develop a keener understanding of how to make self-government respond to the environmental concerns shared by millions more people around the world each year" (p. 180). That will happen, of course, when corruption is eliminated and a majority of the people prefer environmental protection to other alternatives they face. Majorities for environmental protection will exist, at least some of the time but, as Gore recognizes, the temptation for corruption will remain. And even absent corruption, the process of logrolling, or *mutuality* as Gore labels it, will assure that special interests will always dominate in representative democracies. Leadership can make a difference, but as Gore's ecumenical approach to his subject underscores, politicians will not be permitted to lead in a democracy until they demonstrate that they can follow. What dooms Gore's ambition for a political equilibrium is his belief that the public interest is anything other than the result of the hard fought battles among special interests.

It is probably inevitable that politicians who make a career of urging that their particular view is coincident with the public interest will come to believe in the concept of the public interest. It is thus not surprising that Vice President Gore remains optimistic about politics while recognizing its failures. However, it is surprising that he does not have a better understanding of some basics of political theory. Gore endorses the widely held notion that democracy is an opposite political system to communism. Although the communist systems that have now failed in Eastern Europe were by no means democratic, there is nothing about the philosophy of communism that is incompatible with democracy. Nor is there anything about democratic theory that precludes a communist economic system. Because communism calls for centralized micromanagement of the economy, democracy proves to be a cumbersome process of decision making. And democrats are surely chary of the centralization required by a communist economy. But to suggest that they are opposites is to confuse economic systems with political systems.

This confusion of economic and political systems is reflected in Gore's equation of collective choice with politics. Collective choices are merely aggregates of individual choices. In a majoritarian democracy, it is supposed to be an aggregation of at least 50 percent plus one. Individual choices are also aggregated in the market, often with very different results for society and for the individual. Gore claims to be a proponent of free markets, but he sees them as part and parcel of democracy. In his conception, the collective choices are made by democracy, and individual choices are made in the market. This conception provides politicians with a long agenda and greatly limits the role of markets.

Vice President Gore's confusion of political with economic theory is also reflected in his equation of democracy with capitalism. "[I]t seems obvious that both democracy, as a political system, and capitalism, as an economic system, work on the same principle and have the same inherent 'design advantage' because of the way they process information" (p. 359). It is true that the individual is the initial information processor in both capitalism and democracy, but the similarity ends there. In a capitalist system, individuals do all the information processing and all the decision making. Because the individual gets precisely what he or she chooses, subject to wealth and capacity limitations, the individual has incentives to acquire information relevant to clear alternatives. In a democratic system, information is also processed by individuals, but for very different purposes. Individuals know they will seldom get precisely what they would choose and that they are not necessarily limited by wealth or capacity. Their incentives are to acquire and generate information, as much for the purpose of influencing the decisions of others as for informing their own decisions.

But information processing is not the central strength of either capitalism or democracy. The strength of each is that it permits autonomy to the individual. However, individual autonomy is far more restricted in democratic decision making than it is in capitalist decision making. As methods for aggregating individual choices, they are fundamentally different. Political aggregations of individual choices are like capitalist ag-

16

gregations only under a rule of unanimity. As a political system moves from a rule of unanimity to a rule of majoritarianism, it makes enormous inroads on the autonomy of the individual. This is not an argument against democracy; rather, it is an argument for thinking carefully about what decisions to permit to government and what decisions to leave with freely transacting individuals. By treating democracy and capitalism as philosophical equivalents, Gore perpetuates a widely held view that if democracy is the best way to make some decisions it is the best way to make all decisions.

Dysfunctional Civilization

"What we are up against," says Vice President Gore, "is nothing less than the current logic of world civilization" (p. 269). Our civilization has become *dysfunctional* in Gore's judgment. The evidence is everywhere but nowhere more obvious than in our relation to the earth. Waste is growing in the Third World because of the "pattern of conspicuous consumption that has been exported to these countries along with Western culture and its consumer products" (p. 156). The Exxon *Valdez* oil spill stands "as an indictment of our civilization" (p. 21). We stand indicted, says Gore, of having lost our way in the natural world, and we have responded by pillaging the planet. "Our species used to flourish within the intricate and interdependent web of life, but we have chosen to leave the garden. Unless we find a way to dramatically change our civilization and our way of thinking about the relationship between humankind and the earth, our children will inherit a wasteland" (p. 163).

Desperate as our situation is, according to Gore, he is not pessimistic because he thinks he understands how we got this way and therefore how we can make amends. Gore believes that there are "deep social and attitudinal causes of America's relative economic decline, some of which also contribute to the environmental crisis" (p. 351). Our dysfunctional civilization, says Gore, is like the dysfunctional family. "Just as children cannot reject their parents, each new generation in our civilization now feels utterly dependent on the civilization itself" (p. 231). Like the children who blame themselves for their dysfunctional families, "we quietly internalize the blame for our civilization's failure to provide a feeling of community and a shared sense of purpose in life" (p. 231). "[W]e internalize the pain of our lost sense of connection to the natural world, we consume the earth and its resources as a way to distract ourselves from the pain, and we search insatiably for artificial substitutes to replace the experience of communion with the world that has been

17

taken from us" (p. 231). Thus we have a civilization addicted to consuming itself into oblivion.

This is all very interesting, and Gore's understanding of dysfunctional family theory is impressive, but it is really quite fanciful. Our civilization, particularly the industrialized countries of Europe and North America, have made enormous strides in protection and restoration of the natural environment. Through our political systems, we have imposed all manner of restraints on our consumption, often at costs many times greater than any conceivable benefits. We have also imposed immense costs on the planet, more often than not through those same political institutions. Rather than being addicted to the consumption of the planet due to "[t]he cleavage in the modern world between mind and body, man and nature" (p. 220), it seems we are addicted to centralized mismanagement of the planet due to a cleavage between mind and experience.

Vice President Gore suggests that Nazi Germany, fascist Italy, the Stalinist Soviet Union, and Maoist China are examples of dysfunctional civilizations. Indeed they are, and millions of destroyed human lives remain to remind us. The destroyed environment of Eastern Europe should also remind us of the dysfunctional politics of centralized management that grew out of these human tragedies. These, not the Exxon *Valdez*, are indictments the human jury should attend. At worst the Exxon *Valdez* should lead to an indictment for drunkenness by an individual and perhaps inadequate supervision by a corporation. It was an accident sobriety might have prevented, but oil spills will inevitably occur in a civilization that has discovered how to turn petroleum to the service of human welfare. It is oil hauled in tankers like the Exxon *Valdez* that permitted the Clinton–Gore campaign bus to traverse the American byways spreading the news of dysfunctional civilization.

SOLUTIONS TO CRISIS

Objectives

Consistent with his ecumenical approach, Vice President Gore has numerous objectives for a reformed and functional civilization. Biodiversity is the first priority as it has been ever since God commanded Noah: "Thou shalt preserve biodiversity" (p. 245). Central to maintaining biodiversity is an understanding of the proper relationship between humans and nature. Gore is not one to say that humans are external to nature, rather he believes that "the way we currently relate to the environment is wildly inappropriate" (p. 238). The Jeffersonian approach he advocates will lead us to an ecological perspective that will permit us to restore the earth to its proper balance. This ecological perspective "is rising powerfully from the part of our being that knows better, that knows to consolidate, protect, and conserve those things we care about before we manipulate and change them, perhaps irrevocably" (p. 215).

As luck or providence would have it, the pursuit of biodiversity and natural balance is consistent with other important objectives, "including our interest in social justice, democratic government, and free market economics" (p. 270). Gore does not explain exactly how natural balance serves these social goals, but perhaps it is nothing more sophisticated than that without a viable planet to live on society will not be able to pursue the traditional objectives of liberal society. Certainly, without something like our planetary ecosystem, future generations will not be able to secure those blessings, and Gore devotes considerable attention to the rights and prospects of future inhabitants of the earth.

It is interesting and somewhat puzzling that many of the things Vice President Gore seeks to achieve by restoring the earth's balance are central values of Western civilization. He even comes to the defense of national sovereignty, which may be the most significant obstacle to the global environmental future he imagines. Why would one who claims that our central problem is a dysfunctional civilization repeatedly rise to the defense of the basic philosophical values of that civilization? The answer is that he totally misconceives Western civilization as being centrally concerned with consumption and waste. Consumption is a manifestation of the remarkable success of Western civilization. Waste, where it exists, is often the result of institutional arrangements that have abandoned the central values of liberal individualism. Unfortunately, Gore is so firmly rooted in orthodox environmentalism that he cannot even imagine the perversity of his commitment to centralized environmental management.

Solutions

Gore's solution to the environmental crisis is to restore the functionality of our civilization through the adoption of a new central organizing principle. "[W]e must make the rescue of the environment the central organizing principle for civilization" (p. 269). It will be news to some that civilizations have central organizing principles, but Gore assures us that they do and that it is possible to consciously embrace a "single shared goal as the central organizing principle for every institution in society" (p. 270). We have done so "several times" in the past, he suggests, at least among the free nations of the world (p. 270). The decline and fall of communism was made possible, asserts Gore, by a "conscious shared decision by men and women in the nations of the 'free world' to make the defeat of the communist system the central organizing principle of not only their governments' policies but of society itself" (p. 271). Gore goes on to argue that "virtually every policy and program was analyzed and either supported or rejected primarily according to whether it served our basic organizing principle" (p. 272). To suggest that communism collapsed because of a concerted, multidecade effort by everyone in the free world is to overestimate both communism and the free world. By definition, the free world would not be party to such uniformity of purpose. The principle contribution of the free world was for its citizens to go about their business of improving their lot, while communism rotted from within.

Even if Vice President Gore could make a case for the abstract concept of a central organizing principle, the one he suggests does not serve the argument for his new central organizing principle. As he points out with reference to World War II, "[o]ur resources, our people, our art, and even our gardens played a role in the struggle to save civilization as we knew it" (p. 272). One can imagine a unified effort to save the civilization we have; it is more difficult to imagine a unified effort to jettison our civilization. But Gore plans to have his cake and eat it too. "Ultimately, a commitment to healing the environment represents a renewed dedication to what Jefferson believed were not merely American but universal inalienable rights: life, liberty and the pursuit of happiness" (p. 270). Will apocalyptic environmentalism sell better when wrapped in the flag?

"What does it mean to make the effort to save the global environment the central organizing principle of our civilization?" asks Vice President Gore (p. 273).

> Adopting a central organizing principle—one agreed to voluntarily—means embarking on an all-out effort to use every policy and program, every law and institution, every treaty and alliance, every tactic and strategy, every plan and course of action—to use, in short, every means to halt the destruction of the environment and to preserve and nurture our ecological system. (p. 273)

It is a tall order, admits Gore, but it can be done. The first thing we have to do, particularly since it is to be voluntary, is to educate people. "So with time running out, the real source of hope still lies in the prospect of a change in the way people at the grass roots think about the global environment" (p. 354). We must "secur[e] widespread agreement that it

20

should be the organizing principle" (p. 273), which will be accomplished by exposing people to "the harsh light of truth" (p. 236). Although he says it is a matter of "lasso[ing] our common sense" (p. 114), there is a disquieting self-assurance in his use of the term *truth* and in his cautioning against confusing "sophisticated imbecilities" with "serious analysis" (p. 195). Gore has that confidence in his own perceptions so common to orthodox environmental advocates. He knows what the content of this global education must be.

Vice President Gore places his hope for the adoption of his new central organizing principle in leadership, grass roots commitment, and spiritual conversion. From President Bush there was a "refusal to provide leadership," which in Gore's view is "a historic failure that will, if not soon remedied, be regarded by future generations as unforgivable" (p. 176). Not surprisingly, he finds precedent for such leadership in the battles against Nazism and communism. Indeed, in his mind it is all part of the same battle.

Gore is careful to insist that leadership does not mean dictatorship. Rather "the real work must be done by individuals, and politicians need to assist citizens in their efforts to make new and necessary choices" (p. 179). He is confident that there will be a "large shift in public opinion about the global environment" (p. 305) if "men and women who care . . . [are] politically empowered to demand and help effect remedies to ecological problems wherever they live" (p. 179).

Education, leadership, and grass roots politics will not matter, in Gore's view, unless something far more fundamental happens. "We have a kind of collective identity crisis," says Gore; "a spiritual crisis . . . that seems to be based on an emptiness at its center and the absence of a larger spiritual purpose" (p. 367). For Gore this all has a lot to do with God and traditional religion, but he recognizes that for many, ours is a secular world. He thus seeks to marry traditional religion with environmentalism, an effort by no means unique to Vice President Gore. "For civilization as a whole, the faith that is so essential to restore the balance now missing in our relationship to the earth is the faith that we do have a future" (p. 368). Few will disagree with a desire for a future on a healthy planet, but there is little reason for faith if Gore's prescriptions are the best we can do. With all the weaknesses in this book, its greatest failing, and one for which a politician must be held accountable, is its lack of proposals for institutional remedies that will achieve the objectives he seeks. This failing is not surprising in light of Gore's analysis of both political and economic theory, but it is nevertheless disappointing.

CONCLUSION

Vice President Gore's ideas about the institutional remedies for the environmental crisis are as ecumenical as his attribution of blame. He calls for individual responsibility, community action, governmental intervention, international cooperation among sovereign nations, spiritual commitment, and the invisible hand of nature. He leaves no strategy unmentioned but places his confidence in the good sense of good people to follow the leadership of those who understand the serious nature of the problem. The reform of a dysfunctional civilization is to be achieved on a global scale while preserving most of the central foundations of that civilization.

Gore states that "with personal commitment, every individual can help ensure that dramatic change does take place" (p. 12), but he is not so naive as to think that the well-intentioned actions of billions of individuals will make the difference. He correctly concludes that "influencing the criteria and values used to inform and guide these billions of everyday choices represents the real key to changing the direction of human civilization" (p. 338).

Gore notes that some corporations have discovered they can benefit from environmentally friendly actions. He also is seemingly amazed by the realization that incentives matter to individual and business decisions. Twice he cites the example of a successful tree planting program in Kenya that compensated those who participated only after they had nurtured the seedlings for a period of time sufficient to assure their survival. What is surprising is that Gore finds this surprising. Any successful entrepreneur could have predicted the outcome Vice President Gore considers a "discovery" (p. 288).

Gore seems to have little appreciation for the importance of individual rights to the actions taken by individuals. He does not recognize the role of property rights in avoiding the tragedy of the commons, which explains many of the environmental problems that concern him. Rather than focusing on how the clear definition and enforcement of property rights can promote environmental protection, Gore suggests that "[t]he emphasis on the rights of the individual must be accompanied by a deeper understanding of the responsibilities to the community that every individual must accept" (p. 277). Like so many of Gore's points, he believes this one can be understood in ecological terms, "in the sense that it involves a balance between rights and responsibilities" (p. 278). Gore believes that "we have tilted so far toward individual rights and so far away from any sense of obligation that it is now difficult to muster an adequate defense of any rights vested in the community at large or in the

22

nation—much less rights properly vested in all humankind or in poster-ity" (p. 278). Gore offers no suggestion as to what the meaning of commu-nity or national or humankind or posterity rights might be, but he is clearly of the view that "a global problem can only be solved on a global basis" (p. 295).

The problem, says Gore, is not only that individuals act without any sense of responsibility to their community or their environment, but also that "something . . . has gone terribly wrong in the way we collectively determine our mutual relationship to the earth" (p. 226). Gore believes that individuals have become separated from their communities in part because of their separation from the earth (p. 278). As a result, communi-ties become dysfunctional and unable to properly relate to their environ-ment. He makes no mention of the impacts of various social policies that have promoted separatism and community division, nor does he give any indication of what he means by community. He does seem to have the naive view that, through education and with leadership, all the residents of the globe can come to view themselves as members of a global commu-nity. They can learn, in words often used by environmentalists, to think globally while acting locally.

Vice President Gore, like the orthodox environmentalists whose views he espouses, has got it backwards. There is a reason for the NIMBY effect. People think locally, even when their leaders endeavor to get them to think in broader terms. Gore urges that we educate people to realize that the globe is their backyard, but few will be persuaded. People respond to what affects their lives. For the vast majority of people, that will be what occurs in their backyards. Relatively few of the globe's inhabitants have the leisure to invest time and energy in protection of tropical rainforests or endangered species. But as studies of African elephant protection efforts have demonstrated, people can become interested in protecting species and habitats when they have clear incentives to do so.

Although Vice President Gore pays much lip service to the impor-tance of individuals and of decentralized solutions, his prescriptions are for centralized regulations made acceptable by appealing to spiritual and communitarian values. He insists that world government is "both politi-cally impossible and practically unworkable" (p.301), but his proposal for a "Global Marshall Plan" could only be realized through centralized global institutions. Gore argues that "we must negotiate international agreements that establish global constraints on acceptable behavior but that are entered into voluntarily—albeit with the understanding that they will contain both incentives and legally valid penalties for noncompli-ance" (p. 302). Who, one might ask, will enforce these penalties? Vice

23

President Gore sees a limited role for the United Nations and suggests creation of a "Stewardship Council" (p. 302) as the appropriate institution. He also imagines an annual environmental summit, presumably like the one held recently in Rio. No doubt Gore and many other world leaders would welcome such meetings, but the experience in Rio suggests that not much will be accomplished.

The central obstacle to the kind of international cooperation envisioned by Gore is national sovereignty. For decades some nations have struggled to overcome the detrimental effects of national sovereignty on international trade. The solutions that have been reached, such as the European Community, have been dependent for success upon the willingness of the participating states to relinquish some amount of their sovereignty to a central authority. But Gore insists that national sovereignty must be respected. If he is serious about his proposals, he will have to choose enforceable environmental mandates over national sovereignty.

Vice President Gore's Global Marshall Plan will have a "scope and complexity . . . [that] far exceed those of the original" (p. 297). In Gore's words:

> [W]hat's required now is a plan that combines large-scale, long-term, carefully targeted financial aid to developing nations, massive efforts to design and then transfer to poor nations the new technologies needed for sustained economic progress, a worldwide program to stabilize world population, and binding commitments by the industrial nations to accelerate their own transition to an environmentally responsible pattern of life. (p. 297)

Gore goes on at great length to elaborate on the content of this plan, but he says virtually nothing about who will do it, how they will know what to do, or how it will be made effective in nations whose sovereignty he wishes to protect.

Gore's grand plan for international action will exceed anything ever attempted by the now failed economies of Eastern Europe. Presumably the difference is that this plan will be implemented in a democratic world populated by well-educated, public-spirited global citizens. This is precisely the kind of naive thinking that has led many a people down the primrose path to economic disaster and political oppression. Gore cannot conceal the essentially centralist nature of his proposals by repeated insistences that he believes in markets, liberty, sovereignty, and all the other central values of the civilization he has diagnosed as dysfunctional.

Although Vice President Gore offers a laundry list of substantive objectives, *Earth in the Balance* is a vague prescription for the internationalization of environmental regulation. It is inspired by pessimism about our civilization and confidence that we are in a grave environmental crisis. Neither the pessimism nor the confidence are justified. The environmental problems we face, and there are many of them, will often be better solved by decentralized institutional arrangements that recognize and exploit the incentives for the billions of individual decision makers who inhabit the globe. Vice President Gore is right to insist upon the importance of the environment to human freedom. If only he understood the importance of human freedom to the environment.

CHAPTER 2

Toward a New
Environmental Paradigm

Robert W. Hahn

INTRODUCTION

Albert Gore, Jr. is a man with a mission. He wants to save the planet. Nothing short of a complete overhaul of the world economic system and a redefinition of our relationship to nature will satisfy him. Whether you agree with his plan for saving the planet or not, his recent book *Earth in the Balance* is a "must read." It is a *reveille* for environmental action in the same way as was Rachel Carson's *Silent Spring*,[1] except it calls for action on every front. As he noted in his acceptance speech for the Vice Presidential nomination, Mr. Gore believes that "[t]he task of saving the Earth's environment must and will become *the central organizing principle* of the post Cold-War world."[2] Coming from a politician who may have the power to act on his vision, this is heady stuff.

Readers expecting to find an unreadable book, written by a coterie of senate staffers and full of platitudes, are in for a surprise. *Earth in*

This review essay of *Earth in the Balance: Ecology and the Human Spirit* by Albert Gore, Jr., (Boston: Houghton Mifflin, 1992) first appeared in *The Yale Law Journal*. It is reprinted by permission of The Yale Law Journal Company and Fred B. Rothman & Company from *The Yale Law Journal*, vol. 102, pp. 1719–1761.

the Balance is written by the author himself, beautifully argued, and truly thought-provoking. Mr. Gore's book is structured as a dual quest to restore the "natural balance of the earth's ecological system" (p. 270) and to restore the appropriate balance between man and nature. It proceeds from an exposition of the crisis in the first two sections of the book to recommendations for addressing it, at the book's end.

Earth in the Balance is mostly about the perception of large patterns. Seeing about him a global environmental holocaust, the author strives to help his readers see it too. The book is unified by a series of computer generated pictures of the earth, with each successive snapshot bringing the planet into sharper focus.[3] In helping his readers to perceive the global crisis, the author is self-consciously eclectic in approach. He does not exaggerate when he claims to draw upon "perspectives offered by the earth sciences, economics, sociology, history, information theory, psychology, philosophy, and religion" (p. 269–270). To borrow the words of Ivan Illich, a philosopher whom Mr. Gore admires, the Vice President is "searching for a language to speak about the shadow our future throws" (p. 47).

Mr. Gore's elegance and breadth of reference put the specialized reviewer at something of a disadvantage. As an economist, however, I feel particularly qualified to evaluate the last third of the book. For in this section, the Vice President avowedly speaks from the vantage point of a politician (p. 270). And as a politician proposing solutions to problems in the real world, Vice President Gore necessarily speaks the language of economics. My focus on the prescriptive portion of the book is justified because—no matter how persuasive—the book must be adjudged a failure if its policies are misguided. A leader must not only identify problems and move the public to action, but also must ensure that the action adopted is timely and effective given existing constraints. In this last task, economics is indispensable.

The Vice President is not oblivious to economics, but he cannot bring himself to embrace its premises fully. My essential difference with the author is contained within the ambiguity of the book's title. The phrase "earth in the balance" may be, and is, used in the loose metaphorical sense that the planet is in grave danger.[4] But it may also be used in the crude, strict metaphorical sense that the earth may be placed in a merchant's balance, and weighed against competing considerations—balanced against the proverbial six bars of gold. Mr. Gore recognizes this meaning of the phrase too, but he attributes it to the Bush administration, and dismisses it as "absurd" (p. 193). This essay is written from the perspective of an economist who accepts both meanings of the phrase. It does not deny

28

that the earth may lie "in the balance," but neither does it shirk from the necessity of *placing* the earth "in the balance."

After an attempt to give the reader a flavor of the book as a whole, this review essay undertakes a detailed critique of Vice President Gore's plan for action, the Global Marshall Plan. It then notes what is most sorely lacking in the book, a realistic discussion of the political dynamics, and attempts to fill the gap. Finally, this essay analyzes the concept of sustainable development that is the ostensible goal of environmental policy, and compares two roads to its attainment: the "visionary" approach taken by Mr. Gore, and the "policy analytic" approach preferred by economists.

THE ENVIRONMENTAL
AND SPIRITUAL BREAKDOWN

In the first two-thirds of the book, Vice President Gore paints a grim picture of how we are destroying the planet. He goes through a litany of problems ranging from the loss of the Aral Sea (pp. 19–20) to the disappearance of rainforests at the fantastic rate of 1.5 acres per second (p. 118). The Vice President describes the strategic environmental threats posed to our air, water, and land. At the heart of the book lies the contestable claim that a consensus is forming in the scientific community about the likelihood and severity of global warming. Mr. Gore bolsters this claim by pointing out that in the past climate changes have caused political instability and disrupted activities throughout the world.[5]

Mr. Gore claims that the twin evils of technology and population growth exacerbate the strategic environmental threats (p. 30). Rapid population growth puts ever-increasing pressures on the world's resource base and intensifies our vulnerability to potential changes in climate (p. 78). While Mr. Gore does not ignore the potential mitigating impacts of technology, he claims to foresee projected climate changes sufficiently large to dwarf our ability to deal with them.[6] In his view, we are conducting a massive unethical experiment on patient earth, where we are the guinea pigs (p. 92). We can manipulate nature, "but our notions of how to consolidate and protect the environment against unintended consequences are still rudimentary" (p. 214). The basic problem is that we now have "godlike powers," but we have failed to exercise "godlike wisdom" (p. 240).

Vice President Gore believes that the global environmental crisis is an outward manifestation of a spiritual crisis (p. 12). People, especially politicians, have avoided taking moral responsibility for their actions. We

29

are no longer in balance with nature. This disharmony in our relationship to the earth has led to a no-deposit, no-return society. "Our insatiable drive to rummage deep beneath the surface of the earth . . . is a willful expansion of our dysfunctional civilization into vulnerable parts of the natural world" (p. 234). We must recognize that man is spiritually linked with the natural world rather than separate from it. The argument is reminiscent of Thoreau's *Walden Pond*[7] and Schumacher's *Small Is Beautiful*.[8]

Mr. Gore's solution lies in two simple ideas—first and foremost, in developing structures that limit environmental harm and lead to a resurgence in environmental productivity; second, in educating the wayward masses and misguided elites as to the folly of our ways. Rethinking man's relationship to the environment will require a new kind of "eco-nomics" that counts the environment as an investment in the future rather than simply an additional cost of doing business. Ultimately, however, the prime mover for change must be a heightened awareness of the current imbalance between nature and man. This sensitivity can come only through concerted efforts in education. "Our challenge is to accelerate the needed change in thinking about our relationship to the environment in order to shift the pattern of our civilization to a new equilibrium—before the world's ecological system loses its current one" (p. 48).

But simply to state Mr. Gore's argument does not do it justice. Like Rachel Carson, the author moves us more by rhetoric than by logical persuasion. The Vice President has the journalist's appetite for anecdotes, yet the novelist's gift for rendering them true. He will draw from any source to illustrate a point, from *Principia Mathematica* (p. 47) to *Saturday Night Live* (p. 153)—all to great effect. The only constants in the book are the references to Gore's personal experience ("In the course of one human lifetime— mine"),[9] and to the folks back home in Tennessee.[10] This latter tendency stands in stark contrast to his reticence about his friends at Harvard, who go unmentioned with the exception of one oblique reference to a "college" professor (p. 4).

One of the most memorable, and revealing, passages in the book tells the story of a valiant group of Soviet scientists during World War II:

> [E]ven during the bombardment of Leningrad, Vavilov's colleagues bravely planted new generations of crops in order to freshen their genetic stock. And when hungry rats learned to knock the metal boxes of seeds off the shelves to get to the contents, the scientists took turns standing watch to protect their genetic treasures.

> Surrounded by edible seeds and sacks of plants such as rice and potatoes, fourteen of the scientists died of starvation in December rather than consume their precious specimens. Dr. Dmytry S. Ivanov, the institute's rice specialist, was surrounded by bags of rice when he was found dead at his desk. He was reported to have said shortly before his death, "When all the world is in the flames of war, we will keep this collection for the future of all people." (pp. 281–282)

The story of the Vavilov institute is representative not only for its power and poignancy. Mr. Gore's admiration for these martyrs also manifests, in extreme form, his preference for personal changes in behavior over technological fixes. At one point or another, Mr. Gore casts his scorn upon the science of genetic engineering (p. 141), and upon various schemes for desalinizing water (p. 114), incinerating garbage (p. 156), and fertilizing the oceans (p. 215).

Furthermore, the Vavilov story exemplifies Mr. Gore's fondness for military analogy. In Mr. Gore's view the world's areas of genetic diversity were "under a siege of their own" in the 1940s—the only difference being that the environmental siege, rather than lifting by the war's end, has tightened its grip in the decades since (p. 281). Elsewhere, Mr. Gore likens the world's environmental insensibility to its deafness on the night of *Kristallnacht*,[11] and, repeatedly, to Chamberlain's appeasement of Hitler (pp. 196, 274–275). Such analogies underscore not only the moral dimensions of the danger perceived by the Vice President, but also the magnitude of the threat, and its global nature. We should thus not be surprised to discover that it is strategic nuclear defense, the Vice President's first love, that provides the paradigm for his analysis of ecological issues (pp. 7–8). Our energies, he insists, should be devoted to defusing "strategic" global conflicts, rather than local skirmishes or regional battles (pp. 28–29).

In advancing these arguments, and employing the rhetorical strategies illustrated by the Vavilov passage, the first two-thirds of *Earth in the Balance* makes a powerful case that the earth is indeed in the balance. Though the purpose of this review essay is not to quarrel with that conclusion, I cannot recount Mr. Gore's argument without two serious caveats.

First, the discussion of climate change, while lucid, is hardly balanced. Vice President Gore admits there are disagreements among reasonable scientists and economists, but tends to view science (and the world's welfare) through a very narrow lens. The Vice President has given a fair portrayal of the environmentalist position on climate change,[12] but fails to acknowledge that it is far from universally accepted.[13] For example, Mr. Gore showers compliments on Roger Revelle, his Harvard professor, as a man who sensitized him to the importance of climate change, yet he does not relate Revelle's recent opinions on the subject (pp. 4–6). In fact, Revelle's recent view is far more cautious than that of his star pupil: "The scientific base for a greenhouse warming is too uncertain to justify drastic action at this time. There is little risk in delaying policy responses to this century-old problem since there is every expectation that scientific under-standing will be substantially improved within the next decade."[14]

Second, Mr. Gore's discussion of global resource depletion is sim-plistic, for it neglects the essential underlying issue—the vitality of the price mechanism. Questions raised concerning the "sustainability" of the world's current growth path are reminiscent both of Malthusian argu-ments that the world was running out of food,[15] and the more recent panic over energy articulated in the "limits to growth" literature.[16] Malthus and Meadows have thus far been proved wrong, because the price mechanism works adequately in communicating information on scarcity.[17] One of course may argue that markets do not work so well when particular goods and services are not priced directly in the marketplace. Indeed, this is a frequently used and abused rationale for government regulation of the environment.[18] My point is simply that the vitality of the price mechanism in this context is a question that requires further research. Malthusian despair may be once again premature.

This is not to say, however, that Vice President Gore's entreaties should be ignored. Even if the horrors of global warming and resource depletion are overdrawn, there remains ample reason for alarm. The threat to biodiversity alone may be cause for action.[19] Vice President Gore has made a persuasive argument that the future of the earth lies in the balance. The question is what is to be done.

THE POLICY PRESCRIPTIONS: A REVIEW AND CRITIQUE

The policy recommendations for this book are neatly laid out in the penultimate chapter of the book, entitled "A Global Marshall Plan." There are five key aspects of the plan: (1) to stabilize population; (2) to develop and apply "environmentally appropriate technologies"; (3) to introduce a "new global eco-nomics"; (4) to develop new international treaties to deal with the myriad environmental problems that are global in scope;

and (5) to educate the world's population about global environmental issues (pp. 305–306).

The First Pillar of the Marshall Plan: Population Stabilization

One can certainly imagine a situation in which too many people inhabit the earth and impose sufficient strain on the earth's resources that civilization as we know it comes to a screeching halt. Vice President Gore traces the exponential rise in population over the last few thousand years, noting that up until the time of Caesar there were fewer than one quarter of a billion people on the planet (pp. 30–31). By 1945 there were about 2 billion people. Today there are 5.5 billion and by about 2030, the population is expected to be around 9 billion (p. 31). He believes that we must stop the growth in population as a way of arresting the earth's environmental decline.

An economic argument frequently offered to support Mr. Gore's position asserts that, at some point, adding additional people to the earth is likely to result in a net drain on accumulated wealth.[20] More specifically, if the focus is on environmental and natural resource wealth, the notion is that at some point an additional person will contribute to a net decrease in these resources, thus possibly limiting opportunities for future generations. It may make sense to think about an appropriate "scale" for human activity, which would include a measure for the appropriate size of the population.[21] This measure would depend on a number of things, including technology and social, political, and economic institutions.[22]

Suppose we take Mr. Gore's thesis at face value for the moment—that population increase will lead to environmental degradation if something is not done. If the planet cannot "sustain" this increase at current levels of consumption, how should the problem be addressed? One approach would regulate population directly, either through a pricing mechanism or a quantity mechanism. A second approach would regulate the "externalities" associated with population growth, such as increased pollution, congestion, and garbage. The two approaches are not mutually exclusive. Moreover, they both may be required to achieve a kind of economic optimality.[23]

Vice President Gore believes that population control policies are needed. He prefers a multifaceted approach that would target illiteracy in developing countries, educate populations on birth control, supply birth control devices to people who want them, and reduce infant mortality (p. 312). The motivation for a program to reduce infant mortality is that it will give parents greater assurance that their children will grow up, and thus decrease the motivation for having large families (p. 311).

As with virtually all of his proposals, Vice President Gore makes no attempt to ascertain whether the plan he endorses represents the best way of achieving his objective. If one were solely interested in slowing the rate of growth in population, there are a variety of programs that can achieve that goal, including a tax on childbearing or more draconian measures, such as a limit on the number of children in conjunction with forced sterilization. One might also consider the introduction of a market in the right to bear children by distributing rights to have children to members of the population and allowing these rights to be traded.[24] There are obvious strengths and weaknesses to these different proposals.

It is premature, in my view, to suggest that population controls are a needed or even a desirable mechanism for reducing the rate of global environmental change. If, for example, the objective is to limit net carbon dioxide emissions in the atmosphere, the most efficient way to accomplish this is through a tax or marketable permit scheme that puts a price on these emissions and provides an equivalent subsidy for activities that increase the storage of carbon dioxide in "sinks," such as trees. Controlling population is an ineffective and inefficient way of addressing most environmental issues involving definable physical or economic objectives.

The linkage between population and various aspects determining the quality of life is complex. It is simplistic to suggest that an increase in population will necessarily result in a decline in environmental quality or an increase in the use of certain resources. Problems need to be clearly specified and key feedbacks need to be identified. For example, as societies become more wealthy (in a material sense), there appears to be a reduction in family size and an improvement in local environmental quality. This may suggest that an alternative strategy for dealing with global environmental issues is to focus on introducing market institutions that generate wealth and also take account of global environmental issues.

There is evidence that in poor countries population growth has an adverse impact on resource degradation. Large families are needed to carry out tasks necessary for subsistence, such as gathering fuelwood, cooking food, and obtaining water.[25] There is a cycle of poverty that is exacerbated by the interplay between resource degradation, population growth, and the need to survive. On the other hand, economic growth can improve local environmental quality. Mikhail Bernstram argues that "as economies grow, discharges to the environment increase rapidly, then decelerate, and eventually decline."[26]

There may be an economic case for regulating population in the interest of preserving or enhancing local or global environmental assets. Vice President Gore does not make that case, however. The first step in making the case for global issues, such as climate change, is to show why it is more efficient to focus on an indirect variable affecting the problem rather than its immediate cause.

There may be other reasons for ensuring access to birth control devices. As a matter of principle, some would argue (myself included) that women and men, particularly in developing countries, should have greater access to birth control technologies that would give them a richer choice over whether or not to have children. Limiting population in some developing countries might also promote political stability. In some instances, it could help slow the rate at which valuable wilderness areas are developed or defiled.[27]

The potential linkage between population and environmental degradation deserves further study. It is often asserted that human beings tend to use environmental resources at a rate that is faster than some "optimal" path.[28] This assertion is based on the view that the environment is a type of commons.[29] The problem with this argument is that the environment is multi-dimensional. Some parts of our environmental wealth may be depleted too rapidly, while others may not be depleted rapidly enough.[30] There is a strong case to be made that global problems are not receiving adequate attention, and Mr. Gore makes it. His discussion provides a useful basis for a research agenda. Such an agenda is likely to show, however, that the linkages between specific environmental problems and policies controlling population are subtle, and in many instances, counterintuitive.[31] Vice President Gore's solutions are not convincing, because they fail to account for this complexity.

The Second Pillar of the Marshall Plan: Appropriate Technologies

Vice President Gore tries to make a strong case for an environmental and economic policy aimed at the rapid development and diffusion of appropriate technologies. He believes that a "Strategic Environmental Initiative" should be launched to deal with global environmental issues (p. 319), which would be patterned after the Strategic Defense Initiative and have similar levels of funding. The Strategic Environmental Initiative would have several components, including: tax incentives and funds for research and development that would encourage new technology and discourage old technology; government purchasing programs to stimulate the introduction of new technologies; a guarantee of large profits for new technology; sophisticated technological assessment procedures for determining the economic and ecological impacts of proposed technologies; training centers for educating an elite group of environmental planners and technicians; export controls on environmentally unfriendly technology; and improvements in laws protecting inventions and ideas (p. 320).

This is an incredible laundry list. It could easily result in central planners selecting environmentally and politically correct products and technologies. It is nothing less than environmental socialism. Imagine bureaucrats trained at our best universities deciding what technologies are environmentally appropriate. These products and technologies would not necessarily have to pass a market test, because Vice President Gore believes that a market with guaranteed profits should be created for them. How sweet it would be if your product were the lucky winner. Environmental bureaucracies around the world would be in seventh heaven. Whether the environment would improve is another matter, since the bureaucratic renaissance could have a numbing impact on the world economy, which in turn would dampen enthusiasm for making the kinds of "investments" Vice President Gore wants for an environmental star wars offensive.

Vice President Gore goes further. He provides a list of recommended technologies and regulations—many of which are right out of the environmental do-gooders' songbook. These include the promotion of cost-effective photovoltaic cells (p. 327) (who could be against cheap solar power—ignoring the environmental impact of the materials used in the production of these cells?); the promotion of wind-generated energy (p. 330); the introduction of building codes that require more energy-efficient materials (p. 333); the required use of energy-efficient light bulbs (p. 332); the introduction of information superhighways (p. 327); the further subsidization of mass transit and the promotion of telecommuting (p. 326); and the advancement of recycling and waste reduction technology (pp. 333–334).

Any or all of these ideas may have merit for achieving a particular social objective, and some of them may even be economical. But the reader is rarely told about either the costs or benefits of these technologies,[32] or the particular reason for choosing a specific policy. Evidently, the Vice President has been through enough hearings that he feels confident picking the winners and losers and creating the necessary markets to prime the proverbial environmental pump.[33] The problem with this kind of policy prescription is that it is devoid of analysis—thus requiring the reader to have a great deal of faith in the judgment of the politician endorsing these ideas.

36

I, for one, am not persuaded. This is an industrial policy without a well-defined mission. Even if one were willing to buy into the Vice President's premise that the environmental apocalypse has arrived, there are likely to be better ways to respond. A carbon tax may be a less onerous method of reducing carbon than assembling a panel of distinguished experts to pick the most promising technologies. Similarly, a gasoline tax may be more effective at reducing gasoline consumption than a hike in the fuel economy standards. The thrust of my argument, developed at greater length later, is that the government should, where possible, set the broad ground rules for environmental protection rather than microman-age individual decisions in the private sector. Vice President Gore some-times seems to recognize this argument, but his foray into the appropriate technology game[34] suggests that he supports a huge expansion in govern-ment bureaucracy and regulation.

Once the appropriate technology is developed, there is the equally important matter of diffusion. There are folks in the real world as well as in bureaucracies, such as the State Department, who believe that technol-ogy should be given away for free. Needless to say, the requirements one places on the providers of technology could have a dramatic impact on their willingness to invest in the development of new technology. Vice President Gore seems to understand the problem of incentives and tech-nology transfer. To solve the problem, he proposes creating a new stream of revenues by using green taxes—a clever application of the new disci-pline of eco-nomics.

The Third Pillar of the Marshall Plan: The Eco-advocate's View of Eco-nomics

Vice President Gore believes that economic decisions "are bringing us steadily closer to the brink of ecological catastrophe" (p. 85). He correctly identifies two root causes of the problem: national income statistics that do not adequately reflect environmental changes and misguided govern-ment policies that encourage the over-exploitation of natural and environ-mental resources.

Accounting Frameworks for a Sustainable World

Economists generally agree that national income statistics, such as Gross National Product (GNP), do not adequately account for environmental benefits.[35] They differ, however, on how best to remedy this defect. Moreover, it is unclear whether the inclusion of environmental resource costs and benefits will have a large or small impact on output measures.

37

Vice President Gore obviously believes the effect will be large because "for all practical purposes, GNP treats the rapid and reckless destruction of the environment as a good thing."[36] He believes that "to accomplish the transition to a new economics of sustainability, we must begin to quantify the effects of our decisions on the future generations who will live with them" (p. 339).

Including estimates of environmental degradation and resource use in national income accounts is not a straightforward exercise, even in theory. Economists begin by defining a measure of welfare, Net National Product (NNP), which represents the sum of the value of all goods and services the economy produces, net of depreciation. When measured at appropriate (optimal) prices, this measure can be shown to correspond to a measure of welfare that maximizes the present value of consumption over time.[37] Karl-Goran Mäler applies these ideas to the case of environmental resources.[38] He argues that NNP needs to be adjusted by deducting environmental damages and adding the value of net changes in the environmental resource base as well as other resources.[39] At the same time, he suggests that defensive expenditures to avoid pollution, such as the cost of doing laundry more frequently, should be included. Interestingly, Mäler also finds that wages paid in producing goods should *not* be included as part of the net national product since, at the margin, workers are indifferent as between receiving an extra hour's wages or taking that time off, in which case they would not be contributing to the NNP.[40]

The formulation suggested by Mäler is sensible from a theoretical perspective, but quite complicated. It would require fundamental changes in the statistics currently used to describe economic activity. Most decision makers look at GNP as a measure of economic performance.[41] The measure suggested by Mäler corresponds to a highly stylized version of NNP. Thus, assuming the concept could be implemented, decision makers would need to be reeducated on the relevance of the measure.[42]

The implementation of an elegant version of NNP that includes environmental and resource degradation creates profound measurement problems. Mäler's framework would require that NNP be calculated at optimal prices, that the marginal value of environmental resources in consumption and production be estimated, and that the optimal levels of consumption of all resources be estimated. The algorithm for implementing this idea would involve three basic steps. First, "correct" prices and marginal valuations in a world with no market failures would need to be defined. Second, net national product would be calculated along an optimal path. Third, net national product would be recalculated along the path currently traveled at the optimal prices. This is a bit much to swallow, even for an economist.

Two fundamental problems arise from this approach. First, the equilibrium associated with optimal prices may not be attainable. That is, there may not be political institutions in the real world that allow such an equilibrium to be attained. Even if such an equilibrium were attainable, a second problem is that a move to that equilibrium may not be desirable. For example, the amount of lobbying activity might differ under the new and old equilibria.[43] These costs are routinely ignored in economic analyses of income accounts, but they are quite important. Suppose it was found that environmental policies led to a 5 percent shortfall in output or welfare relative to some "optimal" policy. Would it then be desirable to pursue the optimal policy, even in the narrow sense of increasing output or welfare? The answer depends on the costs of transition and the costs of maintaining the new equilibrium.

This concern is more than a quibble, particularly in the case of developing economies where the issue of including environmental impacts in national income accounting has been most extensively studied.[44] What should the political baseline be? Should it be a stable political structure, which yields a stable investment climate along with competitive markets? If so, are we not assuming away some of the most fundamental problems faced by developing countries?[45] There are no simple answers to these questions. They involve fundamental choices about the theoretical baseline from which to measure changes in output or welfare.

In making comparisons, we should restrict our attention to the range of feasible alternatives, rather than comparing the status quo with Nirvana. Many theoretical economists argue that a price vector be used that corresponds to the case of perfectly competitive markets. An alternative would be to identify those aspects of the economy subject to the policy-maker's control and compare the actual policy with the optimum that could be achieved subject to the constraints imposed on the policy-maker.[46]

The preceding critique highlights how little we, as economists, know about proper accounting when we move away from the theoretical ideal of perfectly competitive markets to the realities introduced in a real world in which politics is central. The problems are exacerbated by resources that are not priced adequately in markets, which is the typical case for environmental resources, and is sometimes the case for other natural resources, such as energy.

There have been two basic approaches for implementing environmental accounting. One, used by Robert Repetto, is to adjust gross domestic product for depreciation of natural resources.[47] This adjusted measure reduces gross domestic product by about 6 percent in Costa Rica,[48] 9 percent in Indonesia,[49] and 4 percent in the Philippines.[50] The clear implication is that these countries are consuming their natural resource base at an alarming rate and are not on sustainable growth paths.

Shantayanan Devarajan and Robert Weiner note two problems with this kind of analysis. First, GNP and GDP measures do not include depreciation, so it is arbitrary to include depreciation of one set of resources, but not others, such as machinery.[51] Second, the depreciation measure, which is equal to the difference between the price of the resource and its production cost, is only valid when the resource is being used optimally, but this is frequently not the case for environmental and natural resources. These authors suggest an alternative approach, which adjusts GNP for over- or under-exploitation of a resource.[52] Applying this framework to Mali and Thailand, they find that traditional measures overstate gross domestic product between 0.3 percent and 2 percent, which is significant, but not necessarily alarming.[53]

This cursory review of the issues involved in accounting for changes in the environment suggests that it is much more easily said than done. While there is some convergence among economic theorists about how to measure things, these techniques tend to work in a world in which human beings do not exist. Actual applications of these theories, estimating the adverse impacts of particular resource policies in specific countries, have serious deficiencies when measured against the theoretical constructs. Moreover, to my knowledge, no serious empirical work has been done regarding some of the critical challenges posed by the fact that it will be costly to change resource management policies in the ways Vice President Gore might desire.

Just because we are low on the learning curve does not mean that we should not explore this issue, however. Vice President Gore is correct in calling for rethinking. Research funds should be provided to explore how national income accounts could be constructed and implemented. In some cases, I suspect, we will find that environmental and natural resources are being exploited in ways that mortgage the future, particularly in developing countries and highly centralized economies. In the developed countries, we may find the opposite; that is, some of our environmental resources may be underutilized, in a narrow economic sense. In sum, the claim that conventional national income accounting overstates the health of an economy, because it fails to account for environmental impacts adequately, is not warranted at this time.

Any measures of income and wealth are likely to be imperfect. The analysis by Mäler suggests that different measures may need to be tailored for different purposes.[54] For example, traditional GNP may be useful as a measure of how people think they are doing, but more refined measures, which include the costs of using resources and environmental services, may be more useful for describing the actual state of the economy. I use "may" because proposed conceptual improvements will not necessarily result in actual improvements, given the enormous measurement problems. This will depend on how the ideas are implemented. Moreover, a trade-off between analytic rigor and ease of estimation is common.[55]

Given the difficulty in constructing conceptually attractive and easily implemented measures of output and welfare, one should consider whether introducing a new set of national income statistics is likely to be worthwhile. The primary value to be derived from changes in national income statistics should be their impact on private and public decision making. I conjecture that a change in standard accounting procedures could have an impact on international lending institutions, but is unlikely to have a significant impact on politicians in the short term. Only if this new information serves to mobilize interest groups in a way that affects voters or the existing power structure will such measures have a pronounced impact. Politicians have little reason to change their behavior in response to new ways of looking at the world unless they are pressured.[56]

Policy Measures for a Sustainable World

The second thrust of Vice President Gore's eco-nomic strategy is to introduce a variety of measures that induce people and businesses to take better account of the impact of their decisions on the environment. The recommendations include: eliminating subsidies for environmentally destructive activities (p. 346), introducing economic incentive-based instruments for environmental protection (pp. 345–346), extracting additional information from companies on their pollution (p. 346), helping companies evaluate the costs and benefits of environmental efficiency, developing government standards for green labels (p. 341), introducing environmental standards in trade negotiations (pp. 346–347), incorporating environmental concerns in international lending activities (p. 346), and extending the antitrust laws (pp. 342–343).

The elimination of subsidies that encourage over-exploitation of resources is a good idea. For example, why should the general public be asked to pay for roads that directly benefit only logging companies (p. 194)? The logging companies should pay. Introducing economic incentive-based approaches is also a good idea; examples include debt-for-nature swaps and the use of marketable permits to reduce acid deposition.

41

When using economic incentives, it is important to select problems that merit attention.[57] For example, Vice President Gore argues that nations should adopt a marketable emission credit approach for limiting carbon dioxide emissions (pp. 317–337). The desirability of such an approach depends in part on the damages one believes are likely to be associated with this greenhouse gas, a point on which there is a great deal of disagreement.[58]

Providing additional information on pollution activities sounds good in theory. But the benefits of providing new information on emissions should be weighed against the cost of imposing additional paperwork requirements on businesses, which can be substantial.[59] In addition, the quality of the information provided may be subject to question. The United States has imposed substantial requirements on individual firms to report their emissions.[60] There is anecdotal evidence suggesting that some firms have responded to this information by reviewing their activities and cutting their emissions.[61]

Additional information may also tilt the balance toward some groups in the environmental community who desire to play a greater role in the day-to-day operations of businesses. There is a move afoot to place environmentalists on the boards of major corporations.[62] If environmentalists are successful in intervening in day-to-day operations of businesses, this is likely to have a deleterious impact on economic activity.[63]

The government should also actively promote environmental efficiency, according to Vice President Gore. He would like to see the government help private companies assess the costs and benefits of environmental efficiency. Such efforts would presumably build on recent efforts by the Environmental Protection Agency to promote energy efficiency and voluntary reductions of toxic pollution. The basic problem with this approach is that it ignores the fact that the private sector is likely to be able to do private cost/benefit calculations far better than government bureaucrats, who are rarely asked to pass a market test to ensure their survival. Instead, government bureaucracies should provide easy access to information on emerging technologies, which may be costly for private firms to obtain. Even here, however, such information may be provided more effectively by private firms.[64]

The notion of having the government set standards for green labels is appealing. After all, consumers would like to have confidence that the products they are purchasing are environmentally friendly. Unfortunately, this standard is often very difficult to set, as the debate between disposable and cloth diapers demonstrates.[65] The government would be well-advised to stay out of the business of making such difficult decisions.

42

If it feels the need to provide standards, it should provide broad guidelines concerning the kinds of information that should be used in making claims about products. We simply do not know enough, and may never know enough, for the government to prescribe detailed labeling standards for environmentally correct products. This, of course, will not stop government from engaging in this activity because there will be pressure from all sides to do so.[66]

Environmental standards are becoming increasingly important in trade negotiations. Vice President Gore says that environmental policies should be considered when the United States is exploring liberalizing trade with a country, and that standards of environmental responsibility should be defined. Where there are global externalities, such as depletion of the ozone layer, I would agree. When countries have primarily local pollution problems, they should be allowed to decide on an appropriate trade-off between the provision of environmental amenities and other goods. Vice President Gore singles out weak enforcement of environmental laws as a potential unfair trading practice. The economic case for limiting trade in this way is weak. Both countries are likely to be better off with trade, even if one has different environmental policies than the other. Moreover, if per capita income in developing countries rises, the residents of these countries are likely to increase their demand for improving the local environment because they will have more discretionary income. The case for American paternalism is not overwhelming in light of these market dynamics.[67]

International lending institutions can play an important role in affecting the environmental policy in developing countries. It is important for these lending institutions to consider environmental impacts when making their lending decisions. While the World Bank has done much good work on the general subject of the environment, it is unclear at this point whether this work is being translated into substantive changes in the way it finances projects.

A final approach that Vice President Gore suggests is to factor in environmental concerns in decisions regarding antitrust law. He uses as an example a paper firm that opposes recycling because of extensive forest holdings and a chemical company that owns a seed company, but will not develop seeds that do not use fertilizers produced by the company (p. 343). In both cases, if the industries were competitive, other firms could presumably develop the kinds of products that are environmentally friendly, such as recycled paper and new strains of seeds that require fewer pesticides. Problems may arise when there is market power, but these problems are no different qualitatively than standard problems encountered in

43

antitrust. Thus, if antitrust laws can satisfactorily address other forms of market power, they should handle the kinds of examples that Vice President Gore raises. And if they don't, then they should be modified on general principle, and not as a result of environmental policy.

Just as James March developed the garbage can theory of organizations,[68] Vice President Gore has developed the "kitchen sink" theory of environmental policy design: Use everything you've got in attacking the "problem" and hope for the best. It is an approach that is consistent with the views articulated by many environmental groups who fail to consider carefully how their proposed policies are likely to interact with each other to impact the public. To an economist, this is downright frightening. While there are undoubtedly many good proposals in Mr. Gore's environmental program, he has made no attempt to separate the wheat from the chaff, leaving the reader with no guide as to how to assess the priorities of these prescriptions.

There are signs of hope that the Vice President recognizes the critical weaknesses in the kitchen sink approach. For example, in articulating the American role in the grand environmental policy design, he points out the importance of using prices to induce people to account for environmental externalities imposed on others (p. 348). Yet, at the same time he provides a bold new vision allowing the United States to exercise "leadership," he embraces the kitchen sink approach. His proposals include: an environmental security trust fund, which would simultaneously subsidize "good" technology and be revenue neutral;[69] a virgin materials fee on products to encourage recycling (p. 349); governmental programs that purchase environmentally correct products (p. 350); higher mileage standards for cars and trucks sold in the United States (p. 350); more stringent efficiency standards for buildings, appliances, and motors (p. 350); utility rate reform to encourage conservation (pp. 350–351); tree planting programs (p. 351); and the accelerated phase-out of chlorofluorocarbons that deplete stratospheric ozone (p. 351).

Without giving a detailed description of each proposal, suffice it to say that many can do more harm than good. A virgin materials fee on products may or may not promote environmental improvement. Recycling is not a good in and of itself. Moreover, proposals for recycling fees frequently ignore other aspects of recycling, such as the increase in energy use and pollution and the possible decline in product quality or the fact that many government programs already promote recycling. It is not clear that we have the insight to know which products are environmentally correct, and even if we did, it is not clear a government would make judicious use of those insights. Higher mileage standards encourage

44

consumers to defer the purchase of new vehicles and are a very expensive way to reduce petroleum consumption. Utility rate reform can be implemented in ways that promote efficient conservation, but there is a real danger that these programs will be poorly designed.[70] A more reasonable approach is to rationalize pricing in the electric utility industry by increasing competition and defining broad environmental rules with which utilities must comply. More "efficient" standards may be appropriate if energy is underpriced, but why not increase the price of energy if that is the problem? A tree planting program sounds good, but what problems is it likely to solve, and what would the costs be? Moreover, President Bush implemented one, though this does not seem to satisfy Mr. Gore. And finally, there is already an accelerated phase-out of chlorofluorocarbons, so Mr. Gore should be partly satisfied (though I doubt he is).

The Fourth Pillar of the Marshall Plan: Treaties Are the Answer, But What Was the Question?

Dealing with global and regional environmental problems presents difficult political and economic choices. On the one hand, nations would like to preserve their sovereignty and economic way of life. On the other, coordinated action may be required to address the problem successfully. A way out of this dilemma is to develop an international treaty that requires countries to take specified actions. The Montreal Protocol, which reduces the production of ozone-depleting substances, is considered to be an excellent example of such a treaty. Vice President Gore is proposing to expand this model to deal with a host of other global issues, including the limitation of greenhouse gases.

Such treaties have the advantage that they allow for the continuation of the apparent trend toward democracy and capitalism throughout the world. Vice President Gore recognizes the value of both democracy and capitalism as a way of processing information. He also recognizes the severe limitations of statism. In this regard, he seems to be in tune with the great economist, Friedrich von Hayek.[71] There is a fundamental tension that is bound to occur when one admits the existence of a global environmental problem.[72] In order to address such problems, countries will need to cede some authority to a supra-national group for an agreement to be effective. The reason is simple: When each country has an incentive not to enforce an agreement, it is not sufficient to ask each country to enforce the agreement unless there are external monitoring and enforcement mechanisms.

Vice President Gore believes the United States should take a leader-

ship role in developing a new round of environmental treaties. He casti-
gates the Bush administration for allegedly dragging its feet. In my view,
the Bush administration should be praised for taking a politically *coura-
geous* position at the Rio Earth Summit in 1992. While the European
countries were succumbing to pressure from the environmental community on global warming, the Bush administration decided that the environmentalists were too far ahead of the science. The point is simply that
leadership is largely in the eyes of the beholder and should not be
measured by the number of new environmental treaties signed by the
United States.[73]

Before launching headlong into signing a series of treaties to protect
the environment, the United States should carefully examine the politics,
economics and the underlying science that should be the driving force.[74]
Here, it would be wise to note two political realities. First, international
environmental treaties are likely to be adhered to more rigorously in this
country than in most others. Second, the pressure to sign such agreements
is likely to increase over time as the green movement becomes more
popular and effective in pursuing its agenda. Real political leadership in
this area, in my view, lies in turning attention towards those environmental problems that are important and truly global in scope, and crafting
treaties with appropriate incentives to address the issue while rewarding
innovation.

The Fifth Pillar of the Marshall Plan: Education and the Thought Police

There are two basic ideas underlying the Vice President's policy suggestions. First, measures are needed to force people and institutions to be
more sensitive to the impact of their behavior on the environment. In
economic parlance, this means that the cost of pollution must be internal-
ized. All but one of Vice President Gore's proposals, ranging from population controls to carbon taxes to mandated mileage standards for
automobiles, fall into this category. The fifth and final pillar of the Global
Marshall Plan represents the Vice President's second approach to policy,
which involves an attempt to reshape the attitudes of the public through
a massive education campaign.

Mr. Gore wants to design and implement a "worldwide education
program to promote a complete understanding of the crisis" (p. 355). As
part of the program, children would be asked to collect data, which would
allegedly be used to monitor the global environment.[75] The Vice President
believes we need to teach environmental values in the home and in the
46

school so that we can restore the sense of balance between man and nature. With changed values, people would relate to each other differently, and most importantly, they would have a greater reverence for the earth, treating it with respect and placing a higher economic value on preserving the environment. Indeed, the logical outgrowth of this education process is to think about the planet in terms of "spaceship earth," a notion introduced by Kenneth Boulding to illustrate how the economics of a closed system and an open system are fundamentally different.[76]

The author's pitch for education is really about teaching different values. While one can imagine useful educational programs on the environment, one suspects that Vice President Gore's program would resemble religion more than education.[77] The book's energetic tone and partisan fervor have the flavor of a revival meeting rather than a kindergarten. Though the Vice President's passion is to be praised, his approach does not seem particularly receptive to dissenting views.[78]

WHAT HAPPENED TO POLITICS?

Environmental politics is a key to understanding the type of changes that could take place in environmental policy. Regrettably, Vice President Gore's treatment of the subject is superficial and one-sided. It is incumbent upon the reviewer to complete the picture.

Politics in Mr. Gore's Fantasy World

The Vice President presents a radically asymmetrical view of environmental politics. Industry lobbyists are described as "self-interested cynics . . . seeking to cloud the underlying issue of the environment with disinformation."[79] Environmental lobbyists, on the other hand, are portrayed romantically. They appear only as individual men and women of humble backgrounds, members of the environmental "resistance," who have "taken the fight for the environment from the scientific journals and symposia to their own backyards and from there to corporate board rooms and the halls of Congress" (p. 292).

Mr. Gore's presentation of environmental politics is incomplete, and—frankly—wrong. While he correctly points out that industry has an axe to grind, he chooses to ignore strategic manipulation of the process by the environmental community. Not once in the book does the author suggest that environmentalists may use information to their own advantage. On the contrary, he accepts their debating points without question.[80]

47

This skewed picture does not reflect naivete on the part of the author, but cunning. Mr. Gore wishes to avoid offending the many environmentalists who embrace him as a folk hero. He knows that his proposals will appeal to them, not least because they amount to a full-employment act for environmental interest groups. At the same time, Mr. Gore renders his proposals more palatable to the general public by fostering the illusion that they would be painless to implement.[81] Thus, while the Vice President claims to have grown impatient with his tendency to test the "political winds" (p. 15), his unrealistic analysis of the political scene suggests that his weather vane is still working quite well.

Politics in the Real World

In the real world, environmental groups are key players in the formulation of policy. Among mainstream groups, two important trends may be identified: the continued resort to public relations as the weapon of choice, and an increased willingness to use economic instruments.

Green and Yellow Journalism

Environmental groups have become increasingly skilled at manipulating the media. Consider the alar scare,[82] the Love Canal "disaster,"[83] and the Arctic ozone hole.[84] In the first case, apples sprayed with alar were removed from the market despite the fact that there was widespread agreement that the risks were de minimis and the costs of this action were large.[85] In the case of Love Canal, an entire neighborhood was closed down only to find that the risks were overstated—people are now moving back in;[86] in the case of the North American ozone hole, the press reported the preliminary finding with great fanfare, but was characteristically subdued in reporting its retraction.[87]

Global warming is the ultimate example of media alarmism. Aaron Wildavsky has called it "the mother of environmental scares."[88] As Richard Lindzen has observed:

> [C]urbing 'global warming' is identified with saving the whole planet. . . . [T]he threat of warming fits in with a variety of preexisting agendas—some legitimate, some less so: energy efficiency, reduced dependence on Middle Eastern oil, dissatisfaction with industrial society (neopastoralism), international competition, governmental desires for enhanced revenues (carbon taxes), and bureaucratic desires for enhanced power.[89]

Proponents of these various agendas use the issue to justify massive changes in manufacturing, forestry, and agricultural practices, transportation policy, and natural resource use.

Unfortunately, these are not isolated examples,[90] and there is no reason to believe the dynamic will change any time soon. Environmentalists will continue to compete for contributions, the press will continue to need stories, and politicians will continue to recognize the advantages of using the environment as an issue for gaining broad public support.

The Environmentalists and Adam Smith

Many environmental groups are beginning to appreciate that the basic economic system is here to stay, and that price signals are a potent mechanism for changing behavior.[91] In tune with this trend, Mr. Gore advocates the use of incentive-based approaches to environmental control such as marketable permits and taxes. He also argues that we should move away from taxes on labor, and toward taxes on pollution. In this regard, he is likely to be supported by many environmentalists.[92]

But while there is some consensus on the theoretical desirability of using economic instruments, there is less agreement on which problems most urgently require attention.[93] Even within the environmental community, there is widespread disagreement on this question. This disagreement rarely surfaces because environmentalists are unwilling to rank the importance of environmental issues in a public setting. If they did so, they might give the public the dangerous—and correct—impression that some of their issues are less important than others.[94]

The great appeal of economic instruments is that they help delay fundamental disagreements over goals. By lowering the cost of achieving particular objectives, they allow society to enjoy increased environmental protection along with economic growth. Accordingly, we may expect to see greater experimentation with these approaches over the next decade.

This is not to say that the right and the left will coalesce any time soon. Fundamental differences on the desirability of centralized solutions remain. At one extreme lie the "free market" environmentalists, who argue that private property rights in conjunction with the common law can successfully address most problems.[95] At the other extreme lie the deep ecologists and the members of Greenpeace, who reject the ideal of linking improved environmental quality with economic growth. Nothing short of a move back to pre-industrial civilization would satisfy this wing of the movement.[96] Though Vice President Gore flirts with deep ecology, he ultimately recognizes the futility of trying to put the genie back in the bottle (pp. 216–237).

SUSTAINABLE DEVELOPMENT
AS A UNIFYING THEME

Questions involving complex environmental issues such as global warming and the preservation of species diversity cry out for a unifying framework. If I had to attribute an underlying rationale for the prescriptions offered in the book, it would be the promotion of "sustainable development." The problem is that sustainable development is difficult to define and operationalize. After providing several definitions of sustainable development, I compare two approaches to policymaking—one which I call the "policy analytic approach," and a second, embraced by Vice President Gore, which I call the "visionary approach." While the two approaches are markedly different, they are both useful ways of groping toward a sustainable future.

Defining Sustainable Development

The notion of sustainable development was highlighted in the Brundtland Report.[97] Since that time a large literature has emerged on its meaning and application to environmental issues. It is a wonderful, "politically correct" concept, which attracts adherents from across the political spectrum. Part of its political appeal lies in the fact that it can mean different things to different people. Unfortunately, the fuzziness of this concept is precisely what makes it difficult to evaluate rigorously.

There is not to my knowledge a widely accepted definition of sustainable development, yet there is no dearth of candidates.[98] For example, some economists have argued that a sustainable policy is one that maximizes a discounted sum of utilities across generations.[99] Others have suggested that this maximization be modified to include the constraint that each succeeding generation enjoy a higher level of utility than the preceding one.[100] The advantage of the utilitarian framework is that it formally links changes in policies to changes in "well-being" of specific individuals or generations of individuals. The principal drawback from the policy standpoint is the difficulty in measurement. How do we measure whether a modest tax, say on carbon, is likely to improve or hurt future generations? Moreover, much of what people are concerned about here are zero-infinity type dilemmas, in which there is a very low probability of a high consequence event, such as the earth no longer being habitable.[101] This could be accommodated in a utilitarian framework by maximizing some function of a stream of utilities (say the discounted sum), subject to the constraint that the probability of extinguishing life as we know it does not increase with time.[102] Yet, it is by no means obvious that

TOWARD A NEW ENVIRONMENTAL PARADIGM / HAHN

discounting makes sense as a decision rule for dealing with such events, even if we could measure these outcomes.

A second group of definitions focuses on opportunity.[103] Ideally, one might like to afford a larger set of opportunities to future generations than those afforded to us. This may mean greater access to different kinds of experiences, including those involving environmental amenities. Like utility, however, the idea of opportunity presents measurement problems. Moreover, the evolution of technology and use of resources means that some opportunities are likely to be more difficult to experience. For example, it is less likely that people in the twenty-first century will be able to "get away from it all" in a Walden Pond-like setting without fax machines or portable telephones. Thus, the objective may not be attainable.

Related to the notion of opportunity is the preservation of various kinds of capital—most notably natural capital.[104] Typically natural capital is divided between renewable resources, such as forests used for logging, and nonrenewable resources, such as fossil fuels and the ozone layer.[105] Some scholars have argued for the preservation of natural capital, on the theory that it is fundamentally different from man-made capital and the general stock of human knowledge that is transmitted from one generation to the next.[106] I am sympathetic to this argument. Yet, the environment is only one part, albeit an important one, in the formation of values and lifestyles. Economic, political, and social institutions also play prominent roles. These institutions, of course, both shape and are shaped by the environment in which we live.

Narrow and formal interpretations of utility or an ad hoc definition of the resource base are inadequate to define sustainability. Sustainability is about maintaining or enhancing the quality of life for each successive generation while not threatening life as we know it. Quality of life, however, is intrinsically difficult to define as is the threat to life as we know it. Nevertheless, I think the definition underscores several important points. First, the environmental concerns highlighted by Mr. Gore are likely to be only one factor in determining the quality of life and the threat to life as we know it. For example, the threat of nuclear war is a critical issue in assessing the future habitability of the planet. Second, quality of life depends on more than the environment. Economic, political, and social institutions all play a critical role.

This brief review of sustainable development suggests that it is difficult to determine, except in extreme instances, whether a particular set of policies are more or less sustainable than the status quo. The narrower the definition, the easier it is to determine, but the less satisfactory the concept.

Even if we cannot determine in any deep sense whether most policies enhance sustainable development, economics offers two useful insights about the nature of policies that could affect sustainability. The first is that productive investment leads to greater consumption in the future at the expense of less consumption today. Thus, if we believed that the quality of life could decline, we should search for productive investments to improve that quality of life. The second insight is that prices of environmental and natural resources that do not include their external costs, such as the impact of pollution on health, are likely to result in excessive consumption of these resources.[107]

Using Policy Analysis as an Aid to Achieving Sustainable Development

To address the problems that lie ahead, we need to move beyond mere platitudes concerning sustainability and improvements in the quality of life and begin to provide a concrete definition of the problems we wish to solve along with a serious analysis of the kinds of tools we might use. For example, if our major concern were preventing global warming, that would imply a very different strategy than if our major concern were reducing the number of people whose lives are not satisfying (in a material or spiritual sense). Vice President Gore says both of these problems are urgent: the "strategic threat, global warming, is the most dangerous of all" (p. 89); and "the worst of all forms of pollution is wasted lives" (p. 162, emphasis omitted). Elsewhere, Vice President Gore has identified yet a third problem, hazardous waste, as "the most significant environmental health problem of the decade."[108] Even allowing him some leeway for rhetorical flourish, Gore seems oblivious to the necessity of making trade-offs.

Among the most difficult trade-offs that must be made are between today's environmental problems and those of the future. Buying an "insurance" policy, such as a modest carbon tax, may make sense for addressing climate change, depending on your degree of risk aversion and your views on the theory. It makes no sense if the primary concern is with helping the have-nots who are alive today. Even if the concern is with promoting environmental quality, a strong case can be made for implementing policies that alleviate human suffering and promote economic growth. The challenge is to promote such policies in a way that also improves the local environment. Approximately 1.7 billion people lack

52

access to basic sanitation, leading to widespread disease in children and adults.[109] Problems also arise because of lack of clean water. These are basic human problems, and they are also environmental problems.

Vice President Gore does not lose sight of such immediate problems; he simply fails to make the hard choices. Since the hard choices will be made one way or another, it makes sense to develop a strategy for thinking about them. Here, policy analysis and economics provide a useful guide.

Policy analysis, broadly construed, involves two key components— a description of the state of a system of concern to humans, and a theory that defines the relationship between that system's inputs and outputs. For example, if one were concerned about the impacts of the 1990 Clean Air Act Amendments, one would attempt to measure the state of the "system" before and after the law was implemented. The state of the system could be measured in many ways, including direct measures of environmental quality, the number of regulations, the costs of the regulations, and the nature of the regulations. Thus, policy analysis provides a way of summarizing a complicated system using a few key variables that are of interest to the policymaker. It is thus analogous to a standard accounting system that could be used to summarize the health of a business.[110]

First, one needs to define the nature of the problems that need to be examined. For example, one might consider different ways to operationalize notions of sustainability and different objectives for environmental policy.

A second logical step, in the case of sustainability, would be to explore the strengths and weaknesses of various policies in achieving environmental objectives. It might be useful to know, for example, the cost of a policy to stabilize carbon dioxide emission levels at 1990 levels and its likely effect on the global temperature profile. The focus here should be on "policy-relevant" research rather than the pursuit of science to push back the frontiers of knowledge. While I am a great supporter of both endeavors, the United States government does not always organize its research efforts in ways that produce useful and timely policy insights. With the potentially staggering resources we could spend on reducing greenhouse gas emissions, it is important to have a strategy to spend research dollars in ways that will produce useful insights.[111] It is also important to consider policies in light of the political constraints likely to be imposed on policymakers.[112] Developing "optimal" economic approaches may be of little value to policymakers who are constrained by political forces. Finally, the linkages between policies need to be explored

53

more fully, including the linkages between population growth and resource use, and freer trade and the environment.

A pervasive feature of many of the problems in the environmental area is an uncertain relationship between policies and outcomes. Take, for example, the problem of estimating the impact of a $100/ton carbon tax on climate change. First, one must estimate how the tax is likely to change fuel use patterns in the short and long term. Then, one must estimate how these changes are likely to be translated into changes in temperature. Both of these exercises are subject to great uncertainty. These uncertainties should be analyzed and their significance should be effectively communicated to decision makers.[113]

Since different decision makers will have different criteria for a particular problem, it would be useful to spell out how preferred policies are likely to change with different criteria. For example, suppose three decision makers are assigned the task of choosing a carbon tax. The first is risk-neutral, the second is risk-averse, and the third is particularly concerned with preventing an environmental catastrophe. Suppose further that these three decision makers are in agreement on the distribution of benefits and costs from various tax levels in terms of their effect on the environment and the economy. The risk-neutral decision maker might select a modest tax or no tax, the risk-averse decision maker would select a higher tax, and the decision maker concerned about avoiding the unlikely event of a catastrophe might select a still higher tax.[114]

After linking objectives and outcomes for various problems, one has to prioritize problems and decide how to proceed. While this prioritization is, of necessity, highly subjective, it can be aided by analysis. Moreover, this prioritization could take place using a number of criteria, which may or may not relate to economic efficiency.

This kind of analytical process is likely to yield several insights that are conveniently glossed over in Vice President Gore's presentation. First, and most important, the Vice President's policy prescriptions are likely to be quite expensive—I suspect they would cost hundreds of billions of dollars annually for the United States alone.[115] Second, while a few of his suggestions may enhance our international competitiveness (read our standard of living), the lion's share of his policies are likely to reduce the material quality of life that most Americans enjoy, at least in the short term.[116] Third, the appropriate or preferred strategy for addressing a particular issue will depend on a variety of factors. Only in rare instances is a kitchen sink approach justified when one considers the costs.

Policy analysis has room for a wide range of perspectives. It includes conventional cost–benefit analysis as practiced by economists, but it is far broader. Thus, people not comfortable with the objectives specified in conventional economic analysis can substitute their desired objectives. Moreover, if we place suitable constraints on the problem, we can include issues related to political feasibility in policy analysis. For example, we could design an energy tax in such a way as to ensure that producers and/or specific consumer groups are likely to be better off than they are now. In the age of personal computers, quantitative policy analysis offers a useful guide for developing and evaluating policies to promote sustainable development.

The Visionary Approach to Sustainable Development

Vice President Gore's visionary approach to sustainable development is a curious blend of religion, revolutionary zeal, and homespun economics. In this section I critically examine four defining characteristics of this visionary approach: (1) its religious dimension; (2) its assumption that attitudes are malleable; (3) its reliance upon big government; and (4) its ambivalent attitude toward economics.

Religious Aspects

Visionary approaches are almost of necessity religious in nature.[117] Vice President Gore's religious zeal emerges most clearly when he depicts environmental politics as an epic battle between good and evil. There is something disturbing about the author's use of military imagery in this context. Mr. Gore's green activists are "comrades in arms"—and like the Marxists before them, they are fighting the excesses of capitalism (p. 293). One fears that, also like the Marxists before them, they will demonstrate little tolerance for opposing views.

Faint hints of such intolerance may be detected in the book. Vice President Gore occasionally shows a lack of respect for people who do not share his perspective, or conclusions. For example, he implies that skeptics on global warming are less than "reputable" (p. 89). Yet, as several scientists have noted, the debate is far from settled.[118] Ironically, while Vice President Gore expresses disdain for the skeptics on global warming, he praises one of the greatest skeptics of all time—Galileo—for daring to change our views of the earth's relation to the universe (p. 40).

There are two key dangers in Mr Gore's absolutism. First, it may foster among his followers a culture of intolerance, characterized by a distorted view of reality. Second, it may dampen the enthusiasm of serious social scientists and natural scientists to engage in the environmental

55

policy debate, where their input could be critical to designing policies that help promote sustainable development.

The Difficulty in Reshaping Attitudes

Vice President Gore wants to ameliorate environmental policy by prompting changes in public attitudes. "[A]s changes in our thinking about the environment take place, we can expand the range of what is politically imaginable" (p. 178). In a sense, he is correct—changes in paradigms can have a dramatic impact on policies and human behavior. And as Keynes pointed out, we are often prisoners of the ideas of defunct academicians.[119]

Unfortunately, this part of the visionary approach is based on a false view of human nature. It is likely to fail because people tend to resist fundamental change, especially when it conflicts with their narrow self-interest. Moreover, the Vice President's recipe for changing the views of key decision makers does not adequately reflect political realities.

Vice President Gore believes that a main source of our crisis can be traced back to the decision makers. "The problem is not so much one of policy failures: much more worrisome are the failures of candor, evasions of responsibility, and timidity of vision that characterize too many of us in government" (p. 11). The solution, Mr. Gore believes, lies in dramatically changing attitudes "to remove constant pressures exerted by population growth, greed, short-term thinking and misguided development" (p. 125).

The problem is that politicians have little incentive to change their behavior. Mr. Gore disarmingly notes the irony in his own behavior. For example, he uses chlorofluorocarbons in his automobile "on the way to a speech about why they should be banned" (p. 15). While Senator, Mr. Gore also failed to vote his environmental conscience on many issues where his interest in reelection evidently dominated. He has voted to continue sugar subsidies, and to fund construction of the Clinch River Breeder Reactor and the Tellico Dam—two projects that happen to be located in Tennessee, but were opposed by environmentalists.[120] Apparently, Mr. Gore's personal and political actions have not yet caught up with his bold vision.

None of these decisions should surprise us. Vice President Gore is a politician and a human being. As such, he is largely governed by self-interest. Unfortunately, Vice President Gore seems to have forgotten this in painting his picture. He envisions a wonderful public policy heaven, but fails to explain why it will serve the interests of powerful groups (other than environmentalists) to embrace his vision. He may have succumbed to a sort of *Field of Dreams* logic—if you build it, they will come—but this logic works better in Hollywood than in the real world.

Using Government to Lead the Way

Vice President Gore exhibits some ambivalence about the role of government in addressing environmental problems. At one level, he recognizes the potential excesses associated with government and government intervention. He realizes that nations are unlikely to give up their sovereignty (p. 301). He also notes that "world government" is definitely not the solution (p. 302). Moreover, he recognizes that some government policies have been disastrous for the environment, noting:

> The most serious example of environmental degradation in the world today are tragedies that were created or actively encouraged by governments—usually in pursuit of some notion that a dramatic reordering of the material world would enhance the greater good. And it is no accident that the very worst environmental tragedies were created by communist governments, in which the power of the state completely overwhelms the capabilities of the individual steward. Chernobyl, the Aral Sea, the Yangtze River, the "black town" of Copsa Mica in Romania—these and many other disasters testify to the severe environmental threats posed by statist governments. (pp. 247–248)

Despite this sensitivity to the excesses of government, Vice President Gore seems not to care that his proposals would lead to tremendous growth in bureaucracy throughout the world. Organizing a worldwide education network, passing regulations on appropriate labeling, deciding which products the government can purchase, and implementing many new taxes, including a carbon tax, are nontrivial exercises that would expand bureaucracy significantly.

The Vice President's position can be explained only by a naively optimistic view of bureaucracies and their power to improve conditions.[121] Anyone who has dealt with the Environmental Protection Agency knows that bureaucracies have strong vested interests in maintaining the status quo and little incentive to promote the kind of cost-effective innovation needed to improve living standards.[122] Bureaucrats rarely get credit for approving process or product innovations that succeed; but they can get blamed for approving a gadget or process that fails. Thus, regulators frequently have an incentive to stifle innovation rather than promote it.[123]

The Love-Hate Affair with Economics

Vice President Gore may like living things, but he has very little patience with conventional economics or economists. He derides the conclusion from the 1989 *Economic Report of the President*,[124] assembled by the Council of Economic Advisers, that "there is no justification for imposing major costs on the economy in order to slow the growth of greenhouse gas emissions" (p. 195). The statement undoubtedly rested on a comparison of subjective estimates of the benefits and costs of taking major action now to reduce greenhouse gas emissions versus the benefits and costs of waiting. Waiting has several drawbacks, as Vice President Gore is quick to point out, but it also has several advantages.[125]

The Vice President's approach talks about using economics, but remains weak on the details. This reflects, in part, his propensity for big-picture thinking. Unfortunately, the devil often lurks in the details. Economics, science, engineering, and law provide useful tools and frameworks for understanding how those details interact.

The Vice President's tin ear for economics is evidenced by his position on the issue of "dead zones." He expresses outrage that companies wish to buy property around their manufacturing plants to reduce public exposure to extremely low levels of airborne toxic emissions. Vice President Gore asserts that such firms would be creating "dead zones"; yet the data strongly suggest that the health benefits of reducing air toxics emissions are minuscule, while the costs are in the billions of dollars annually.[126]

When the Vice President embraces different solutions, he fails to note potential interactions associated with different policies. For example, he overlooks the possibility that raising fuel economy standards would increase pollution by providing an incentive for people to extend the life of their old clunkers before purchasing a new, cleaner vehicle. A second example relates to his prescriptions for controlling carbon dioxide, a key greenhouse gas. Vice President Gore advocates both a domestic tax to raise money for his trust fund and an international marketable permit system. He fails to recognize that these two instruments are really aimed at doing the same job within the United States, since they both place an explicit price on limiting the amount of carbon dioxide going into the atmosphere.[127]

Vice President Gore exhibits a love–hate relationship with economics. While he pays lip service to cost–benefit analysis, he is disdainful of approaches taken by conventional microeconomists. Mr. Gore notes that there is no better method of reducing pollution "than finding ways to put a price on the environmental consequences of our choices, a price that would be reflected in the marketplace" (p. 348). He exhorts the nation to harness "the power of market forces to help save the global environment" (p. 346). And he expresses an interest in identifying "the most effective and least costly solutions [to the] crisis."[128] These sentiments are music to an economist's ears.

Unfortunately, the author never defines the "crisis" very carefully. Absent a clear definition of the problem, it is difficult to evaluate the proposed policy prescriptions. In any case, he makes no attempt to identify the costs or benefits of these prescriptions. The reader is left with a partial vision and a full bag of policy tools. But what would happen if these tools were actually used? Are we to assume that it would be all gain and no pain on the part of the citizenry?

Vice President Gore views economics as a method for selecting the best means to an end. This is a perfectly valid use of economics. The problem the economist confronts in implementing Mr. Gore's vision is that it is difficult to talk about appropriate means until the ends are more clearly specified. Mr. Gore's failure to make the hard calls on prioritizing problems, even within the environmental arena, makes it virtually impossible to implement his vision.

The Two Approaches: Complements or Substitutes?

I believe a constructive alternative vision can be offered. It is an inclusive vision, acknowledging a wide range of perspectives on complex environmental issues. It is a synthetic vision, melding the strengths of the visionary and the policy analytic approaches. Finally, it is a pragmatic vision, which would portray politics realistically when designing policies to enhance our quality of life.

In a sense, the policy analytic approach and the visionary approach can be viewed as complements. The visionary approach aims primarily to help reshape attitudes toward saving the earth. The policy analytic approach aims primarily to highlight the ramifications of achieving a state closer to Nirvana, however defined. The visionary approach may be best viewed as a way to stimulate discussion by playing on our emotions. The policy analytic paradigm can help ground that discussion in reality. In practice, both may be needed to resolve successfully the major challenges that confront humanity.

While the two approaches can complement each other, they differ in important respects. The policy analytic approach is likely to make concepts of sustainability lose much of their luster. Indeed, I suspect that the policy analytic approach will eventually reduce sustainability to a matter of trying to internalize environmental costs and then hoping for the best. That is, we will never be able to be sure that we are on a sustainable path unless the definition or the analysis trivializes the problem. The policy analytic approach makes a serious attempt to link inputs to outputs, an exercise that is sorely lacking in the Vice President's vision. It does not solve the world's problems, but it does help provide a roadmap for concerned decision makers.

Both the policy analytic approach and the visionary approach are highly abstract. They represent different perspectives on the universe— one in which analysis guides the making of decisions which help identify further problems for analysis; and a second, in which the time for analysis has come and gone, and the time for action is long overdue. Both abstractions are useful, but limited.

To someone who believes "we already know more than enough" (p. 37) to act on a variety of global environmental issues, including climate change, the hard-headed criticism contained in this review essay must be frustrating. But, and this is key in my opinion, such views should not be omitted from the discussion, as I fear they would be in the massive educational campaign Mr. Gore envisions. Through a judicious dose of analysis combined with common sense, we may have the good fortune to continue enjoying higher standards of living in successive generations, even as we assume the mantle of environmental stewardship.

CONCLUSION

Perhaps I have been unfair in my evaluation of this book. Rachel Carson's *Silent Spring* would not have received good grades as an exercise in policy analysis; yet, it would receive a high mark for consciousness raising. So, too, should *Earth in the Balance*. As a wake-up call for environmental activists, this book makes for great reading. And perhaps this is Vice President Gore's mission. As a politician and leader, part of his job is to help provide vision and shape our preferences. But the Vice President goes further. He defines a Global Marshall Plan that would make the original Marshall Plan pale by comparison.

The author sees the environment in black and white terms. For Mr. Gore, "you are either on the bus or you are off the bus."[129] "Adopting a central organizing principle . . . means embarking on an all-out effort to use every policy and program, every law and institution, every treaty and alliance . . . to halt the destruction of the environment and to preserve and nurture our ecological system" (p. 274). Vice President Gore derides people who do not share his perspective, most notably mainstream econo-mists, scientists who beg to differ with his conclusions, and people who would be hurt by his proposed policies. There is something troubling to me as a policy analyst about all this religious fervor. Most troubling is the apparent unwillingness to consider opposing points of view. This tactic works well in spewing forth sound bites on television. It works less well in devising a grand plan to save the world.

Politicians who seek power can have both visions and delusions; it is the task of the public to tell one from the other. To change the world, Mr. Gore must first convince us that his belief system is more vision than delusion. This book represents the first critical step in that process. In my view, we are unlikely to be persuaded, for several reasons. First and foremost, whether or not the fate of the earth lies in the balance, human nature is not going to change. Consciousness raising was an unmitigated disaster in the communist "experiment" over the last century, and it will continue to fail, at least until genes can be manipulated to change human nature. Second, the changes Mr. Gore is talking about are hardly modest, and thus are likely to meet fierce political resistance. Third, his evidence is vastly overstated. Humanity would hopefully require more evidence before agreeing to such massive changes.

My principal criticism of this book is that it is long on rhetoric and short on policy analysis. It is true there are encouraging signs that politi-cians are learning to consider new ideas. But in the end Mr. Gore's policy prescriptions do not fit neatly within the economist's framework. Pricing and markets are the exception rather than the rule in the Global Marshall Plan.

So if you agree that we are falling off a cliff, this book is the perfect manifesto. But even if you disagree, this book has much to offer. The reality is that we face serious environmental problems at the local, re-gional, and global levels. The reality is that we are experimenting with our planet on a massive scale.[130] We do not know very much about what we are doing to the planet; and while so far we seem to have "muddled through,"[131] we are not infallible. Mr. Gore sensitizes us to our fallibility.

Vice President Gore correctly points out that we need "a searching reexamination of the ways in which political motives and government policies have helped to create the crisis and now frustrate the solutions we need" (p. 11). At present, we have a limited understanding of how different interest groups—including environmentalists, business, politi-cians, and bureaucrats—affect the evolution of environmental policy. Research that sheds greater light on these issues would be most useful. I would hope the Vice President promotes public support for such research.

PART I: CIVILIZATION IN THE BALANCE

It is essential that we understand the forces that shape the status quo to determine the ideas that will be needed to move us in a new direction.

The central theme of this book is that we need a new perspective—particularly in thinking about our relationship to the earth. Mr. Gore uses many examples to demonstrate the importance of perspective, but the one that I found most compelling was the story about artists in ancient Peru who drew figures on the ground that could be recognized only from the air (p. 43). Looking at things in new ways is one of the trademarks of human intellectual progress.

Over the next century we will be compelled to rethink our relationship to the environment, as well as to one another. The emergence of new technology connects us in ways few could have imagined thirty years ago. The beauty of this book is that it stimulates the reader to take a new perspective. While I do not adhere to Mr. Gore's vision, I do agree that we need to move toward a new paradigm. I hope politicians and scholars seize upon this vision as a starting point for discussion. Who knows? The future of the earth may lie in the balance.

Notes

I would like to thank Marilyn Arnold and Shantayanan Devarajan for their helpful comments and suggestions, and Elizabeth Baldwin for her research support. Financial support was provided, in part, by the National Science Foundation. This review essay represents my views and does not necessarily reflect the views of any individuals or institutions with which I am affiliated.

1. Rachel L. Carson, *Silent Spring* (1961).
2. Albert Gore, Jr., "America is Ready to Be Inspired and Lifted Again," *Wash. Post,* July 17, 1992, at A28 (emphasis added); see also Albert Gore, Jr., *Earth in the Balance: Ecology and the Human Spirit* 269 (1992) [hereinafter cited by page number only] ("[W]e must make the rescue of the environment the central organizing principle for civilization.").
3. Pp. 17, 165, 267.
4. See, for example, the concluding words of the book: "We can believe in th[e] future and work to achieve it and preserve it, or we can whirl blindly on, behaving as if one day there will be no children to inherit our legacy. The choice is ours; the earth is in the balance." P. 368.
5. Some time between 1150 and 1136 B.C., for example, the Hekla 3 volcano in Iceland erupted. Mr. Gore claims that this event may have caused unusually harsh weather in China and Scotland the following winter. Pp. 58-59.
6. For example, Mr. Gore notes that previous climate changes are in the range of 1 to 2 degrees Centigrade, but he believes we are moving toward changes that are 3 to 4 times that amount. P. 73
7. Henry D. Thoreau, "Walden," in *Walden and Other Writings of Henry David Thoreau* 3 (Brooks Atkinson ed., 1965).
8. E. F. Schumacher, *Small is Beautiful: Economics as if People Matter* (1973).
9. P. 31; on the link between Mr. Gore's ideological and psychological growth, see pp. 14, 364.
10. Pp. 2, 4, 15, 16, 38, 153, 288.
11. P. 177; see also Mr. Gore's comparison of environmental indifference to the "moral blindness implicit in racism and anti-Semitism," p. 189.
12. See, e.g., Michael Oppenheimer & Robert H. Boyle, *Dead Heat: The Race Against the Greenhouse Effect* (1990); Stephen H. Schneider, *Global Warming* (1989); Jessica Matthews, "Science, Uncertainty and Common Sense," *Wash. Post,* Nov. 3, 1991, at C7.
13. Richard S. Lindzen, "Global Warming: The Origin and Nature of the Alleged Scientific Consensus," *Regulation,* Spring 1992, at 87, 95.
14. Fred S. Singer, et al., "What to Do About Greenhouse Warming: Look Before You Leap," *Cosmos,* vol. 1, no. 1, at 28 (1991).
15. Thomas R. Malthus, *An Essay on Population* 5-11 (J.M. Dent & Sons 1914) (1798).
16. See, e.g., Donella H. Meadows et al., *The Limits to Growth: A Report for the Club of Rome's Project on the Predicament of Mankind* (1972). For an insightful and amusing account of how the prophets of doom hedge their

bets, see Gregg Easterbrook, "Propheteers: Environmental Problems are Alarming Enough Without the Doomsayers' Exaggerations," *Wash. Monthly*, Nov. 1991, at 43-46.

17. See, e.g., Julian L. Simon, *The Ultimate Resource* 17-22, 90-110 (1981).
18. See, e.g., Charles Wolf Jr., "A Theory of Nonmarket Failure: Framework for Implementation Analysis," 22 *J.L. Econ.* 107 (1979).
19. See generally Edward O. Wilson, *The Diversity of Life* (1992).
20. See *Malthus, supra* note. I purposely leave the definition of wealth vague here. In this context, wealth could be defined narrowly to include material wealth or more broadly to include other components that might affect the quality of life.
21. Herman Daly argues that just as economists think about the optimal scale for a particular industry, they should also think about the optimal scale for all economic activity in relationship to the planet. See Herman E. Daly, "Sustainable Development: From Concept and Theory to Operational Principles," in *Resources, Environment, and Population: Present Knowledge, Future Options* 25, 28-29 (Kingsley Davis & Mikhail S. Bernstram, eds., 1991) [hereinafter *Resources, Environment, and Population*].
22. This measure might differ across societies at a given point in time. For example, in wealthier or less densely populated societies, increases in population might increase the stock of environmental wealth, whereas in poorer societies, increases might lead to greater stress on the resource base.
23. Ronald Lee suggests both sets of policies would be needed to achieve economic optimality in theory; however, he notes that there may be severe technical and political problems in designing and implementing a tax. Ronald D. Lee, "Comment: The Second Tragedy of the Commons," in *Resources, Environment, and Population, supra* note, at 315.
24. Kenneth E. Boulding, *The Meaning of the Twentieth Century*, 135-136 (1964).
25. Partha Dasgupta & Karl-Goran Mäler, "The Environment and Emerging Development Issues" 23 (1990) (unpublished manuscript, on file with the author).
26. Mikhail S. Bernstram, "The Wealth of Nations and the Environment," in *Resources, Environment, and Population, supra* note, at 333. Bernstram does not examine carbon dioxide emissions, but does review data on per capita energy consumption. Bernstram also provides some interesting data comparing energy use and pollution in market and socialist economies. *Id.* at 363-369. The data support the view that socialist economies use more energy per person for a given level of output per person and they also suggest that energy per capita increases and then eventually declines as GNP per capita grows in market economies. Such aggregate analysis masks the importance of particular policies towards energy pricing and pollution control in individual countries. Nonetheless, it strongly suggests that increased energy use is *not* a prerequisite for conventionally defined economic growth.
27. Population growth could also affect the politics between nations. At pre-

sent, roughly 85% of all the world's children live in third world countries. Kingsley Davis, "Population and Resources: Fact and Interpretation," in *Resources, Environment, and Population, supra* note, at 1, 9. In a world that is becoming more interconnected all the time, this percentage is staggering. As this group ages, there may be extreme pressures on developed countries to increase assistance and liberalize immigration policies.

28. See Lee, "Comment: The Second Tragedy of the Commons," in *Resources, Environment, and Population, supra* note, at 320, arguing that we select an environmental standard that is lower for the future than we might like if we could register our true preferences in terms of trading off population and environmental quality. Lee also makes an important argument about the need to tax reproduction in order to have optimal use of environmental and natural resources. In a population that is changing, it is not sufficient simply to charge a price for the resource or limit access through the use of transferable property rights. The problem is that the optimal level of usage of these resources is linked to the number of people who might use the resource. Thus, for example, with more people, the optimal level greenhouse gases could be higher, since the cost of reducing these gases would likely be higher (for a given level of technology). The solution for optimal resource usage is not only to adopt an appropriate allocation mechanism for the resource itself, but also to charge for births an amount that reflects the costs imposed on the society at large. *Id.* at 318. This argument, while theoretically elegant, may be difficult to apply because of difficulties in computing an appropriate birth tax. Moreover, the argument does not consider the linkage between technology and population, which could be positive or negative. The challenge for research is to identify and measure those externalities related to population that are likely to be important.

29. See Garrett Hardin, "The Tragedy of the Commons," 162 *Science* 1243 (1968).

30. Moreover, the politics of environmental decision making is often overlooked. Politics may drive countries or regions to make environmental decisions that result in excessive regulation relative to an economist's notion of optimality. I believe this happened in the initial round of the Montreal Protocol (though subsequent evidence justified a more stringent standard), and in recent acid rain legislation in the United States. I hasten to add that there is a great deal of uncertainty in even estimating the narrow concept of net economic benefits. See, e.g., Robert W. Hahn & John Hird, "The Costs and Benefits of Regulation: Review and Synthesis," 8 *Yale J. Reg.*, 233, 241-243 (1991).

31. The impact of population on resource use will vary as a function of income of the individual, region, and consumption patterns. For example, one fewer human being in a developed country may result in a greater reduction in greenhouse gas emissions than one fewer human being in an undeveloped country. At the same time, one fewer human being in an undeveloped country may have a greater salutary impact on local en-

vironmental quality than one fewer human being in the developed country.

32. But see p. 332 for a brief discussion of the trade-off between capital costs and operating costs in purchasing more energy-efficient light bulbs. My point is not that such purchases might not be economical; in some cases, they very well may be, and some kinds of light bulbs may be good examples. The problem is that there are costs to regulatory programs that require or encourage such technologies, and the costs of these programs need to be weighed carefully against the benefits. Blanket mandates are not likely to be effective or efficient. In many cases, the proposed cure may be worse than the disease. See, e.g., Bruce A. Ackerman & William T. Hassler, *Clean Coal/Dirty Air* (1981).

33. See, e.g., pp. 320-32 (singling out a number of emerging technologies for praise).

34. As Vice President Elect, Mr. Gore had already shown a propensity to get involved in the appropriate technology debate. Recently he decided to try to block the siting of a hazardous waste incinerator in Ohio. This plant would have provided jobs in an economically depressed area while applying state-of-the-art technology for reducing hazardous wastes. Despite the fact that known health risks were de minimis, Mr. Gore believed that blocking the siting of this facility was desirable. While such stands may ingratiate the Vice President with environmental groups such as Greenpeace, they make one question his commitment to preserving environmental quality while promoting jobs and economic growth. See, e.g., "Environmental Preview?," *Wall St. J.*, Dec. 30, 1992, at 6; "Gore on a Von Roll," *Wall St. J.*, Jan. 8, 1993, at A14.

35. See, e.g., Robert Repetto et al., *Wasting Assets: Natural Resources in the National Income Accounts* (1989); Shantayanan Devarajan & Robert J. Weiner, "Natural Resource Depletion and National Income Accounting" (May 1992) (unpublished manuscript, on file with the author).

36. P. 185. Vice President Gore quotes Herman Daly, one of the more thoughtful critics of our current resource policy, as saying that "[t]here is something fundamentally wrong in treating the earth as if it were a business in liquidation." P. 191.

37. See Martin Weitzman, "On the Welfare Significance of National Product in a Dynamic Economy," 90 *Q.J. Econ.* 156 (1976) (showing perpetual stream of income equal to net national product equals present value of stream maximizing consumption).

38. Karl-Goran Mäler, "National Accounts and Environmental Resources," 1 *Envtl. & Resource Econ.* 1 (1991).

39. Id.

40. Id. at 6.

41. Devarajan & Weiner, *supra* note, at 4.

42. According to Mäler, implementation is no small feat. For a formal statement of the rules for constructing a theoretically sound measure, see Mäler, *supra* note, at 6–7. In the case of uncertainty (i.e., the real world), the analyst must also distinguish anticipated from unanticipated

changes in prices, resource levels, and technologies, *id.* at 13, a daunting task that is beyond most mortals I know.

43. Consider the case of industry structure changes, such as the deregulation of airlines. There is no reason to expect the same amount of lobbying before and after regulation. It is sometimes asserted that the amount of lobbying or "rent-seeking" activity will decrease as markets become more competitive. This is an empirical question. See Robert W. Hahn & John A. Hird, "Letter to the Editor: Computing the Costs of Regulation," *Regulation*, Fall 1991, at 6. In contrast, transition costs in moving from one equilibrium to another are positive and quite real, as is clear from observing the wrenching transition the citizenry in Eastern Europe and the former Soviet Union are now encountering.

44. See, e.g., *Repetto, supra* note; Devarajan & Weiner, *supra* note.

45. For an insightful analysis of the instability issue, see Jose Edgardo Campos, The Political Economy of the Rent-Seeking Society Revisited: Cronyism, Political Instability and Development (Sept. 1991) (unpublished manuscript, on file with the author) (arguing that instability may exist in dynamic equilibrium, so that rent-seeking societies may be inherently unstable).

   Instability may mean that entrepreneurs use a higher discount rate, thus squeezing out investment that would have occurred in a more stable environment. Moreover, they may choose to use wasteful production technologies in order to get the most out of their resource in the limited time frame. In such cases, the best environmental and resource policy would provide a different institutional structure for defining and trading property rights. How one moves to that institutional structure in the real world is a critical issue about which little is known.

46. It would be useful to explore the difference between first-best estimates of welfare or output, constrained estimates that reflect political considerations, and where we are now. The estimates are likely to be highly dependent on the welfare or output measure used. For example, one could estimate how output or economic efficiency would change with or without OPEC influencing the price of oil.

47. Gross national product for a country "is defined as the market value of all goods and services produced during a particular year" by residents of that country, whether produced outside the country or inside the country. Gross domestic product for a country is the "value of output produced by people, government, and firms in that country," including citizens of that country and foreign citizens. See *Economic Report of the President* 246 (1992).

48. Raul Solorzano et al., World Resources Inst., *Accounts Overdue: Natural Resource Depreciation in Costa Rica* 7 (1991) (taking average of ratio of natural resource depreciation to gross domestic product from 1970 to 1989).

49. *Repetto, supra* note, at 6.

50. Wilfrido Cruz & Robert Repetto, World Resources Inst., *The Environmental Effects of Stabilization and Structural Adjustment Programs: The Phil-*

ippines Case 18 (1992) (averaging ratio of resource depreciation to gross domestic product from 1970 to 1987).

51. Devarajan & Weiner, *supra* note 78, at 4.

52. Id. at 7-9. This measure, when defined in terms of GNP, is not related to welfare; however, an analogous measure defined for NNP would be related to welfare in the desired ways. Interview with Shantayanan Devarajan, World Bank, in Washington, D.C. (Sept. 1, 1992).

53. Devarajan & Weiner, *supra* note, at 17.

54. Mäler, *supra* note.

55. A great deal of research is needed on the empirical relationship between different measures of output and welfare to determine where there are important differences in overall levels as well as the rate of change of these measures.

56. I suspect we will eventually run the experiment in some form, so we will be able to see how politicians respond.

57. Market-based approaches have increased in popularity for a number of reasons. See, e.g., Robert W. Hahn & Robert N. Stavins, "Incentive-Based Environmental Regulation: A New Era from an Old Idea?", 18 *Ecology L.Q.* 1 (1991). Some advocates of these ideas tend to ignore the importance of choosing problems for which the benefits of controlling pollution exceed the costs. See, e.g., Robert W. Hahn, "A Recipe for Sustained Environmental Growth," *Regulation,* Spring 1991, at 17.

58. It also depends on the ease of implementing such a system. Dudek, Hahn, and Stavins argue that there are formidable obstacles in implementing an international system of marketable permits. Daniel J. Dudek et al., International Trading in Greenhouse Permits (Mar. 1992) (unpublished manuscript, on file with author). On the other hand, Dudek and LeBlanc suggest that the United States is a logical place to experiment with a market-based approach for limiting carbon dioxide emissions. Daniel J. Dudek & Alice LeBlanc, "Offsetting New CO_2 Emissions: A Rational First Greenhouse Policy Step," *Contemp. Pol. Issues,* July 1990, at 29.

59. It is interesting to note that neither Vice President Gore nor the environmentalist community has asked for information on the polluting activities of individuals. I conjecture that they have avoided this because they realize such reporting could be expensive and could result in a political backlash. The environmental community would rather perpetuate the myth that industry and government, and not the public, are responsible for pollution. Politicians embrace this view as well. See generally Robert W. Hahn, "U.S. Environmental Policy: Past, Present, and Future" (Dec. 1991) (unpublished manuscript, on file with the author).

60. Id.

61. The 3M company instituted a Pollution Prevention Pays program as a result of increased sensitivity to its pollution. P. 342.

62. "Valdez Principles: Aiming for Fortune 500's," *Greenwire,* Aug. 19, 1991, available in LEXIS, Nexis Library, Greenwire file.

63. Most businesses need to respond quickly to changes in the increasingly

competitive global marketplace. To the extent that environmentalist intervention reduces the ability of business to respond, it is likely to have an adverse impact on business performance.

64. The rationale for considering government involvement is that information is a public good; however, there are several private organizations that collect and publicize information effectively. One well-known one is *Consumer Reports* magazine.

65. Robert J. Samuelson, "The Way We Diaper," *Wash. Post*, Mar. 14, 1990, at A17.

66. Consumer groups are likely to find the idea of green labels attractive. Business groups would like the government to set standards that they can live with (or use to gain a competitive advantage). Bureaucrats stand to gain from the emergence of a growth industry within the government. Whether consumers or the environment will benefit remains an open question.

67. But note, there may be a case for paternalism in some cases. See Peter Passell, "Tuna and Trade: Whose Rules?", *N.Y. Times*, Feb. 19, 1992, at D2.

68. James G. March & Johan P. Olsen, *Rediscovering Institutions: The Organizational Basis of Politics* 13-14 (1989).

69. This proposal is intriguing for several reasons. First, it suffers from the appropriate technology disease. The examples used by the Vice President suggest that he believes a reduction in energy consumption is desirable. If that is the goal, why not just tax energy instead of using a kitchen sink approach? Second, it calls for a revenue neutral tax change that would substitute a carbon tax for income and payroll taxes, while changing the progressivity in the tax structure and changing the constituency that benefits from this stream of revenues. I do not know whether this is politically feasible (as Senator Gore suggests, p. 349), but I have my doubts because of the large visible wealth transfers that would be involved.

The suggestion of using the tax structure to improve policy raises a broader issue that seems to have been lost in the environmental shuffle. There are a host of analyses that suggest that the tax structure could be modified to help the environment as well as the economy by moving away from inefficient taxes, such as income and payroll taxes, and towards a tax structure that encourages investment and preservation of the environment. See, e.g., Robert Shackleton et al., "The Efficiency Value of Carbon Tax Revenues" (March 27, 1992) (unpublished manuscript, on file with author). These analyses point out that our current tax structure is inefficient, but they fail to explain why green taxes would, in fact, improve efficiency given the underlying political structure in which they would be implemented.

70. See Alfred E. Kahn, "Environmentalists Hijack the Utility Regulators," *Wall St. J.*, Aug. 7, 1991, at A10 (questioning whether utility commission and companies are proper agencies to promote and subsidize conservation).

71. See, e.g., Friedrich A. von Hayek, *The Road to Serfdom* (1944) (warning that extended collectivism implied in "social planning" is incompatible with the preservation of a free society).

72. Even so-called Free Market Environmentalists who endorse private property solutions for almost all environmental and resource problems are at a loss to define such solutions for problems in which there are difficulties in defining and enforcing individual property rights. See Terry L. Anderson & Donald R. Leal, *Free Market Environmentalism*, ch. 11 (1991). Their approach to these problems is either to downgrade their importance or to admit reluctantly that some form of government-sanctioned market may be appropriate.

73. For an articulate defense of the Bush position at Rio, see C. Boyden Gray, "Put the Forests First," *Wash. Post*, June 2, 1992, at A19, and Clayton Yeutter, "Letters to the Editor: The President's Trip to Rio," *Wash. Post*, June 12, 1992, at A22.

74. For an analysis of how various factors, including domestic politics, affect the development of international environmental agreements, see Robert W. Hahn & Kenneth Richards, "The Internationalization of Environmental Regulation," 30 *Harv. Int'l L.J.* 421 (1989).

75. P. 357. I hope for the Vice President's sake that children are more reliable than graduate students. Otherwise, the difficulties in obtaining useful data from this endeavor will be immense.

76. Kenneth E. Boulding, "The Economics of the Coming Spaceship Earth," in *Environmental Quality in a Growing Economy* (Henry Jarrett ed., 1966). As a metaphor, Boulding's spaceship earth has a certain appeal. The analogy should not be taken too far, however, since earth is not a closed system with respect to energy. Nonetheless, it reminds us that the earth should be treated as our home for the foreseeable future and we should not squander the earth's resources.

77. For works discussing examples of dogma masquerading as environmental science, see Robert W. Hahn, "The Politics and Religion of Clean Air," *Regulation*, Winter 1990, at 21; Lindzen, *supra note*, at 87.

78. See *supra* Part V(C)(1).

79. P. 360 (describing attempts by the National Coal Association to persuade parts of the electorate that global warming is not an important issue).

80. For example, see Mr. Gore's discussion of Love Canal at pp. 209-10.

81. The Vice President here ignores one of the key insights of economics, the "TANSTAAFL" principle: there ain't no such thing as a free lunch.

82. The Natural Resources Defense Council received substantial publicity when it orchestrated the ban on Alar with the help of actress Meryl Streep. Michael Weisskopf, "From Fringe to Political Mainstream: Environmentalists Set Policy Agenda," *Wash. Post*, April 19, 1990, at A1, A16.

83. Lois Ember, "Love Canal: Uncertain Science, Politics, and Law," in Christoph Honenemsen & Jeanne X. Kasperson, *Risk in Technological Society* 77-95 (1982).

84. See Gregg Easterbrook, "Green Cassandras," *New Republic*, July 6, 1992,

at 24. ("It's just that, ummm, there never was any Northern ozone hole.")

85. Eliot Marshall, "A is for Apple, Alar, and . . . Alarmist?", 254 *Science* 20 (1991).

86. See Laurie Goodstein, "Back to Love Canal: A Symbol of Toxic Waste Hazards," *Wash. Post*, June 21, 1990, at A3.

87. See Elizabeth M. Whelan, *Toxic Terror* 87-105 (1985); Bob Davis, "Hole in Ozone Didn't Develop, NASA Reports," *Wall Street J.*, May 1, 1992, at B12; "Letters to the Editor: Big Holes in the Ozone Studies," *Wall St. J.*, Apr. 15, 1992, at A21; "Letters to the Editor: The Dreaded Ozone Hole," *Wall St. J.*, Mar. 10, 1992, at A19; "Press-Release Ozone Hole," *Wall St. J.*, Feb. 28, 1992, at A14.

88. Aaron Wildavsky, "Global Warming as a Means of Achieving an Egalitarian Society: An Introduction," in Robert C. Balling, Jr., *The Heated Debate: Greenhouse Predictions Versus Climate Reality* xv-xvi (1992).

89. Lindzen, *supra* note, at 96.

90. For a recent article exposing the environmental camp's subordination of rational policy to public relations, see Raymond Bonner, "Crying Wolf over Elephants," *N.Y. Times*, Feb. 7, 1993, § 6 (Magazine), at 16 (describing how conservation groups reversed their position on the advisability of banning ivory when they discovered that hyping the threat to elephants is a highly effective device for obtaining funds and publicity).

91. See Dudek & Leblanc, *supra* note; Jessica Mathews, "Science, Uncertainty, and Common Sense: Greenhouse Warming is the Moral Equivalent of the Cold War," *Wash. Post*, Nov. 3, 1991, at C7.

92. See Robert Repetto et al., *Green Fees: How a Tax Shift Can Work for the Environment and the Economy*, World Resources Institute, Washington, D.C. (1992).

93. There is also substantial disagreement about how broadly these instruments might be applied and how effective they are likely to be. See, e.g., Anderson & Leal, *supra* note (offering a conservative view).

94. The problem is analogous to that of organizing a cartel, where each individual member may have an incentive to produce beyond the allocated quota. In the case of environmental groups, there is an incentive to maintain a posture suggesting that improving the environment is the most important challenge facing mankind, and that most, if not all, environmental issues should be viewed as crises. This position helps increase the pool of resources going to environmental groups and environmental problems. At the same time, these groups compete, sometimes fiercely, within this large tent. They do so in a variety of ways by offering different kinds of services to their supporters. See, e.g., Riley E. Dunlop & Angela G. Mertig, "The Evolution of the U.S. Environmental Movement from 1970 to 1990: An Overview," 4 *Soc'y & Nat. Resources* 209-18 (1991).

95. See Anderson & Leal, *supra* note.

96. For example, Paul Watson, former leader of Greenpeace, suggests that human beings are "the AIDS of the Earth." Robert H. Nelson, "Unorig-

inal Sin: The Judeo-Christian Roots of Ecotheology," *Pol'y Rev.*, Summer 1990, at 52, 57.

97. *World Commission on Employment and Development, Our Common Future* 8-9 (1987).

98. See, e.g., Robert Goodland, et al., "Environmentally Sustainable Economic Development Building on Brundtland" 1-4 (World Bank Environment Working Paper No. 46, 1991); "Inheriting the Earth," *Economist*, Sept. 16, 1989, at 77; Robert M. Solow, "Sustainability: An Economist's Perspective," Lecture at Woods Hole Oceanographic Institute (June 14, 1991) (unpublished manuscript, on file with author); Michael A. Toman & Pierre T. Crosson, "Economics and Sustainability: Balancing Trade-offs and Imperatives" (Jan. 1991) (unpublished manuscript, on file with author).

99. John Pezzey, "Sustainability, Intergenerational Equity, and Environmental Policy" (August 20, 1989) (unpublished manuscript, on file with author).

100. Id.

101. Talbot Page, "A Generic View of Toxic Chemicals and Similar Risks," 7 *Ecology L.Q.* 207, 208-12 (1978).

102. I ignore the formidable problems of defining "life as we know it," but one could relate it to extinction or catastrophic losses in human life or cultures.

103. See Pezzey, *supra* note; Toman & Crosson, *supra* note.

104. There are substantial problems in defining and measuring natural capital, but they are more readily addressed than abstract utilitarian notions of sustainability. The natural resource stock will have to be translated into a common metric, such as monetary units, to compare the impacts of different policies.

105. The distinction between renewable and nonrenewable resources is somewhat arbitrary. Most resources can be renewed or replenished, but the time it takes to do so may be long relative to a human's life span. Thus, the ozone layer can be preserved through the reduction of chlorofluorocarbon production, but it will take decades for this policy to have an effect because of the long residence times of these chemicals in the atmosphere.

106. See, e.g., David Pearce et al., *Blueprint for a Green Economy* (1990).

107. A standard environmental economics text would argue that there are private costs and external costs, the sum of which yield social costs. See Tom Tietenberg, *Environmental and Natural Resource Economics* 45-47 (1988). Optimality is sometimes defined as the point at which marginal social cost is equal to marginal social benefit. This notion of optimality is central to microeconomic analysis of environmental problems, yet the measurement of an external cost is not straightforward. For example, how do we estimate and measure the impact of an additional ton of carbon dioxide in the atmosphere? People disagree on the impact of projected CO_2 emissions on climactic conditions. Moreover, the analysis typically assumes that the existing income distribution is appropriate

for determining the so-called optimal policy. This assumption on distribution can be modified by imposing different weights on people with different income classes.

108. Ronald Bailey, "Captain Planet for Veep," *Nat'l Rev.*, Sept. 14, 1992, at 40, 43.

109. World Bank, *World Development Report 1992*, at 5 (1992).

110. For a more detailed discussion of technical approaches to policy analysis, see Edith Stokey & Richard Zeckhauser, *A Primer for Policy Analysis* (1978). For an insightful discussion of policy design, see David L. Weimer, "Claiming races, broiler contracts, heresthetics, and habits: ten concepts of policy design," 25 *Pol'y Sci.* 135 (1992).

111. See, e.g., Edward S. Rubin et al., "Keeping Climate Research Relevant," *Issues in Sci. & Tech.*, Winter 1991-92, at 47.

112. See, e.g., Robert W. Hahn & Robert N. Stavins, "Incentives for Environmental Protection: Integrating Theory and Practice," 82 *Am. Econ. Rev.* 464 (1992); Robert W. Hahn, "The Political Economy of Environmental Regulation: Towards a Unifying Framework," 65 *Pub. Choice* 21 (1990).

113. See, e.g., M. Granger Morgan & Max Henrion, *Uncertainty: A Guide to Dealing with Uncertainty in Quantitative Risk and Policy* (1992).

114. The tax example is used for illustrative purposes only. I am not endorsing taxes as the preferred instrument for addressing this issue.

115. This is a crude estimate based on the view that significant reductions in greenhouse gas emissions could be comparable to the current cost of environmental programs, which are in this range. See, e.g., Alan S. Manne & Richard S. Richels, *Buying Greenhouse Insurance: The Economic Costs of Carbon Dioxide Emission Limits* 45-66 (1992). Of course, Gore's prescriptions merely start with global warming. Thus, an estimate of $100 billion annually would probably be a lower bound. Moreover, the cost to the world could be several times that amount. See *Report of the Administrator, Environmental Protection Agency, Environmental Investments: The Cost of A Clean Environment* (1991) for estimates of current environmental expenditures in the United States.

116. There is a popular mythology to which Vice President Gore and many of his followers adhere that tighter economic standards will increase U.S. competitiveness. See, e.g., Michael Porter, "America's Green Strategy," *Sci. Am.*, April 1991, at 168. While there is not much data to support or refute this argument, it is questionable on first principles. Define U.S. competitiveness by the average standard of living of the U.S. citizen. (Whether this standard of living is measured by income per capita or some adjusted measure that includes environmental degradation is not particularly important for this argument.) I can imagine two basic reasons why tighter standards would increase the average standard of living. The first is that we are under-regulating particular pollutants relative to some optimum that economists might define. A good example of such a pollutant would be airborne lead emissions from burning leaded gasoline. Indeed, this was a primary motivation for removing the lead from gasoline. Unfortunately, the data suggest that, at least for

the United States, a large class of pollutants tend to be over-regulated rather than under-regulated, which is the main reason why the incremental costs of most proposed environmental regulations tend to exceed the benefits.

A second rationale for supporting tighter standards as a way of promoting competitiveness is based on a dynamic argument. The argument assumes the government has the ability to identify industries in which the United States has comparative advantages *and* is able successfully to stimulate their development. Thus, some people believe that the United States has or can have a comparative advantage in producing pollution control equipment and other environmental products. The proposition that government can redirect investment to its most highly valued uses is highly dubious in most cases. Indeed, the U.S. government has not been particularly astute in choosing economic winners in the marketplace and frequently continues projects even after it is obvious they are economic losers. See, e.g., Linda R. Cohen & Roger G. Noll, *The Technology Pork Barrel* (1991). Thus, while the data are limited, arguments based on first principles suggest the burden of proof should lie with those who believe that tighter standards will improve living standards.

117. See Nelson, *supra* note, at 52 (arguing that "environmental policy-making often turns out to be a battlefield for religious conflict"); see also Hahn, *supra* note, at 21-30. For an insightful critique of the inherent biases in economic thought, see Robert H. Nelson, *Reaching for Heaven on Earth: The Theological Meaning of Economics* (1991).

118. See, e.g., Lindzen, *supra* note, at 87-98. Mr. Gore also conveniently fails to note that many scientists were deeply concerned about global cooling just twenty years ago. Moreover, chlorofluorocarbons (CFC's), thought to be one of the most potent greenhouse gases just a year ago, are now thought to have a negligible *net* impact on the problem of warming because the impact of the CFC's is counter-balanced by the reduction in stratospheric ozone. CFC's still are thought to be a critical factor in the depletion of stratospheric ozone. See World Meteorological Organization, "Global Ozone Research and Monitoring Project Report No. 25," *Scientific Assessment of Ozone Depletion* xi, xv (1991).

119. "[T]he ideas of economists and political philosophers, both when they are right and when they are wrong, are more powerful than is commonly understood. Indeed the world is ruled by little else. Practical men, who believe themselves to be quite exempt from any intellectual influences, are usually the slaves of some defunct economist. Madmen in authority, who hear voices in the air, are distilling their frenzy from some academic scribbler of a few years back." John Maynard Keynes, *The General Theory of Employment Interest and Money* 383 (1936).

120. See Bailey, *supra*, note 174, at 43; see also 34 *Cong. Q. Almanac* 117-H (1978) (vote in favor of HR-12928); 35 *Cong. Q. Almanac* 71-H (1979) (vote in favor of HR-4388).

121. See Steven Kelman, *Making Public Policy* (1987).

122. See Francis S. Blake, "The Environment: Does Washington Know Best?", *Am. Enterprise*, Mar.-Apr. 1990, at 6-7.

123. See, e.g., Fred L. Smith, "Conclusion: Environmental Policy at the Cross-roads," in *Environmental Politics: Public Costs, Private Rewards* (Michael S. Greve & Fred L. Smith eds., 1992).

124. Council of Economic Advisers, *Economic Report of the President* (1989).

125. For example, waiting allows money that would have been spent on reducing greenhouse gas emissions to be spent on other pressing needs; it allows new, more effective technology to emerge; and most importantly, it allows new information to surface that could provide a better basis for decision making.

126. See, e.g., Hahn, *supra* note, at 21; Paul R. Portney, "Economics and the Clean Air Act," *J. Econ. Persp.*, Fall 1990, at 173; Frederick H. Rueter & Wilbur A. Steger, "Air Toxics and Public Health: Exaggerating Risk and Misdirecting Policy," *Regulation*, Winter 1990, at 51.

127. Indeed, if the tax were higher than the market price of a permit without such a tax, then the market price for a permit would plummet to zero. I am ignoring distributional considerations here, which could be addressed through a suitable distribution of permits.

128. P. 37. Vice President Gore glosses over the fact that the most effective solution and the least costly solution may not be the same.

129. Tom Wolfe, *The Electric Kool Aid Acid Test* 74 (1968).

130. The real question is what kinds of experiments should be allowed, not whether we will do them.

131. Charles E. Lindblom, "The Science of Muddling Through," 19 *Pub. Admin. Rev.* 79 (1959).

CHAPTER 3

Gore's Environmental Views and the Economy?

John R. Lott, Jr.

One of the many remarkable facts about the 1992 presidential election was the complete absence of hard news stories on Albert Gore's book *Earth in the Balance*. When Mr. Gore's views on the environment were mentioned he was characterized as a "moderate." The Bush campaign can surely attest to difficulty generating any serious scrutiny of Gore's beliefs, and when attacks were made they frequently resulted in the press accusing the author of false caricatures of Gore's views. Yet, to Mr. Gore, environmental problems are seen as arising from capitalism's unrestrained exploitation of the earth and humankind's addiction to consumption. Despite his proclaimed belief in markets, he sees government intervention through a vast array of new laws and expanded bureaucracies as the only solution to environmental problems.[1] Reducing the world's population along with command-and-control solutions for humankind's wasteful use of water and energy form the central focus of Gore's policy concerns.

If taken at his own word, Vice President Gore is surely one of the smartest people around. He claims to have figured out many ways to vastly improve the efficiency of everything from American businesses to farms. If his proposed solutions are correct, his devotion to public service surely implies that he has sacrificed a great deal—a consulting business that would have reaped vast wealth. Gore predicts that prices for resources will soar in the future as man continues to use them "uncaring" of the consequences. No one seems to realize that if this were true, vast sums of money could be made by buying resources today while they are relatively cheap and selling them in the future when he expects them to be so dear. He argues that stockholders supposedly compensate their managers to maximize current profits rather than the present value of the firm, yet no one seems to realize that they could make money by buying up these ill-run companies and correcting their mistakes. Farmers are so stupid that they water their crops to such an extent that they are actually stunting plant growth and reducing farm output, and alas, no one is there to correct their mistakes.

One thing is for sure, however. Vice President Gore so frequently states his faith in the free market and refers to his proposals as market-oriented that one would think him a not so distant relative of Milton Friedman or F.A. Hayek. Yet, the reliance he places on "market mechanisms" (such as taxes) to alter activities he deems harmful to the environment are not proposed as a replacement to traditional command-and-control restrictions but simply as a supplement to them. Mr. Gore also seems to deny the notion that there are trade-offs in life. He has mastered the political rhetoric that there are only benefits and no pain to the changes that he proposes. Reducing air conditioning and increasing automobile gas mileage will supposedly not only help the environment but will also create new jobs and increase income.

In this review I will first examine the theoretical foundation for Mr. Gore's view of people as the destructive creatures he paints them. Then I will turn to Gore's views on central planning and Malthus and provide some examples of his economic analysis. Finally, I will identify some of his incorrect "facts." Given that Mr. Gore is not only the Vice President of the United States but that he also has been allowed to place his former aides in charge of several aspects of environmental policy, Gore's views on the relationship between the environment and the economy may give us some preview of the Clinton administration's environmental policy preferences.

GORE VERSUS THE ECONOMIST'S CREED OF CONSUMER SOVEREIGNTY

Economists are modest in one sense: When they discuss what will maximize society's wealth, they take the preferences of people as given. Whether some people buy Mercedes-Benzes because they want very safe cars or because of the less noble notion that they like to feel superior to their fellow human beings is irrelevant to economists. Theoretically, an economist's advice on what actions will maximize the consumer surplus from buying Mercedes-Benzes is unaffected by the economist's personal feelings about whether people's reasons for buying that type of car are "acceptable."

Vice President Gore's position on what constitutes acceptable preferences for consumers is diametrically opposed to the approach used by economists. If you are going to read only one chapter to get insight into how Gore thinks about consumer sovereignty and how he views those who disagree with him about the environment, look at Chapter 12, Dysfunctional Civilization. The good news from this chapter is that humankind is not an inherently evil "virus," the bad news is that we are "mentally ill" and this has manifested itself in our "addiction" to consumption and the "momentary 'rush' experienced by drug addicts" that we obtain from progress. The scope of this theory is as broad as it is bizarre. It starts with the notion that with the "scientific era" God's importance in people's lives began to recede and God's authority was replaced with that of the family's patriarch. In Gore's own words:

> Before the scientific era, children almost certainly found it easier to locate and understand their place in the world because they could define themselves in relation both to their parents and to a God who was clearly present in nature. With these two firm points of reference, children were less likely to lose their direction in life. But with God receding from the natural world to an abstract place, the patriarchal figure in the family (almost always the father) effectively became God's viceroy, entitled to exercise godlike authority when enforcing the family's rules. As some fathers inevitably began to insist on being the sole source of authority, their children became confused about their own roles in a family system that was severely stressed by the demands of the dominant, all-powerful father. . . . One of the ways dysfunctional families enforce adherence to rules and foster the psychic numbness on which they depend is by teaching the separation between mind and body and suppressing the feelings and emotions that might otherwise undermine the rules. Similarly, one of the ways our civilization secures adherence to its rules is by teaching the separation of people from the natural world and suppressing the emotions that might allow us to feel the absence of our connection to the earth. (p. 227)[2]

This "cleavage" between mind and body supposedly results in an emptiness in people. To fill this void created by their parents, individuals become addicted to consumption. This "mental illness" creates the illusion for people that they want "the food on the supermarket shelves, the water in the faucets in our homes, the shelter and sustenance, the clothing and purposeful work, our entertainment" (p. 231). This addiction is pervasive: "I believe that our civilization is, in effect, addicted to the consumption of the earth itself" (p. 220) or "I believe our civilization must be considered in some basic way dysfunctional" (p. 230). Like child abuse, this psychological plague is supposedly passed from generation to generation. The "good news" to Mr. Gore is that identifying a "particular family member as bad" is unnecessary and that the psychological "harm" parents inflict is probably not done "consciously" (p. 229).

Gore would like to eliminate the amenities most of us think make life more pleasant. He writes of "a false world of plastic flowers and Astroturf, air conditioning and fluorescent lights, windows that don't open and background music that never stops, . . . Walkman and Watchman, . . . frozen food for the microwave oven" (p. 232). These products may be man-made, but in what sense are they "false" or wrong? If we had real grass instead of Astroturf in a football stadium, would Gore complain that it was wrong to mow the grass? There is no discussion of trade-offs. Frozen foods are wrong because they use packaging and require energy to keep them cold, and most important, they separate man from nature (that is, we do not have to do the food gathering ourselves). These products represent "our apparent obsession with inauthentic substitutes for direct experience with real life" (p. 232).

What Vice President Gore thinks of those with whom he disagrees is equally worrying. After defining "denial" as a serious mental illness, Gore claims that those who describe the environmental programs as "statist" are themselves suffering from "a well established form of denial" (p. 225). This is an extremely dangerous and intolerant attitude for a national leader. Those who oppose him are not merely wrong but sick (p. 223). While he definitely does not take the final step of rationalizing force or coercion against those who disagree with him, his discussion is like arguments used to rationalize such actions.

After describing how our society is awash in mental illness, Gore argues that "The idea of a dysfunctional civilization is by no means a theoretical construct" (p. 232). As evidence of this, he points to Nazi Germany and Stalinism. His point, however, is not clear. Are we like or becoming like Nazi Germany? Or, is drastic government action justified to prevent us from this final solution?

This remarkable chapter ends by demonstrating Gore's complete lack of perspective—he compares Italy's ruthless attack using poison gases on Ethiopia to the exploitation of natural resources and equates both with civilization's dysfunctional "expansionist tendencies" (p. 234).

During the 1992 presidential campaign, *The Wall Street Journal* (August 13, 1992, p. A14) ran a copy of a memo from a Democratic National Committee staffer detailing possible problems with Gore's book, particularly how the public may perceive it. Yet, despite all the allusions to Gore being a "Luddite" and his lack of proportion (both of which are evidenced in his book), the memo fails to mention his strange theories of the emotional damage inflicted by parents on their children and his beliefs that those who disagree with him are mentally ill. Was the memo an attempt at misdirection?

Only after reading this chapter does the reader really get a good feeling for why Gore feels so justified in advocating self-censorship by the press (p. 39) and why his book is so grim and exaggerated. If people are addicts who have lost control over their actions, a truly paternalistic government might censor the news in the public's best interest.

PRICES AND PROPERTY RIGHTS VERSUS CENTRAL GOVERNMENT PLANNING

Ironically, this book contains many environmental horror stories from the former Soviet Union and Eastern Europe (for example, p. 81) yet fails to draw any connection with central planning. Gore sees what happened in those countries as resulting from a lack of democracy (p. 179)—that is, the central planners had the wrong motivations. His inability to see the distinction between markets and central planning is contained in virtually all his policy discussions. He relies primarily on command-and-control rather than property rights and prices to protect the environment.

Gore exhibits this inability to comprehend how markets work in his extensive discussions of water shortages. He argues that models of global warming predict higher temperatures, which will result in less rain fall (p. 103),[3] and claims that, given current water usage, huge shortages of fresh water will result. California's recent water shortages serve as an example of what the future will hold. The concern that 85 percent of California's water goes to farming (with such questionable uses as growing rice in desert areas) is real and legitimate. But, while economists would point out that the problem lies with the huge subsidies for farmers' water, Gore's approach is to micromanage how farmers water their crops. He argues that "open ditch irrigation also typically leads to the waterlogging of the 'root zone,' which paradoxically deprives the plants of oxygen and stunts their growth" (p. 112) and that reducing the amount of water devoted to agriculture would not only allow more water for other uses but would improve agricultural output. Gore's claim seems to be that the water shortage is simply due to farmers making mistakes in how they use their water allocation rather than the economist's normal refrain that farmers use water until the marginal return equals the marginal cost.

Another example involves Gore's concern about overfishing where "the total annual catch . . . is now assumed to be higher than the replenishment rate in most areas" (p. 143). He movingly writes of the damage done by drift net fishing or of the congregation of "Asian fishing fleets" in the ocean east of New Zealand. To Gore this is a problem of overpopulation—the world is providing fish for more people than it is able to sustain in the long run. The solution, then, is to limit the world's human population. Isn't it more realistic to prevent overfishing by extending property rights to that portion of the ocean? There is a great deal of evidence supporting that when a fishery is owned, and not open to anyone or any country that desires to fish there, the owners maximize the value of that property by managing the fish stocks. The more likely it is that fish will become scarce in the future, the greater is the return on cutting back on fishing today.

REHABILITATING MALTHUS

To Gore, population is the source of most of these supposed environmental problems. He worries that "It took more than ten thousand generations to reach a world population of 2 billion people. Now, in the course of one human lifetime—mine—the world population will increase from 2 to more than 9 billion" (p. 31).[4] It appears that we are quite lucky not to have already met the fate Malthus predicted because "without some interference in the natural evolution of plants, Malthus's prediction of disaster would almost certainly have come true" (p. 129). While continued plant selection will still allow us to escape Malthus's prediction "for a long while yet" (p. 127), plant selection places us in a very precarious position of depending on a "tiny genetic reservoir" that will eventually result in disaster as new diseases outrace our ability to come up with new strains of crops. Supposedly heedless to this impending disaster, we are destroying what were once vast plant genetic pools in rainforests and other centers of genetic diversity that could provide new strains resistant to

82

prevalent diseases. Farming methods increase current yields but at the expense of a "sharp reduction" in future output (p. 128).

Unfortunately, unlike Malthus or his more recent imitators, such as Paul Ehrlich, who have made predictions and been proven wrong,[5] Gore makes no testable predictions. He concentrates instead on predictions he claims will eventually come true. If some fortuitous events intervene, the calamity will merely come later than if they do not. Some points are plainly silly however. If a danger exists that disease will wipe out existing commercial strains, and if preserving strains that exist in the wild is the solution, there is an easy way for Gore to make lots of money—buy up many different strains of these crops that exist in the wild. On the question of disappearing farm land, it is clear that if the price of food is going to rise in the future because of reductions in farming land, farmers would make more money ensuring that their farm land will remain productive in future years.

THE NOTION OF TRADE-OFFS

Mr. Gore's book is written from an absolutist point of view—virtually everything is either good or bad. Either something helps preserve the earth in its natural state (read: the condition that would exist in the absence of humankind) and this is good, or it alters the proper order of things. Gore laments how refrigerators and air conditioning generate chlorofluorocarbon emissions and use energy, but no mention is made about how refrigerators lower the cost of feeding people and air conditioning prevents heat strokes and possible death. Aren't the facts that some elderly people or babies might die in the absence of air conditioning, or even that worker productivity will decline, worthy of consideration?

Buildings are "inefficiently designed" because they do not have "sufficient" insulation (p. 333), but Gore fails to note that sealing buildings tighter serves as breeding grounds for disease and trap gases that can harm health. Gore advocates government subsidies to encourage tree planting (p. 351) while he ignores that recycling paper products reduces the demand for forestry companies to plant new trees. Despite his frequent concern about the number of trees in the United States, he seems unaware that the number of trees in this country is higher now than at the beginning of this century. While Gore is concerned about preserving old growth forests, he makes no mention that young vigorously growing trees will remove five to seven tons more CO_2 per acre per year than old growth.[6]

Gore doesn't seem to realize that not all good things go together, that trade-offs are inherent to responsibility. "The government must establish higher mileage requirements for all cars and trucks sold in the United States" (p. 350), yet more fuel efficient cars will tend to be lighter and smaller and therefore may increase death rates due to accidents. Smaller cars will also impose other costs on people. For example, it may take drivers more trips to move things from one place to another. Apparently, Gore doesn't consider an individual's time as representing as much of a real cost as does fuel usage.

Gore's discussion on global warming is fairly typical. He lists only exaggerated claims of the costs of global warming, and he mentions no benefits that might even slightly offset these costs. Benefits such as the resulting longer growing seasons, the effect of increased CO_2 and precipitation on plant growth rates, and the fact that to the extent warming occurs it will be during the colder seasons and night time that we will see the greatest increases in temperatures are completely ignored.

One of the few exceptions where Gore accepts that both costs and benefits exist is in the development of new technology. He proposes "the establishment of rigorous and sophisticated technology assessment procedures, paying close attention to all of the costs and benefits—both monetary and ecological—of the new proposed substitute technologies" (p. 320). Gore essentially proposes a giant FDA type agency (with all the delays that entails) that would be required to sort out new technology to see if it is benign to the environment. Yet, he fails to mention the costs of this review process. Over time, technological improvements have steadily lead to safer and more efficient products in a wide variety of areas. To the extent that these regulations increase the costs of producing new technology, we may find that these restrictions actually increase the total amount of pollution and retard adoption of safety improvements that would have saved lives.

SELECTED ADDITIONAL EXAMPLES
OF NUTTY ECONOMICS

First, pervasive throughout the book is the theme that people today do not take into account the values of future generations. Gore approvingly quotes Brazil's minister of the environment, who argues that selling off wood from the rainforest is "like auctioning the Mona Lisa to a roomful of shoeshine boys: many would-be bidders, like those in future generations, are not able to bid" (p. 120). The problem with this observation is that although future buyers cannot directly bid on a product today the amount that those who do bid today are willing to pay for the good depends partly on how much they will be able to sell it for tomorrow. Since higher future demand increases future prices, it will also increase current prices.

If people are making mistaken decisions and assuming that the government has better quality information, the most efficient response would be to let the government inform people about the choices they face. It is hardly obvious why the government is better at dealing with the multitude of circumstances facing different individuals. Yet, with example after example of customers or firms acting in ways that are supposedly at odds with their long-term financial interests on decisions that directly affect their own well-being, one wonders how Gore can trust a political process where these same people vote on who will make the decisions for them. If anything, the direct incentives to correctly make decisions operate less forcefully in the political market.

Second, Gore states that "many of the largest paper consumers and manufacturers have large investments in forests and tree farms, and they are therefore loath to use recycled paper instead of making additional profit by cutting the trees in which they have invested" (p. 159). While conspiracy theories about firms are hardly uncommon, it is difficult see how firms would prevent all their competitors from using recycled paper if it really were the lowest cost method of obtaining more paper. In any case, even a pure monopolist will find its profits increased by switching to a lower cost method of production. If no switch occurs, its higher profits in its lumber division will be more than offset by lower profits in the divisions that consume the paper products.

Gore builds on his discussion to call for "a new generation of environmental antitrust laws that insist on carefully scrutinizing the ways in which vertical integration, for example, can work to the disadvantage of the environment" (pp. 342–343). Some economists think people finally have begun to understand why government shouldn't meddle in vertical mergers,[7] but reading Gore's book should convince them that old errors have a long life. Not only does Gore insist that purchases of forestland by large paper users should be carefully examined but he is also concerned with chemical companies buying up seed companies because they will selectively breed seeds that maximize the use of their chemical products, as though farmers don't care about or understand the total costs they face.

After reading Gore's book it is quite easy to dream up new reasons why virtually any type of merger should be prevented because it could increase pollution. Despite all his talk about using market mechanisms to prevent pollution, the idea that the government might want to impose a tax on pollution and let firms decide whether to merge does not seem to have registered with Gore.

Third, the placement of a "disproportionate number of landfills and hazardous waste facilities in poor and minority areas" is viewed as evidence of how we discriminate against minorities (pp. 149, 179). The question is: Where would you want to build a dump site? Most likely not on expensive land. Land prices are likely to be relatively low in poor neighborhoods, but causation also runs the other way. Land prices near a dump site are likely to be relatively low, and thus the poor might find property in that area relatively attractive. The assertion of racial discrimination in deciding where to locate dump sites is unsupported by the simple correlation Gore references.

Fourth, economists want to ignore "bad things" like pollution when calculating national income while they only measure "good things" (pp. 188–189).[8] While it is true that measures of national wealth such as gross national product do not measure "bad things" like the social loss from pollution (they are very difficult to measure), the numbers also do not measure many things people value such as the labor spent by women who work in the home raising children. It is difficult to conceive of a motive for economists to systematically exclude bad things so as to increase measures of national income.

Finally, Gore's claim that Americans have followed free trade policies because we are "altruistic" (p. 271) misses the central point that both sides to an exchange are made better off by voluntary transactions.

CONCLUSION

Although Gore often talks of the environment in terms of war, the truth was the first casualty of this battle. Gore requests press self-censorship in his chapter on the Dysfunctional Society. He believes that Americans are "addicts" to consumption and should be spared accurate information on environmental changes if that information encourages denial of the entire problem and inhibits the scale of changes that Gore believes is imperative. He includes only one brief discussion—with faint praise—of recent environmental gains.

Gore is adamant that what people do to the environment is bad, while the pristine state of nature is good. Somehow, we can move back to the farm, raise our own food, and remain in contact with nature while keeping or raising our standard of living and life expectancies. Such wishful thinking is dangerous. The scariest aspect of Gore's book, however, is the utter intolerance for those who disagree with him. To Vice President Gore, those who disagree with him are not simply wrong but ill. Doctor Gore knows what is best for patients and is ready to administer his medicine.

It is interesting to note that it was not until the 1900s that the scientific understanding of modern medicine facilitated saving lives. Unfortunately, for America and for our environment, Gore's understanding of political economy seems to be like the practice of medicine before doctors understood the function and mischief of microbes. His prescriptions should be checked by specialists. Second opinions are surely in order.

Notes

1. A few quotes regarding Mr. Gore's proposed environmental solutions outlined in his Global Marshall Plan: "a Global Marshall Plan, if you will—is now urgently needed. The scope and complexity of this plan *will far exceed those of the original*; what's required now is a plan that combines large scale, long-term , carefully targeted financial aid to developing nations, massive efforts to design and then transfer to poor nations the new technologies needed for sustained economic progress, a worldwide program to stabilize world population growth, and binding commitments by the industrial nations to accelerate their own transition to an environmentally responsible pattern of life" (p. 297, italics added). Gore goes on to state that "the annual U.S. expenditures for the Marshall Plan between 1948 and 1951 were close to 2 percent of our GNP. A similar percentage today would be almost $100 billion a year" (p. 304). It seems very clear after reading this chapter that Gore was proposing that large amounts of money be spent to help Third World countries with their environmental problems. Already the Clinton administration has proposed to fund some of this type of spending in its first budget proposals.

2. Many questions such as exactly when this "scientific era" occurred are never made clear. Another problem involves the lack of even one specific example of how parents create this separation between "mind and body" in their children.

3. This prediction seems at odds with other discussions that argue that higher temperatures will increase evaporation and thus increase rainfall. See Robert C. Balling, Jr., *The Heated Debate: Greenhouse Predictions versus Climate Reality* (San Francisco: Pacific Research Institute, 1992), p. 135.

4. One of Gore's most effective graphs illustrates how population growth has accelerated over time (pp. 32–33). The graph provides a fairly typical example of how Gore's facts tend to be biased toward exaggerating the extent of this acceleration. This occurs because the values illustrated prior to the sudden sharp increase are biased downward, and the high values at the end are biased upward. For example, if you plot the current population on the graph, it appears that the world had only 2.5 billion people in 1992 as compared with the 5.4 billion that actually existed. The scale along the horizontal axis also subtly increases this acceleration by assigning each year a smaller distance as one gets closer to the end of the time line.

5. For an interesting story on a bet won by Julian Simon against Paul Ehrlich on Ehrlich's predictions of overpopulation and scarcity, see John Tierney, "Betting the Planet," *New York Times* (December 2, 1990), pp. 52–53, 74–78.

6. See Dixie Lee Ray with Lou Guzzo, *Trashing the Planet: How Science Can Help Us Deal with Acid Rain, Depletion of the Ozone, and Nuclear Waste (Among Other Things)* (Washington, DC: Regnery Gateway, 1990), p. 36.

7. See Robert H. Bork, *The Antitrust Paradox: A Policy at War with Itself* (New York: Basic Books, 1978).
8. Gore approvingly cites (p. 189) "A mathematician at the University of British Columbia, Colin Clark, has said, 'Much of apparent economic growth may in fact be an illusion based on a failure to account for reduction in natural capital.'"

CHAPTER 4

The Environmental Creed
According to Gore: A
Philosophical Analysis

James G. Lennox

The subtitle of Al Gore's *Earth in the Balance* is "Ecology and the Human Spirit." Subtitles are often more revealing of intentions than are titles, and that is the case here. Albert Gore's aim is not just to claim that the environmental apocalypse is upon us or merely to recommend massive government control to meet it, he wants "to address some fundamental questions about our purpose in life" (p. 238) to promote "a change in our essential character" (p. 239), "an environmentalism of the spirit" (p. 242). These are, as he stresses, philosophical issues. What are Albert Gore's philosophical conclusions, and how well supported are they?

There are two fundamentally different sorts of argument that one commonly hears for joining the environmental bandwagon. *Earth in the Balance* is a confusing mishmash of the two. To foster clear thinking, I will distinguish between the self-interest argument and the sacred earth argument.

The self-interest argument goes like this.

If people who live in advanced technological civilizations continue to behave as they do (drive their own cars, fertilize their lawns with manufactured chemicals, air condition their homes), this will have a harmful effect on air, water, soil, food,

91

and so forth. These effects are a threat to human health and, at the extreme, to human life. Therefore, if we continue to behave as we now do, we will do terrible harm to human life, our own included. To avoid doing terrible harm to human life, we must make fundamental changes in our behavior (ride bicycles, use organic mulch, sweat a lot). This harmful behavior, however, is the result of a certain set of values that we, as products of the scientific, technological, capitalist revolution, tend to accept. Thus to change our behavior, we must change these values.

The self-interest argument is only compelling if there is strong scientific evidence for the two sorts of empirical claims upon which it rests:

⊃ such human behavior changes certain features of the natural environment, and

⊃ these changes are harmful to human life.[1]

Before you accept the self-interest argument and send off a check to the Sierra Club, it is important to examine the scientific evidence for such claims—disinterestedly, objectively, and without assuming that they are true.[2] The other essays in this volume, and the growing number of related books and articles, are appropriate antidotes to the self-interest argument. While Mr. Gore's book is full of appeals to these arguments, it is singularly devoid of the scientific information required for informed judgments about them.

The sacred earth argument is fundamentally different. It goes like this.

> The earth has intrinsic value—it is a sacred trust, God's creation. Since it is an intrinsic good, intruding on its "wildness," its "naturalness," is intrinsically evil, a violation of the divine, no matter how much such intrusions may benefit human life. It is this transformation of the natural world by science and technology for human benefit that constitutes the environmental crisis. This crisis can be avoided only by behaving in ways that leave the natural world as it is—not "violating," "raping," and "dominating" it as we do. But our current behavior is rooted in the values of Enlightenment confidence in reason and science, and in industrial capitalism. To change our behavior we must accept a different set of values.

Earth in the Balance also contains arguments of this sort, not always clearly distinguishable from self-interest arguments.[3] To respond to the sacred earth argument, the basic *philosophical* premise—that the natural world has some sort of intrinsic worth that makes intrusions on it for "merely" human purposes morally suspect—must be questioned. No scientific response to this sort of argument will ever be effective. It is an undeniable fact that the science, medicine, and technology at the core of modern civilization *do* involve transforming the earth's natural resources for "merely" human ends. There is no satisfactory scientific response to an environmental crisis defined in these terms. There is, however, a fully satisfactory *philosophical* response, and that is what I aim to provide.

GORE'S SPIRITUALISM

As noted, Gore's book is typical of its genre in that it slides back and forth between the self-interest and sacred earth arguments. On the one hand, we are encouraged to think of "the environmental crisis" as a *human* catastrophe—as if we are (or will soon be) starving mutants, gasping for our last breath of toxic waste. Yet the *philosophy* of environmentalism, presented in chapters 12 and 13, is a call for the *rejection* of the man-centered morality of enlightened self-interest that is the implicit appeal of the self-interest argument. It is a ringing endorsement of the sacred earth argument.

In chapter 12, entitled Dysfunctional Civilization, Gore presents his vision of Western industrial democracy. He begins with a straightforward rejection of the solution to "the environmental crisis" recommended by the "Deep Ecologists," the dark green fringe of environmentalism— namely, eliminating humanity. Yet while Gore rejects their solution to the "crisis," he accepts their definition of it. He agrees that modern, scientific, industrial civilization is a scourge on the earth. But rather than eradicating human life, he opts for its denaturing.

> The old story of God's covenant with both the earth and humankind, and its assignment to human beings of the role of good stewards and faithful servants, was . . . a powerful, noble and just explanation of who we are in relation to God's earth. (p. 218)

In Gore's eyes, we modern Western humans have become isolated from nature, lonely and dysfunctional. We are addicted to the pleasures of consumer goods—and the authors of books like this are deeply into denial (pp. 222–224).

> The food on the supermarket shelves, the water in the faucets in our homes, the shelter and sustenance, the clothing and

purposeful work, our entertainment, even our identity—all these our civilization provides, and we dare not even think about separating ourselves from such beneficence. (p. 231)

The passive character of this description is revealing—the values that make life for the average American relatively easy, efficient, and enjoyable are "provided" by a "beneficent" civilization. Does Gore forget that it is the productive activities of human beings that provide these goods and services and that the money earned for these activities is exchanged for them? I expect many of Gore's readers, like me, think about living without these goods and services regularly—every time we see news reports of political refugees forced to live without them. It is at such times that I am reminded of how good life in an advanced industrial society is.

This is not, however, what Albert Gore is reminded of. On the contrary, he insists that life lived with running water, air conditioning, abundant food, symphonic music, and films available at our pleasure is turning us all into psychopaths.

We surely experience a painful loss when we are led to believe that the connection to the natural world that is part of our birthright as a species is something unnatural, something to be rejected as a rite of passage into the civilized world. As a result, we internalize the pain of our lost sense of connection to the natural world, we consume the earth and its resources as a way to distract ourselves from the pain, and we search insatiably for artificial substitutes to replace the experience of communion with the world that has been taken from us. (p. 231)[4]

At best, this is a piece of amateur pop psychology—however intended, it is without merit as an argument.

Perhaps the ugliest element of this extended vision of civilized man comes late in the chapter where Gore develops an analogy between the epitome of dysfunctional civilization, the totalitarian state, and the use of resources by industrial producers. He begins with his own characterization of the pathology of such cultures.

The pathology of expansion so evident in modern totalitarian societies results from this dysfunctional pattern, and the sense of wholeness they seek cannot be restored as long as they refuse to confront the dishonesty, fear, and violence eating away at the heart of their national identity. (p. 234)

The language of territorial expansion, aggression, and violation of proper
94

boundaries first associated with totalitarianism is cleverly transferred to the human use of natural resources.

> The *unprecedented assault* on the natural world by our global civilization is also extremely complex. . . . Our *rapid and aggressive expansion* into what remains of the wildness of the earth represents an effort to *plunder from outside* civilization what we cannot find inside. . . . And the destruction by industrial civilization of most of the rain forests and old-growth forests is a particularly frightening example of our *aggressive expansion beyond proper boundaries,* an insatiable drive to find outside solutions to problems arising from a dysfunctional pattern within. (p. 234; emphasis added)

Gore assumes that the citizens of industrial democracies are dysfunctional and that this leads directly to environmental destruction. No argument is provided for these assumptions, though it is the foundation for every other claim made in this chapter. Further, the language of assault, plunder, and territorial expansion beyond proper boundaries invites us to view ourselves as members of a totalitarian society. The natural world possesses "rights" and "boundaries" that we immorally violate when we employ natural resources for human ends. We are "invited" to draw these conclusions—but once again, Gore provides no reason to do so. These concepts depend on ethical/political concepts such as freedom, rights, justice, and legally established boundaries. No philosophical justification is provided for extending their application to water, coal, oil, forests, or schools of fish. There is no grounding for the truly outrageous claims he makes here about the psychology of his readers and the immoral character of their activities.

The next chapter of *Earth in the Balance,* Environmentalism of the Spirit, attempts to explain where we went wrong philosophically. It opens with a history of modern philosophy and science. It is a history unrecognizable to a specialist in this area, but its purpose is quite clear. It aims to erode the moral foundations of science and reason. The *bête noire* of the story is the 17th century English philosopher Francis Bacon.

Before looking at the Vice President's views of Sir Francis, it is useful to remind ourselves about his philosophy. It was Bacon who proclaimed:

> Man is but the servant and interpreter of nature: what he does and what he knows is only what he has observed of nature's order in fact or in thought; beyond this he knows nothing and can do nothing. For the chain of causes cannot by any force be loosed or broken, nor can nature be commanded except by

being obeyed. And so those twin objects, human knowledge and human power, do really meet in one.[5]

To command nature, Bacon declares in this passage, we must obey it; human power over nature comes from understanding and harnessing the natural chain of causation, not from attempting to violate it. Francis Bacon was thus the most outspoken opponent of the rationalistic, a priori approach to knowledge championed by Plato in the classical world and by Bacon's French contemporary René Descartes. Bacon argued that knowledge of nature's causes and their effects was the secret that would turn theoretical science into a practical tool for human improvement. It would allow us to harness those forces and turn them to human ends. The only way to *ensure* such knowledge, Bacon insisted, was through inductive testing of one's ideas.

Bacon propagandized tirelessly on behalf of science, and human reason generally, as practical tools for the betterment of human life. Knowledge, as he put it, is power. But this is true only of knowledge based on careful inductive observation of nature. Useful knowledge would never come by means of deduction from innate ideas, as Descartes claimed. Thus, Bacon systematized the methods of inductive reasoning in his *Novum Organum*, a systemization that continues to be admired by philosophers of science.[6] To quote the editor of a popular edition of Bacon's work:

> The aim of all knowledge is action in the production of works for the promotion of human happiness and the relief of man's estate. Through inductive science man is to recapture his dominion over nature long forfeited and long prevented through the efforts of erring philosophers and men of learning.[7]

Incredibly, Gore considers Bacon to be a follower of Descartes, indeed one who "took 'Cartesian dualism' one step further" (p. 252). He tells us that Bacon believed that "humans were separate from nature" and that "facts derived through the scientific method had no moral significance." This attitude on Bacon's part, we are told, had "a profound implication: The new power derived from scientific knowledge could be used to dominate nature with moral impunity" (p. 253).

Gore cites Bacon's advocacy of vivisection as an example of his amoral attitude toward nature. Yet Bacon advocated vivisection because of his expectation that it would be of enormous service to medicine. And indeed, he was quickly proven correct. A contemporary and countryman of Bacon's, William Harvey, through the systematic practice of experimental vivisection, solved the mystery of the heartbeat and blood circulation, knowledge basic to virtually every further medical advance. (Bacon was Lord Chancellor of England at the same time that Harvey was Chief Physician to the Royal Court).

Assuming Gore has actually read Bacon,[8] what can account for this distortion of his thought? I offer this hypothesis. The Vice President is searching for the roots of the idea, as he puts it, that "the new power derived from scientific knowledge could be used to dominate nature" (p. 252). He *correctly* identifies Francis Bacon as one of those roots. He also needs to blame someone for the alleged separation of the search for this power from consideration of its ethical consequences. To pin the blame on Francis Bacon, Gore portrays him as a believer in the separation of the human intellect from the natural world. The portrait, however, bears no resemblance to its alleged subject. Bacon advocates the use of scientific knowledge to control nature for the improvement of human life—*and to advocate doing something because it promotes human goodness is not to advocate doing it with moral impunity, but exactly the opposite!*

Wherein lies the basic conflict between Mr. Gore's moral vision and that of Francis Bacon's? It is implicit in the meaning of "moral impunity" as Gore uses the term. He considers the natural world to have intrinsic moral worth and, thus, to be a holder of moral claims. It is his view, as we have seen, that we have a basic duty not to "violate" nature. Bacon, on the other hand, provides a moral justification for the use of science and technology to harness the forces of nature, through "obedience" to its laws—we should do this in the interests of improving human life. Albert Gore is presenting a moral code diametrically opposed to his own as if it were, at best, amoral.

It is not, then, Bacon's *lack* of a moral view of man's place in nature that is actually bothering Mr. Gore—it is *precisely* Bacon's moral point of view that bothers him. Gore has evaded arguing with a worthy opponent by painting him as an amoralist on the issue that divides them.

This allows him to get away with some nasty attributions of blame, such as the following:

His [Bacon's] moral confusion . . . came from his assumption . . . that the human intellect could safely analyze and understand the natural world without reference to any moral principles defining our relationship and duties to both God and God's creation. . . . And tragically, since the onset of the scientific and technological revolution, it has seemingly become all too easy for ultra rational minds to create an elaborate

> edifice of clockwork efficiency capable of nightmarish cruelty
> on an industrial scale. The atrocities of Hitler and Stalin . . .
> might have been inconceivable except for the separation of
> facts from values and knowledge from morality. (p. 256)

Here, Gore blames the philosopher who invented the arguments for the power of empirical science to better human life for twentieth century totalitarianism. We saw, in discussing the previous chapter, that Gore has there laid the groundwork for his next step—if Bacon's amoralism is at the root of totalitarianism, it must also be at the root of industrial civilization's "war against nature." (p.285)

> Today we enthusiastically participate in what is in essence a
> massive and unprecedented experiment with the natural sys-
> tems of the global environment, with little regard for the moral
> consequences. But for the separation of science and religion,
> we might not be pumping so much gaseous chemical waste
> into the atmosphere and threatening the destruction of the
> earth's climate balance. (p. 257)

And Mr. Gore insists that we not let him off the hook by supposing this is a mere analogy.

> It is not merely in the service of analogy that I have referred so
> often to the struggles against Nazi and communist totalitari-
> anism, because I believe that the emerging effort to save the
> environment is a continuation of these struggles. (p. 275)

Those of us (including Vice President Gore) who owe our long, comfortable and healthy lives to the accomplishments of modern industry, technology, and medicine—and therefore, to the scientific revolution—ought to be outraged by such claims. But these benefits to human life are not, for Gore, *moral* consequences of industrial activity, since they don't involve our impact on "the earth." The only consequence *he* considers to involve morality is the (alleged) destruction of the earth's climate balance. And why, might I ask, would mixing some religion with our science prevent us from doing this? Because in Gore's view, we would then look at the earth, not as a potential resource for the betterment of human life but rather as God's creation, and thus as something we are duty bound not to harm. "[A] panreligious perspective may prove especially important where our global civilization's responsibility for the earth is concerned" (p. 259).

Gore finds the basis of the environmental crisis in the belief, underlying the scientific and industrial revolutions, that "the human intellect could safely analyze and understand the natural world without reference to any moral principles defining our relationship and duties to both God and God's creation."[9] But Bacon and his followers in the Enlightenment have quite clearly defined principles about our relationship to nature. The principles are these: (a) we should use the methods of empirical science to understand nature's mechanisms, and (b) we should harness those mechanisms for the improvement of human life. Though he would like us to think so, it is not a *lack* of moral principles that Gore is taking issue with—*it is the very moral principles of the scientific and industrial revolution, which are profoundly at odds with his own.* Gore is asking us to reject the morality of man's "right" to rational control of nature for his own benefit. By ignoring the moral justification for the scientific and industrial revolutions, he has paved the way for the unopposed advocacy of the sacred earth argument. By using moral terms, such as "violation," "war," and "domination," to describe the scientifically based use of natural resources as property, he adopts the position that those resources are inviolate, good in themselves. This becomes explicit in the claim that we have "duties" toward God's creation—duties, that is, to trees, coal, shrimp, forests, and the like. It becomes clearer still as he ends the chapter with the search for the "panreligious perspective" mentioned earlier.

Gore has managed to invent a myth whereby the scientific revolution *lacked* moral principles. This provides him the high moral ground and eliminates the need to argue about which moral principles ought to define man's place in nature. But this is all a self-serving myth, and in the space that remains, I shall argue that *if human life is the standard of value, it is the values of Bacon and the Enlightenment that have the high moral ground.* On the other hand, if Mr. Gore wishes to rest his morality on a standard *other than* human life, he should identify it explicitly so that people know what it is that is to take priority over their lives.

THE ETHICAL ALTERNATIVES

Chapters 12 and 13 of *Earth in the Balance* reveal the philosophical/theological vision driving Albert Gore's environmentalism. He sees the root of all environmental evil in the scientific and industrial/technological revolutions. Both followed from people heeding Bacon's injunction to use the power of knowledge for human betterment.

The quality and quantity of life in those parts of the world influenced by science, technology, and capitalism is so much better in the late-20th century than at any other time in human history that it cannot be how terrible life actually is that motivates Gore's apocalyptic vision. Rather, it is a deeply held theological attitude toward the natural world. Gore views the scientific use of that world for human gain as evil in itself and as a violation of our duty to God and His creation.

> The more we rely on technology to mediate our relationship to nature, the more we encounter the same trade-off: we have more power to process what we need from nature more conveniently for more people, but the sense of awe and reverence that used to be present in our relationship to nature is often left behind. (p. 203)

Precisely. Every other species treats nature as a source of the values needed to sustain life. Are we, in contrast, duty bound to stand back in awe and reverence of nature?[10] It is not *Bacon's* philosophy that advocates the separation of man from nature but Gore's: Gore views nature, not as a potential source of human value, but as an object of worship; as a temple rather than a dwelling place.

Vice President Gore, like many in the environmental movement, advocates rejecting the philosophical tradition responsible for an unprecedented standard of living (including an enormous amount of leisure to "get back to nature"), while taking the economic consequences of that tradition as a given. This is a tragic mistake. Abandoning that tradition will lead us back to the dark ages as surely as embracing it led us out of them.

The essence of human nature is found, as Ayn Rand has stressed,[11] in our volitional faculty of reason. Humans are able, by the use of proper methods of inductive and deductive reasoning, to abstract scientific laws from our perceptual awareness of the world. But while we are *able* to do this, it is not an automatic process; each individual must put forward the effort to formulate concepts consistent with observation, connect them by induction, and infer their consequences. This ability is of crucial, practical importance to us; human life depends on it. Between the Renaissance and the 20th century, due largely to that period's increase in freedom of thought and action, scientists wrenched the secrets of physics, chemistry, and biology from nature. As a result, doctors, inventors, and entrepreneurs were able to apply this knowledge in ways that made human life longer, easier, safer, and more productive.

The achievement of these values depends upon the rational, purposeful, scientific control of the natural world. Those of us living in a technologically advanced society have no reason to feel alienated either from our own nature or from the rest of the natural world. It is human nature to be able to understand, create, and control natural processes—

that is the only way that creatures with reason can improve their lives. Like every organism, we must "dominate" and "transgress" some part of nature to provide for our own needs. Those humans who find this "unnatural" most likely have an incomplete, inconsistent, or otherwise unworkable theory of human nature. This and Gore's theistic attitude to "the earth" are the basic premises of Mr. Gore's Environmental Creed.

The alternative view of human values sketched here has been articulated and defended by Ayn Rand.[12] On this view, values are neither subjective nor are they intrinsic properties of nature. The value of anything depends on its ability to fulfill the needs of some organism. Living things must take specific courses of action to acquire and transform their environment in the ways necessary for their survival. It is for this reason alone that the environment has value for any organism, including human beings. Nature has no value except insofar as it serves the interests and needs of living things. Therefore, the standard adopted to determine the value of something is the life of the organism for which it has value.

Humans are living things, born ignorant of what is good for us and possessed of the incredible power of reason. It is, as Rand constantly stressed, our principal tool of survival. Without it we are more powerless than any creature on earth. With it, we can determine what in nature is of value to us and discover the laws that govern natural processes. These two abilities combined allow us to *create* an endless stream of values lying dormant in the natural world. In this way have we arrived at a world enhanced by fiber optics, lasers, and genetically engineered bacterial factories. In and of themselves, bacteria are neither good nor bad. Judged by the standard of human life, however, they can be either one—good when "engineered" to produce insulin and bad when invading the bloodstream and causing disease.

This, I submit, is a suitable alternative to the morality into which Mr. Gore attempts to browbeat his readers. It takes natural resources as neither good nor bad in themselves but as potentially one or the other depending on whether or not humans are able to harness them for the satisfaction of human needs and desires. That harnessing is what the scientific and industrial revolutions are all about, what Bacon envisaged when he concluded that "human knowledge and human power really do meet in one." This is a morality that takes human life as the source of human values and denies that the natural world has intrinsic value. There is an obvious sense in which *this*, not Mr. Gore's, is a morality that accepts humans as part of nature, using its resources as all living things do, for our own purposes.

There is, however, a profound sense in which modern industrial society *has* isolated us from nature. Life lived in submission to the natural forces of climate and disease, lived without labor-saving technology, without the fruits of sophisticated agricultural techniques, and without modern medicine is, to borrow a phrase from another of Bacon's contemporaries Thomas Hobbes, "solitary, poor, nasty, brutish, and short." To be "alienated" from nature in *that* sense is, if human life is the standard of value, a supremely good thing. I encourage all those in the environmental movement who disagree to have the courage of their convictions—give life without these things a try. On behalf of those of us who feel natural and comfortable in a civilized, technological environment, I make only one request—*Laissez nous faire, s'il vous plait.*

In this discussion, I have focused exclusively on the philosophical core of Albert Gore's environmentalism. I have ignored Gore's embarrassing attempts to bolster his claims with references to split brain research, chaos theory, the Heisenberg uncertainty principle, the general theory of relativity, and so on. These references display the muddled and undigested lack of comprehension of a bad undergraduate essay and are not worth responding to. But the fact that Gore apparently thinks he understands what he is talking about, when he so obviously does not, should disturb every reader of *Earth in the Balance*. If Gore has the same level of comprehension of the sciences relevant to issues such as "global warming" or "ozone depletion," it goes a long way toward explaining why he is willing to believe in an imminent environmental catastrophe.

CONCLUSION

This essay was begun in Pittsburgh, for many years a symbol of industrial productivity in America, and of the pollution such productivity can yield as a side effect. It was completed in Northern Wyoming, in the shadow of the Absaroka mountain range. Pittsburgh is now largely free of the industrial pollution it once was infamous for. It is also largely free of the steel industry that gave it its life. Many things contributed to the decline of that industry, but a major contributing factor was the use of the coercive power of the state to impose air quality standards on the steel industry unlike those anywhere else in the world. Living in Pittsburgh is a lesson in the costs, as well as the benefits, of state-imposed environmentalism.

Similar lessons can be learned in Wyoming. The National Park Service and the United States Forest Service are busy using their own brand of coercion to mismanage its natural resources, as apparently unconcerned with the costs as was the EPA. Environmentalists who share the attitude expressed by Vice President Gore in *Earth in the Balance* no doubt cheered the demise of the steel industry. They are finding it harder to cheer the demise of wilderness they express such concern for at the hands of the departments of Interior and Agriculture.

And yet the lessons are similar—if people value something highly, they will pay for it without coercion. There is a market for anything of value, whether it is wilderness or clean air. But to take this approach to environmental concerns, we must give up the attitude that "nature is God and technology the devil." We must view nature as a source of human values, whether economic, aesthetic, or recreational. We must reject the gospel according to Gore.[13]

Notes

1. To simplify the discussion I shall ignore the very important issue of weighing the costs *and benefits* of economic activity. *Earth in the Balance,* like most books of its kind, ignores both the costs of environmental legislation and the benefits of the products and productive activity they oppose. Two examples of this come to mind. Gore talks reverently of the (largely anecdotal) evidence presented by Rachel Carson in *Silent Spring* of the toxic effects of DDT (p.3) without mentioning the incontrovertible evidence that where it was used it saved millions of lives worldwide by virtually wiping out many insect born diseases. For correctives, see Elizabeth M. Whelan, *Toxic Terror* (Ottawa IL: Jameson Books, 1985); Dixie Lee Ray, *Trashing the Planet* (Washington DC: Regnery Gateway, 1990.) Gore also refers to the improved air and water quality around Pittsburgh as an environmental success story (p. 82) without mentioning that this is almost entirely due to the collapse of the steel industry in the area. A significant factor in that collapse was the multibillion dollar price tag of meeting ever more stringent EPA air quality standards.

2. These types of claims must be distinguished, since there may be good evidence for [a] but none for [b]. For example, there is good evidence that the amount of CO_2 in the atmosphere attributable to human activity rose dramatically after 1930 but none for a correlation between this rise and that of average global temperature, and no way of predicting whether the net effects of this increase in "greenhouse" gases will be beneficial or harmful to human beings.

3. Since both arguments conclude by enjoining the same change in values, there is a way to combine them, and Gore does so. The idea is to argue first that the moral attitude that it is acceptable to "violate" nature is intrinsically evil, and because it is evil we will be punished for it. If you want to test which argument a person takes most seriously, simply ask whether, if there were nothing but benefits to human beings to come from these "violations" of nature, he would still consider them immoral. As George Reisman has pointed out, the fundamental philosophical premise of the sacred earth argument—that the natural world is something of intrinsic value, an end in itself—is often held implicitly by people who fail to see its radical implications . Cf. "The Toxicity of Environmentalism," in Jay H. Lehr, ed., *Rational Readings on Environmental Concerns* (New York: Van Nostrand Reinhold 1992), p. 821.

4. This passage exemplifies a pervasive stylistic aspect of this book— its constant repetition of the first person plural subject "we." It is entirely unclear whether, in doing this, Gore is providing a speculative and untestable hypothesis about every member of Western civilization, a revealing portrait of his own soul, the results of interviews with his friends and family, or what. No doubt if a reader were to claim to be perfectly happy living in air-conditioned, computerized, well-fed comfort, Mr. Gore would simply insist that he was practicing denial: Indeed, he repeatedly characterizes opponents of environmentalism in precisely these terms.

5. Sir Francis Bacon, *The New Organon and Related Writings*, edited with an Introduction by Fulton H. Anderson (New York: Bobbs-Merrill, 1960), p. 29.

6. Cf. Peter Urbach, *Francis Bacon's Philosophy of Science* (La Salle IL: Open Court, 1987).

7. Bacon, op. cit., p. xxvii.

8. It must remain an assumption since, while Gore speaks with an air of authority about a wide variety of philosophers, he provides no references for the claims he makes.

9. Notice how easily Mr. Gore assumes that lack of concern for moral consequences is due to a separation of science and *religion*—as if there were no secular subject called ethics.

10. In fact, it is not obvious that these are exclusive alternatives. Certainly, I feel something akin to awe when I look at the raw power of Niagara Falls, while appreciating it as a valuable source of hydro-electric power. I feel a similar combination of awe and appreciation when I think about Cray super-computers, fiber optic networks, and satellite images transported millions of miles through space.

11. See "The Objectivist Ethics," in Ayn Rand, *The Virtue of Selfishness* (New York: New American Library, 1965).

12. Rand, op. cit., 1965.

13. It is a pleasure to acknowledge the many valuable suggestions of John Baden and David Kelley incorporated into the final version of this essay.

PART II

CLIMATE ISSUES

CHAPTER 5

Global Warming: The Gore Vision Versus Climate Reality

Robert C. Balling, Jr.

I believe that the best available evidence argues strongly against any rapid and substantial changes to the planetary temperature. Over the past five years, a fascinating spectrum of opinions has emerged in the global warming debate. On one end of this spectrum are scientists and some policymakers suggesting that an increase in greenhouse gases will not create any *catastrophic* climate changes in the decades to come. Their assessment leads to the conclusion that the most probable climatic changes (for example, increasing nighttime temperatures, lowering afternoon temperatures, increasing precipitation) may not be disastrous and could even be beneficial to life on the planet.

Some scientists at this end of the greenhouse-opinion spectrum note that carbon dioxide (CO_2) is not a pollutant at all but rather a valuable fertilizer for the growth of plants (see Idso, 1989). Their view is that increasing concentrations of atmospheric CO_2 levels may result in the direct benefit of increasing productivity throughout much of the biosphere. The scientists who are at this end of the spectrum tend to be driven by data-based arguments—they seem to be more impressed with the facts than with the predictions from theoretical models.

From a policy perspective, many of these same scientists feel that no "corrective" policy is needed at this time; there is no urgency to rush into immediate policy action and that any realistic policies are likely to fail in an attempt to substantially reduce greenhouse gas emissions. In Gore's *Earth in the Balance,* we are led repeatedly to believe that these greenhouse skeptics are: (a) small in number and shrinking in number, (b) less credible than other scientists working on the issue, (c) puppets of industry, (d) over-exposed by the media, and (e) looking for "excuses for procrastination" (p. 37).

At the other end of the greenhouse spectrum we find scientists, many policymakers, and much of the environmental community (including assorted movie stars and rock stars) who see a very real disaster in the winds. This group believes that increasing CO_2 levels will increase planetary temperatures considerably, melting ice caps and raising sea levels around the world. Future droughts will more frequently ravage many agricultural heartlands, super-sized hurricanes will tear away at our coastlines, climate as we know it will change its present day regional structure, and general social and economic chaos will result. Any biological benefits of increasing CO_2 will be lost as the biosphere struggles to cope with the rapidly unfolding changes in regional climate. The individuals at this end of the greenhouse-opinion spectrum feel that corrective policy is needed immediately, and they are confident that policy can work to significantly slow greenhouse gas emissions. Quite clearly, the many themes in Gore's *Earth in the Balance* are driven by the underlying beliefs of those who see the greenhouse effect as a severe and immediate threat to the planet; his book is very well received by those at this end of the spectrum.

As a climatologist, I feel confident that an entire volume could be written addressing the many important climate-related points raised throughout Gore's book. To that end, I would strongly encourage readers to examine my own book *The Heated Debate* (Balling, 1992) before or after reading *Earth in the Balance.* You will find that one major, fundamental difference exists between Gore and me—Gore clearly sees the climate system as a collection of fragile but highly interrelated components. I see the climate system as a collection of robust and highly integrated components.

Over billions of years of earth-atmosphere evolution, fragile systems surely would have been replaced by more robust ones; a system of interdependent and fragile components would have little chance of surviving the eons. Gore believes that human-induced changes to atmospheric chemistry are likely, if not certain, to lead to significant changes in climate comparable to those observed over geological time scales. I firmly believe that the earth-atmosphere system will be able to cope with the human-induced changes (which are actually quite small compared to

110

changes over geological time scales) without, as Gore says, throwing the climate system "out of whack" (p. 97).

Gore raises two central themes about climate change. First, Gore believes that global climate changes are likely to be substantial and rapid as we continue to add greenhouse gases to the atmosphere. Second, he believes that corrective policies are likely to have a substantial impact on future atmospheric CO_2 levels and resulting global temperatures. Here again, I believe that the best evidence available does not support Gore's contention. I will argue that (a) the evidence does not support either Gore's view of likely planetary temperature increases or his view on the impact of policy, and (b) a large number of scientists do not feel comfortable with the extreme positions presented in *Earth in the Balance* (see Michaels, 1992, p. 181–183).

THE UNDISPUTED RISE IN GREENHOUSE GASES

No one denies that human activities are increasing the atmospheric concentration of various greenhouse gases (see Figure 1). We know with great confidence that due largely to fossil fuel burning and tropical deforestation atmospheric CO_2 levels have increased from approximately 295 parts per million (ppm) in 1900 to near 360 ppm at present. These molecules of CO_2 have the ability to absorb some infrared radiation (energy from the heat of the earth and atmosphere) that otherwise would escape to space. This trapping of heat energy has been likened to the effects found in glass-enclosed greenhouses; hence, CO_2 is referred to as a greenhouse gas. However, other gases are also increasing in atmospheric concentration due to human activities, and like CO_2, some of these gases are acting to trap additional heat energy. Most important of these other greenhouse gases are methane, various chlorofluorocarbons, and nitrous oxide. When the thermal effects of these other greenhouse gases are expressed in carbon dioxide equivalents, we find that equivalent CO_2 has risen from approximately 310 ppm in 1900 to over 430 ppm at present.

Herein lies a critical point in the greenhouse debate, and a central reason why the "skeptics" remain important players in the global warming controversy. Given the observed changes in global atmospheric chemistry over the past century, many skeptics ask, "Where is all the warming?" Gigantic numerical models of climate that generate Gore's predicted outcome for continued buildup of greenhouse gases can be used to simulate what should have been observed over the past century. Without fail, these large computer global climate models predicting future

Parts/Million

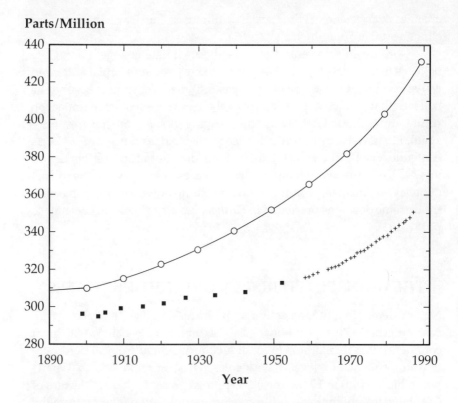

FIGURE 1 Increase in atmospheric carbon dioxide (lower set of boxes and plus signs) and atmospheric equivalent carbon dioxide (upper curve with circles) over the past century. Data are from Boden et al. (1990) and Balling (1992).

disaster suggest that the 40 percent rise in equivalent CO_2 seen over the past century already should have produced a global temperature rise somewhere between 1°C and 2°C (Houghton et al., 1990). Gore claims that global atmospheric temperature has increased by almost 1°C over the past 100 years and that the "upward trend appears to be accelerating as CO_2 concentrations increase" (p. 96, graph). If Gore is correct, the global warming theory and the observations would be in general agreement, and many of the skeptics would probably convert to his position immediately. But if Gore is wrong on this important point, a substantial underpinning of his massive Global Marshall Plan would be seriously eroded. It is on this central issue that I strongly believe that Gore is simply dead wrong.

112

LESSONS FROM PLANETARY TEMPERATURE

Determining a time series of planetary temperature is no simple task, but fortunately scientists at the University of East Anglia have produced such a time series that has been widely used by climate scientists on all sides of the greenhouse debate (see Jones et al., 1986). Jones and his colleagues searched millions of temperature records from land-based and ocean-based stations (including ship reports). They assembled the station-specific time series of monthly temperatures, converted all station data to anomalies (deviations from normal monthly temperatures), and interpolated the temperature data onto a 5° latitude by 10° longitude grid system. These gridded temperature anomalies may then be averaged using a weighting system that accounts for the area of the earth represented by each grid point. The annual planetary temperature anomalies that result from this procedure are shown in Figure 2. With regard to this important depiction of global temperature patterns, the following five points argue very strongly against the greenhouse scare.

First, over the period 1890–1990, the linear rise in planetary temperature was 0.45°C, not the "almost" 1°C claimed by Gore (p. 96). Even if all of the 0.45°C was forced by the buildup of greenhouse gases, the observational record would be pointing to a much smaller greenhouse effect than the one described by Gore. Climate models predicting a greenhouse catastrophe inevitably show that a warming of at least 1°C already should be evident in the temperature record of the past century, and yet the best data we have show less that 0.5°C over this time period (Houghton et al., 1990; 1992).

Second, climatologists are fully aware that urbanization taking place around the globe has created a contaminant to the temperature record. As cities grow, they inevitably get warmer, and thermometers in the urban environment will display a rise in temperature through time that could be mistaken for a greenhouse signal. Somewhere between 5 percent and 25 percent of the global warming of the past century is not real at all—it is a trend that comes from the urban data that contaminates the temperature record.

In addition, overgrazing and desertification, which are taking place over substantial parts of the land area of the planet, have been shown to produce a warming effect that could be mistaken as a greenhouse signal (Balling, 1992). Overgrazing reduces sparse vegetation in arid and semi-arid areas, exposing the thin soils to rapid erosion. Rain that falls in overgrazed areas more quickly runs off the surface, and the incoming sunlight then heats the ground and lower parts of the atmosphere at an

Global Temperature Anomalies (°C)

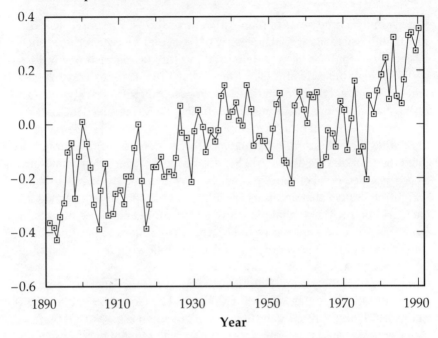

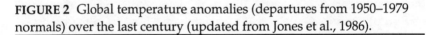

FIGURE 2 Global temperature anomalies (departures from 1950–1979 normals) over the last century (updated from Jones et al., 1986).

accelerated rate. Areas where desertification and overgrazing do not take place will retain the vegetation and soil cover. Here, precipitation does not run off so quickly, and solar energy is used in evaporation and transpiration processes. Less energy goes to heat the ground and air, and near surface air temperatures remain lower than in areas that have been overgrazed. Consequently, areas undergoing overgrazing and desertification are likely to warm through time, and the warming has nothing to do with the buildup of greenhouse gases. Rather, it is due to human-induced activities. Therefore, while the thermometers of the world may show some warming, there is certainly no guarantee that all (or any) of the warming has been forced by the known buildup of greenhouse gases.

Third, planetary temperature is driven by a multitude of factors other than the amount of greenhouse gas in the atmosphere. In particular, solar output and volcanic eruptions are two widely discussed candidates for controlling variations in global temperatures.

Most scientists have agreed that large volcanic eruptions eject massive amounts of dust into the stratosphere that can block incoming radiation (for a review, see Mass and Portman, 1989). When this occurs, less solar radiation reaches the ground, and the planetary temperature drops significantly within a few months of the large eruption. Basic climatological theory predicts cooling from these eruptions, and indeed, the observational global temperature record is in general agreement with the theoretical predictions. Throughout Gore's chapter three, he often refers to this strong linkage between global temperature and volcanic eruptions as evidence of the sensitivity of climate to changes in atmospheric constituents. However, if we statistically control for known variations in stratospheric dust from volcanic eruptions, about 25 percent of the trend in planetary temperature is accounted for over the past century (Balling, 1992). While I totally agree with Gore's assessment that volcanoes control regional, hemispheric, and global climate, I must add that the volcanoes have been responsible, in part, for the observed trends in planetary temperature over the past century.

In addition, varying output from the sun should have an obvious impact on the temperature of the earth. However, in the eyes of many scientists, the magnitude of solar output variations does not appear to be sufficient to have caused the observed variations in planetary temperature. Indeed, in referring to scientists working on the solar-climate linkage, Gore states that "neither measurements of the sun's radiation nor the accepted understanding of solar physics lends any credence whatsoever to their speculation" (p. 90). In my own discussion of this topic in *The Heated Debate* (Balling, 1992, p. 67), I also concluded that the correlation between solar output and temperature has not been particularly strong at the time scale of a century. However, recent results by Friis-Christensen and Lassen (1991) show a strong correlation between the earth's temperature and the length of the solar sunspot cycle (yet another measure of solar intensity). While no one claims to fully understand the physical connection behind the statistical correlation, this remarkable finding has invigorated the debate on the role of solar variations on earth temperature. Irrespective of the outcome of this debate, it should be apparent that urbanization, overgrazing/desertification, volcanic dust in the stratosphere, and variations in solar output have influenced planetary temperature over the past century. Any claim by Gore or others that the warming trend of the past century is uniquely related to the buildup of greenhouse gases dismisses this compelling evidence to the contrary.

Fourth, Gore states that the planetary temperature has shown an accelerated increase in the rate of warming in recent years that has coincided with the increase in the atmospheric concentration of green-

115

house gases (p. 96). However, rather simple analysis of the planetary temperatures over the past century shows that between 1890 and 1940 the rise in global temperature was 0.34°C—fully 75 percent of the total warming of the past century (0.45°C) occurred in the first half of the period! A considerable mismatch clearly exists between the observed timing of the warming and the observed buildup in greenhouse gases.

And fifth, a new measurement of the temperature of the earth further argues against Gore's claim of rapid warming in recent years (in fact, Gore's figure on page 96 shows phenomenal warming of approximately 0.4°C in the most recent 15 years). A fleet of polar-orbiting satellites carries equipment capable of measuring thermal emission of molecular oxygen in the lower part of the atmosphere. This emission of energy is heavily dependent on the temperature of the lower atmosphere, and the emitted energy can escape into space with little disruption from the state of the atmosphere. The satellite-based temperature measurement provides total global coverage, it avoids urban-biases, and appears to be the most accurate method available at this time for computing the true global temperature (Spencer and Christy, 1990).

From 1979 to 1990, and during a time of most rapid buildup in atmospheric concentrations of greenhouse gases, the satellite-based temperature measurements have shown a planetary warming of only 0.001°C (inclusion of the most recent two years of record would lower this value due to the cooling effects of the eruption of Mount Pinatubo). Many of the numerical models of climate suggest that the warming (given the known increase in equivalent CO_2) should be on the order of 0.3°C over that same time period (Houghton et al., 1990; 1992), and Gore's figure on page 96 shows warming of approximately that amount. Unfortunately for the pro-greenhouse argument, the satellites are seeing virtually no warming at all, and certainly they are not supporting the claim of accelerated warming in recent decades.

From the evidence above, along with mounds of hemispheric and regional evidence not covered here (see Balling, 1992), I firmly believe that the observed changes in planetary temperature are *not* broadly consistent with expected changes given the known increases in the atmospheric concentration of various greenhouse gases. Most of the observed warming occurred before the bulk of the greenhouse gases were added to the atmosphere, the amount of warming has been too low to be consistent with Gore's catastrophic predictions, and many factors other than the CO_2 rise account for the trend and variations in planetary temperature. In addition, this warming has not occurred in the right places (for example, the Arctic region) to be consistent with the models, and as discussed by

116

Michaels (1992), most of the warming has occurred at night (not a greenhouse expectation). Very simply, the climate record over the last century or decade is not pointing in the direction of a greenhouse apocalypse.

GASES THAT COOL?

The points raised in the preceding section are well known and widely discussed throughout the climate literature. In the last few years, we have come to realize that future climate will not only depend, in part, on the concentration of greenhouse gases but also on the atmospheric concentration of other gases that may have cooling effects on the planet—most of this new focus has been on the cooling effect of sulfur dioxide in the atmosphere.

Just like the emission of the many greenhouse gases, the global emission of sulfur dioxide has increased exponentially over this past century despite recent reductions in the United States and Western Europe (Moller, 1984). But unlike many greenhouse gases, the sulfur dioxide molecules stay in the atmosphere only a few days or weeks, and they do not get so evenly distributed around the globe. Sulfur dioxide molecules change in the atmosphere to form various aerosol sulfate particles that can cool the earth by (a) reflecting incoming sunlight back to space, (b) brightening existing clouds, and (c) extending the lifetimes of existing clouds (Charlson et al., 1990, 1992). When climate models include these effects, sulfur dioxide increases are shown to cool the earth (Wigley, 1991; Wigley and Raper, 1992). So, quite clearly, the future climate will be functionally related, to some degree, not only to the level of greenhouse gases but also to the level of sulfur dioxide that will be found in the atmosphere. Without fail, the inclusion of realistic future atmospheric concentrations of sulfur dioxide significantly lowers the predicted rise in global temperature (Houghton et al., 1992). The temperature of the atmosphere depends on many factors; simply relating the concentration of CO_2 to planetary temperature overlooks the complications involved in determining the state of the climate system.

POLICY PROBLEMS

From the discussion above, it should be rather clear that enormous uncertainties remain in some of the most fundamental scientific questions associated with the global warming issue. Within the coming decades, numerical models will be vastly improved and will be capable of far more

117

accurate predictions of future temperature levels. Historical climate records are being developed and analyzed at an accelerated pace, and the
high-quality satellite-based global temperature data base is growing in
length and receiving more and more attention. Given the intense interest
in the greenhouse effect, and given the many scientists now involved in
the issue, we should continue to see an explosion of new information on
the subject. What we know today about global warming could be dwarfed
by the knowledge that will be gained in the coming decade.

Yet many greenhouse proponents, certainly Gore included, believe
that we must act immediately to avoid disaster. Despite the uncertainties,
we are told that waiting is too dangerous—we need to error on the side of
caution and take out an insurance policy on our future—we need to stop
global warming! Gore's tactic is to present the greenhouse effect as an
apocalypse and then offer his sweeping policy plans (including the Global
Marshall Plan) to cope with or avoid the disaster. In my own view, the
following two points must be considered before moving toward these
policy decisions.

First, despite all the claims that we must act immediately, several
scientists have shown that implementing policies can wait for a decade
with little climatic penalty. Schlesinger and Jiang (1991) used a numerical
model to simulate the impact of realistic policies hypothetically adopted
in 1990. They then simulated the impact of implementing the same policies
a decade later and found that the future temperature of the earth was
largely unaffected by the delay. They argued that nature has provided a
window of opportunity to get the science right and develop realistic
estimates of policy costs and benefits. Their results have sparked tremendous debate on the policy side of the global warming issue, but despite
the lack of popularity with the policy-driven global warmers, their results
continue to stand.

And second, many policymakers are led to believe that some policy
actions can *stop* global warming, or at least significantly decrease its threat.
However, this may not be true at all. To illustrate this point, Figure 3 was
derived directly from the 1990 Intergovernmental Panel on Climate
Change (IPCC) report (Houghton et al., 1990). The upper line (the top edge
of the dark shaded area) represents the IPCC "Business-as-usual" trend
in planetary temperature over the next century. If we follow the present
path and do not take action to deal with the global warming threat, we
ultimately warm the earth by over 4°C by the end of the next century and
the greenhouse disaster presumably becomes reality. If we adopt IPCC
"Scenario B," which includes (a) moving to lower carbon-based fuels,
(b) achieving large efficiency increases, (c) controlling carbon monox-
118

Global Warming (°C)

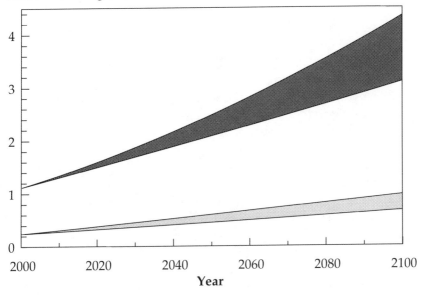

FIGURE 3 IPCC "Business-as-usual" projected warming (upper boundary of the dark shaded area) and IPCC "Scenario B" projected warming (lower boundary of the dark shaded area) for the coming century (Houghton et al., 1990). The lower set of lines (defining the lightly shaded area) are the proportionally reduced "Business-as-usual" and "Scenario B" estimates.

ide, (d) reversing deforestation, and (e) implementing the Montreal Protocol (dealing with chlorofluorocarbon controls) with full participation, we get the line at the bottom of the dark shaded area. Incredibly, we still get nearly 3°C of warming if we adopt this policy. Global warming is not eliminated, it is barely slowed. The IPCC "Scenario B" policy buys us the dark shaded area; by the year 2050, our policies have only saved us 0.3°C.

I have argued that the impact of policy is heavily dependent on the amount of warming predicted over the next century. If we assume that only 1°C will be realized in the next century (and I believe even 1°C is unlikely), we see what happens to our policy impact. Now IPCC "Scenario B" policies save the planet less than 0.3°C by the year 2100; by 2050, these policy options would have spared the earth only something near 0.07°C. The climate impact of various policies is directly related to the amount of warming expected in the future; as we reduce the estimate of future warming

119

for whatever reason (inclusion of SO_2, development of better models), we also reduce the potential climate impact of our corrective policies.

CONCLUSION

Vice President Gore and many others have exaggerated both the threat of global warming and the potential impact realistic policy could ever have on planetary temperature levels. Proponents of global warming call for immediate action based on what is known today. However, rushing into action ignores the findings of Schlesinger and Jiang (1991); immediate action also would be taken before we have the findings of hundreds of ongoing (and expensive) greenhouse-related studies around the world.

Policymakers are moving so far ahead of the scientists that the scientific basis for global warming policy has become somewhat irrelevant. As long as the public believes so strongly in the greenhouse crisis, the global warming issue will remain in the laps of our policymakers. The public may believe that warming is occurring irrespective of the actual trends in local, regional, hemispheric, or global temperatures. For example, Harlin (1990) surveyed 100 full professors, medical doctors, and attorneys in Alabama. He asked them if Alabama was warming or cooling this century. Of the 100 respondents, 98 thought that Alabama was warming, and all 98 blamed the greenhouse effect. However, Harlin showed that Alabama has been cooling steadily throughout this century! These professionals believe that warming is occurring. They blame the buildup of greenhouse gases, and they will likely expect various policymakers to take some type of action. The actual trend in temperature becomes somewhat irrelevant in the process. From this example, we may assume that at least some of our policymakers may be responding more to a global warming perception than to an actual global warming problem.

If we are to adopt the policies suggested by Gore and others, I certainly hope that the policies are constructed using the best science available and not on the hype, hysteria, and exaggerations that are so commonly used to sway opinion on the greenhouse issue. We must gather the facts, unemotionally debate the policy options (including the unpopular option of waiting to "do something"), and be certain that we have evaluated as fully as possible both the costs and the benefits of any proposed actions. Gore's Global Marshall Plan is certainly one direction we can take. But in the best interests of all involved, we need to fully explore a wide range of policy options.

References

Balling, R.C., Jr. (1992). *The heated debate: Greenhouse predictions versus climate reality.* San Francisco, CA: Pacific Research Institute.

Boden, T.A., Kanciruk, P., & Farrell, M.P. (1990). *Trends '90: A compendium of data on global change.* Oak Ridge, TN: Carbon Dioxide Information Analysis Center, Environmental Sciences Division, Oak Ridge National Laboratory.

Charlson, R.J., Langner, J., & Rodhe, H. (1990). Sulphate aerosol and climate. *Nature, 348,* 22.

Charlson, R.J., Schwartz, S.E., Hales, J.M., Cess, R.D., Coakley, Jr., J.A., Hansen, J.E., & Hofmann, D.J. (1992). Climate forcing by anthropogenic aerosols. *Science, 255,* 423–430.

Friis-Christensen, E., & Lassen, K. (1991). Length of the solar cycle: An indicator of solar activity closely associated with climate. *Science, 254,* 698–700.

Gore, A. (1992). *Earth in the balance: Ecology and the human spirit.* New York: Plume Edition, The Penguin Group.

Harlin, J.M. (1990). Warming trends resulting from the greenhouse effect: Fact versus perception. *Program and abstracts of the association of American geographers annual meeting (Toronto),* 95.

Houghton, J.T., Callander, B.A., & Varney, S.K. (eds.) (1992). *Climate change 1992: The supplementary report to the IPCC scientific assessment.* Cambridge, England: Cambridge University Press.

Houghton, J.T., Jenkins, G.J., & Ephraums, J.J. (eds.) (1990). *Climate change: The IPCC scientific assessment.* Cambridge, England: Cambridge University Press.

Idso, S.B. (1989). *Carbon dioxide and global change: Earth in transition.* Tempe, AZ: IBR Press.

Jones, P.D., Wigley, T.M.L., & Wright, P.B. (1986). Global temperature variations between 1861 and 1984. *Nature, 322,* 430–434.

Mass, C.F., & Portman, D.A. (1989). Major volcanic eruptions and climate: A critical evaluation. *Journal of Climate, 2,* 566–593.

Michaels, P.J. (1992). *Sound and fury: The science and politics of global warming.* Washington, DC: Cato Institute.

Moller, D. (1984). Estimation of the global man-made sulphur emission. *Atmospheric Environment, 18,* 19–27.

Schlesinger, M.E., & Jiang, X. (1991). Revised projection of future greenhouse warming. *Nature,* 350, 219–221.

Spencer, R.W., & Christy, J.R. (1990). Precise monitoring of global temperature trends from satellites. *Science,* 247, 1558–1562.

Wigley, T.M.L. (1991). Could reducing fossil-fuel emissions cause global warming? *Nature,* 349, 503–506.

Wigley, T.M.L., & Raper, S.C.B. (1992). Implications for climate and sea level of revised IPCC emission scenarios. *Nature,* 357, 293–300.

CHAPTER 6

Global Warming: The Origin and Nature of Alleged Scientific Consensus

Richard S. Lindzen

Most of the literate world today regards global warming as both real and dangerous. Indeed, the diplomatic activity concerning this issue would have you believe that this is the major crisis confronting humankind. The environmental conference in Rio in June 1992, Earth Summit, focused on development of international agreements to deal with this threat. I must state at the outset that, as a scientist, I can find no substantive basis for the warming scenarios being popularly described. Moreover, according to many studies by economists, agronomists, and hydrologists, there would be little difficulty adapting to such warming if it were to occur.

Many aspects of the "catastrophe" scenario have already been largely discounted by the scientific community. For example, fears of massive sea level increases accompanied many of the early discussions of global warming, but these estimates have been steadily reduced by orders of magnitude, and now it is widely agreed that even the potential contribution of warming to sea level rise would be swamped by other more important factors.

This article first appeared in *Regulation*, Spring 1992, Vol. 15, No. 2, pp. 87–98. It is reprinted with permission of the Cato Institute.

The truly peculiar feature of the global warming debate is that in the popular view the case for warming is virtually self-evident, while according to the so-called skeptics there are neither observational nor theoretical bases for concern. These so-called skeptics usually address all the technical issues. To the public, the technical arguments are typically opaque, and the popular literature continues to present the case for global warming as self-evident, even while admitting that there is some disagreement. The disagreement is usually treated as obscurely technical and unlikely.

As far as I can tell, the global warming debate is not, by and large, a debate about science. There is broad agreement over major scientific facts among experts who therefore have difficulty even understanding the existence of the popular view. There is broad misunderstanding by many, including nonspecialist scientists. The debate is largely a matter of spin control and intentional misrepresentation. The bulk of *relevant* information suggests little warming.

Environmental literature—including Vice President Al Gore's *Earth in the Balance*—relies on the same "arguments" as those presented in popular culture. Gore's book contains a remarkable volume of misinformation, although it offers an amusing discussion of the importance of climate in history. Here we learn of such things as the role of climate in the birth of modern German anti-semitism. While such a lofty view of the importance of climate might warm the heart of any climate scientist seeking funding, it is also the case that Gore regards research with more than a little suspicion. His remark, "Research in lieu of action is unconscionable," has become rather famous. However, the same attitude toward research is endemic in the bulk of environmental literature.

How did this peculiar situation arise? While my focus is global warming, where I have personally followed the phenomenon, what I will describe is similar to what is happening with respect to many other environmental "crises" including ozone depletion, acid rain, diminishing species diversity and contamination by PCBs, dioxin, asbestos, and lead. Nevertheless, there are differences as well—at least in scale.

SUMMARIZING THE SCIENTIFIC SITUATION

⊃ The data provide no evidence of human-induced global warming.

⊃ The models (whatever their other strengths or weaknesses) are predicting large global warming for identifiably artificial reasons.

⊃ There are substantial reasons for expecting the response to increased CO_2 will, in fact, be small.

The increasing acceptance of the above facts has led to a peculiar emphasis on the issue of potential climate "surprises." Here, the claim is that since we do not understand the climate system, it is possible that it may respond in ways we currently have no knowledge of if we subject the system to stress. This is indeed an unanswerable argument. The point, quite simply, is that ignorance is ignorance. It is certainly not a basis for action. If it were, the only logical response would be total paralysis.

CONSENSUS AND THE CURRENT POPULAR VISION

Many studies from the 19th century on suggested that industrial and other contributions to increasing CO_2 might lead to global warming. Problems with such predictions were also long noted, and the general failure of such predictions to explain the observed record caused the field of climatology as a whole to regard the suggested mechanisms as suspect. Indeed, the global cooling trend of the 1950s and 1960s led to a minor global cooling hysteria in the 1970s. All this was more or less normal scientific debate although the cooling hysteria had certain striking analogues to the present warming hysteria, including books such as *The Genesis Strategy* by S. Schneider and *Climate Change and World Affairs* by Crispin Tickell (both authors are prominent in support of the present concerns as well) "explaining" the problem and promoting international regulation. There was also a book by the prominent science writer Lowell Ponte (*The Cooling*) deriding skeptics and noting the importance of acting in the absence of firm scientific foundation. There was even a report by the National Research Council of the U.S. National Academy of Sciences reaching its usual ambiguous conclusions. However, the scientific community never took the issue to heart, governments ignored it, and with rising global temperatures in the late 1970s the issue more or less died.[1] In the meantime, model calculations—especially at the Geophysical Fluid Dynamics Laboratory at Princeton—continued to predict substantial warming due to increasing CO_2. These predictions were considered interesting but largely academic exercises—even by the scientists involved.

The present hysteria formally began in the summer of 1988, though preparations had been put in place at least three years earlier.[2] This was an especially warm summer in some regions, especially in the United States. As I noted in the discussion of observations, there was an abrupt increase in temperature in the late 1970s—too abrupt to be associated with the smooth increase in CO_2. However, in testimony before Senator Gore's

Committee on Science, Technology and Space, James Hansen (Director of the Goddard Institute for Space Studies) said, in effect, that he was 99 percent certain that temperature had increased and that there was *some* greenhouse warming. No statement was made concerning the relation between the two.

Despite the fact that these remarks were virtually meaningless, they led to the immediate adoption of the issue by the environmental advocacy movement. The growth of environmental advocacy since the 1970s has been phenomenal. In Europe, the movement centered on the formation of Green parties; in the United States, the movement centered on the development of large public interest advocacy groups. These lobbying groups have budgets in the hundreds of millions of dollars, and employ about 50,000 people; their support is highly valued by many political figures. As with any large group, self-perpetuation becomes a crucial concern. "Global Warming" has become one of the major battle cries in their fund raising efforts. At the same time, the media unquestioningly accept the pronouncements of these groups as objective truth.

However, within the large scale climate modeling community (a small subset of the community interested in climate), the immediate response was to criticize Hansen for publicly promoting highly uncertain model results as relevant to public policy. Hansen's motivation was not totally obvious, and despite the criticism of Hansen, the modeling community quickly agreed that large warming was not impossible. This was still enough for both the politicians and advocates who have generally adopted the paradigm that any hint of environmental danger is sufficient basis for regulation unless the hint can be rigorously disproved. This is a particularly pernicious asymmetry given that rigor is generally impossible in environmental sciences.

Other scientists quickly agreed that with increasing CO_2 some warming might be expected, and with large enough concentrations of CO_2 the warming might be significant. Nevertheless, there was widespread skepticism. By early 1989, however, the popular media in Europe and the U.S. were declaring that "all scientists" agreed that warming was real and catastrophic in its potential.

Like most scientists concerned with climate, I was eager to stay out of what seemed like a public circus. However, in the summer of 1988, Lester Lave, Professor of Economics at Carnegie-Mellon University, wrote to me about being dismissed from a Senate hearing for suggesting that the issue of global warming was scientifically controversial. I assured him that the issue was not only controversial but also unlikely. In the winter of 1989, Reginald Newell (Professor of Meteorology at the Massachusetts Institute

126

of Technology) lost National Science Foundation funding for data analyses that were failing to show net warming over the past century. Reviewers suggested that these results were dangerous to humanity. In the spring of 1989, I was an invited participant at a global warming symposium at Tufts University. I was the only scientist among a panel of environmentalists. There were strident calls for immediate action and ample expressions of impatience with science. Claudine Schneider (then a congresswoman from Rhode Island) acknowledged that "Scientists may disagree, but we can hear Mother Earth, and she is crying." It seemed clear to me that a very dangerous situation was arising, and the danger was not of global warming itself.

In the spring of 1989, I prepared a critique of global warming and submitted it to *Science* (a magazine of the American Association for the Advancement of Science). It was rejected without review as being of no interest to the readership. The paper was resubmitted to the *Bulletin of the American Meteorological Society* where it was accepted after review, re-reviewed and re-accepted (an unusual procedure to say the least). In the meantime, the paper was attacked in *Science*—prior to publication (in 1990). The paper circulated for about six months as Samizdat. It was delivered at a Humboldt Conference at MIT, and reprinted in the *Frankfurter Allgemeine.*

By this time, the global warming circus was in full swing. Meetings were going on nonstop. One of the more striking of these meetings was hosted in the summer of 1989 by Robert Redford at his ranch in Sundance, Utah. Redford proclaimed that it was time to stop research and begin acting. I suppose that this was a reasonable suggestion for an actor to make, but it is also indicative of the overall attitude to science. Barbra Streisand personally undertook to support the research of Michael Oppenheimer at the Environmental Defense Fund—even though he is primarily an advocate, and not a research climatologist. Meryl Streep made a public appeal to stop warming on Public Television. A bill was even prepared to guarantee Americans a stable climate. By the fall of 1989, some media were becoming aware that there was controversy (*Forbes* and *Readers Digest* were notable in this regard). Cries followed from environmentalists that skeptics were receiving too much exposure. The publication of my paper was followed by a determined effort on the part of the editor of the *Bulletin of the American Meteorological Society*, Richard Hallgren, to solicit rebuttals. Such articles were prepared by Stephen Schneider, and Will Kellogg (a minor scientific administrator for the last 30 years), and these articles were followed by an active correspondence mostly supportive of the skeptical spectrum of views. Indeed, a recent Gallup poll of climate scientists (in the American Meteorological Society and in the American Geophysical Union) shows that a vast majority doubt that there has been any identifiable human-caused warming to date: 49 percent asserted no, 33 percent didn't know, 18 percent thought yes some has occurred. However, among those actively involved in research and publishing frequently in peer-reviewed research journals, zero percent believe any human-caused global warming has occurred so far. On the whole, the debate within the meteorological community has been relatively healthy and, in this regard, unusual.

Outside the world of meteorology, Jeremy Legett (a geologist by training) of Greenpeace published a book attacking critics of warming—especially me. Senator Mitchell (Senate majority leader and father of a prominent environmental activist) also published a book urging acceptance of the warming problem (*World on Fire: Saving an Endangered Earth*). Senator Gore's book (*Earth in the Balance, Ecology and the Human Spirit*) followed, and this barely scratches the surface of the rapidly growing publications on this topic. Rarely has such meager science provoked such an outpouring of popularization by individuals who do not understand the subject in the first place.

The activities of a particular organization, the Union of Concerned Scientists, deserves special mention. This widely supported organization was originally devoted to nuclear disarmament. With the spindown of the Cold War, it began to actively oppose nuclear power generation. This position was unpopular with many physicists. Over the last few years, it has turned to the battle against global warming in a particularly hysterical manner. In 1989, it began to circulate a petition urging recognition of global warming as potentially the great danger to humankind. Most recipients who did not sign were solicited at least twice more. The petition was eventually signed by 700 scientists including a great many members of the National Academy of Sciences and Nobel Laureates. Only about three or four of the signers, however, had any involvement in climatology. Interestingly, the petition had two pages, and on the second page there was a call for renewed consideration of nuclear power. However, when the petition was published in the *New York Times*, the second page was omitted. In any event, this document helped solidify the public perception that "all scientists" agreed with the disaster scenario. This disturbing abuse of scientific authority was not unnoticed. At the 1990 annual meeting of the National Academy of Sciences, Frank Press (president of the academy) warned the membership against lending their credibility to issues about which they had no special knowledge. Special reference was made to the above petition. In my opinion, what the petition did show was that the need to fight "global warming" has become part of the dogma of the liberal conscience—a dogma to which scientists are not immune.

128

At the same time, political pressures on dissidents from the "popular vision" increased. Gore publicly admonished "skeptics" in a lengthy *New York Times* op-ed piece. (In a perverse example of double-speak, he associated the "true believers" in warming with Galileo. He also referred, in another article, to the summer of 1988 as the Kristallnacht before the warming holocaust.)

The notion of "scientific unanimity" is currently intimately tied to the Working Group I report of the Intergovernmental Panel on Climate Change issued in September 1990. This panel consists largely of scientists posted to it by government agencies. The panel has three working groups. Working Group I nominally deals with climate science. Approximately 150 scientists contributed to the report, but university representation from the U.S. was relatively small. This is likely to remain so, since the funds and time needed for participation are not available to most university scientists. Many governments have agreed to use this report as the authoritative basis for climate policy. The report, as such, has both positive and negative features. Methodologically, the report is deeply committed to reliance on large models, and within this report models are largely verified by comparison with other models. Given that models are known to agree more with each other than with nature (even after "tuning"), this approach does not seem promising. In addition, a number of the participants have testified to the pressures placed on them to emphasize results supportive of the current scenario and to suppress other results. This pressure was frequently effective, and a survey of participants reveals substantial disagreement with the final report. Nonetheless, the body of the report is extremely ambiguous, and the caveats are numerous. However, the report is prefaced by a Policymakers Summary written by the editor, Sir John Houghton, Director of the United Kingdom Meteorological Office. This summary largely ignores the uncertainty in the report and attempts to present the expectation of substantial warming as firmly based science.[3] The Summary is published as a separate document and it is safe to say that policymakers are unlikely to read anything further. On the basis of the summary, one frequently hears that "hundreds of the world's greatest climate scientists from dozens of countries all agreed that . . ." It hardly matters what the agreement refers to, since whoever refers to the summary insists it agrees with the most extreme scenarios (which, in all fairness, it does not). It should be added that the climatology community, until the last few years, was quite small and heavily concentrated in the U.S. and Europe.

While the IPCC reports were in preparation, the National Research Council in the United States was commissioned to prepare a synthesis of the current state of the global change situation. The panel chosen was hardly promising. It had no members of the National Academy expert in climate. Indeed, it had only one scientist directly involved in climate, Stephen Schneider, who is an ardent advocate. It also included three professional environmental advocates, and it was headed by former Senator Dan Evans. It should be added that the panel did include distinguished scientists and economists outside the area of climate, and perhaps because of this the report issued by the panel was by and large fair. Their report concluded that the scientific basis for costly action was absent, though prudence might indicate that actions that were cheap and worth doing anyway should be considered. A subcommittee of the panel issued a report on adaptation that argued that even with the more severe warming scenarios, the United States would have little difficulty adapting. Not surprisingly, the environmentalists on the panel strongly influenced the reports, but having failed to completely have their way, they attempted to distance themselves from the reports by either resigning or issuing minority dissents. Equally unsurprising is the fact that the reports of this panel were typically covered on page 46 of the *New York Times* and never subsequently discussed in the popular media—except to claim that the reports support the catastrophic vision. Nevertheless, the reports of this panel were indicative of the growing skepticism concerning this issue.

Indeed, the growing skepticism is in many ways remarkable. One of the earliest protagonists of global warming, Roger Revelle (late Professor of Ocean Sciences at Scripps Institution of Oceanography), who initiated the direct monitoring of CO_2 during the International Geophysical Year (1958), co-authored (with S. Fred Singer and Chauncy Starr) a paper just before his death recommending that action concerning global warming be delayed insofar as current knowledge was totally inadequate. Another active advocate of global warming, Michael McElroy (head of the Department of Earth and Planetary Sciences at Harvard), has recently written a paper acknowledging that existing models cannot be used to forecast climate.

You might think that this growing skepticism would have some influence on public debate, but the insistence on "scientific unanimity" continues unabated. At times, this insistence takes some very strange forms. More than two years ago, Robert White (former head of the Weather Bureau in the United States, and currently president of the National Academy of Engineering) wrote an article for *Scientific American* pointing out that the questionable scientific basis for global warming predictions was totally inadequate to justify any costly actions. He did state that if we were to insist on doing something, we should only do things that we would do even if there were no warming threat. Immedi-
130

ately after this article appeared, Tom Wicker (a columnist for the *New York Times* and a confidant of Vice President Gore) wrote a piece in which he stated that White had called for immediate action on global warming.

My own experiences have been similar. Stephen Schneider, in an article in *Audubon*, states that I have "conceded that some warming now appears inevitable." Differences between expectations of immeasurable changes of a few tenths of a degree and warming of several degrees are conveniently ignored. In a lengthy and laudatory article on James Hansen that appeared in the *New York Times Sunday Magazine*, Karen White reported that even I agreed that there would be warming, having "reluctantly offered an estimate of 1.2 degrees." This was, of course, untrue. When I testified at a 1992 Senate hearing conducted by then Senator Gore, there was a rather arcane discussion of the water vapor budget of the upper troposphere (5–12 km). In 1990, I had pointed out that if the source of water vapor in this region in the tropics were detrained water vapor from deep clouds, then surface warming would be accompanied by reduced upper level water vapor. In subsequent research it has been established that there must be an additional source, which is widely believed to be ice crystals, thrown off by these deep clouds. I noted that this source, too, probably acts to produce less moisture in a warmer atmosphere. Both processes cause the major feedback process to become negative rather than positive. Gore wanted to know if I now rejected my suggestion in 1990 as a major factor. I answered that I did.[4] Gore then called for the recording secretary to note that I had retracted my objections to global warming. There followed considerable argument (involving mostly other participants in the hearing) in which it was explained to Gore that he was confusing matters. However, shortly thereafter Tom Wicker published an article in the *New York Times* claiming that I had retracted my opposition to warming and that this warranted immediate action to curb the purported menace. I wrote a letter to the *Times* indicating that my position had been severely misrepresented and, after a delay of over a month, my letter was published. Vice President Gore, nonetheless, claims in his book that I have indeed retracted my *scientific* objections to the catastrophic warming scenario and also warns others who doubt the scenario that they are hurting humanity.

Why is there such insistence on scientific unanimity on this issue? After all, unanimity in science is virtually nonexistent on far less complex matters. Unanimity on an issue as uncertain as global warming would be surprising and suspicious. Moreover, why are the opinions of scientists sought regardless of their field of expertise? Biologists and physicians are rarely asked to endorse some theory in high energy physics. Apparently,

131

when it comes to global warming, any scientist's agreement will do.[5] The answer almost certainly lies in politics.

It is very risky for politicians to make commitments, such as setting targets and timetables for CO_2 emissions, unless scientists *insist* the threat of not doing so is real.

THE TEMPTATION AND
PROBLEMS OF GLOBAL WARMING

As Aaron Wildavsky (Professor of Political Science at Berkeley) has quipped, global warming is the mother of all environmental scares. Wildavsky's view is worth quoting. "Warming (and warming alone), through its primary antidote of withdrawing carbon from production and consumption, is capable of realizing the environmentalist's dream of an egalitarian society based on rejection of economic growth in favor of a smaller population eating lower on the food chain, consuming a lot less, and sharing a much lower level of resources much more equally." In many ways, Wildavsky's observation does not go far enough. The point is that carbon dioxide is vitally central to industry, transportation, modern life, and life in general. It has been joked that CO_2 controls will permit us to inhale as much as we wish; only exhaling will be controlled. The remarkable centrality of carbon dioxide means that dealing with the threat of warming fits in with a great variety of pre-existing agendas, some legitimate, some less so—energy efficiency, reduced dependence on middle eastern oil, dissatisfaction with industrial society (neo-pastoralism), international competition, governmental desires for enhanced revenues (carbon taxes), and bureaucratic desires for enhanced power.

The very scale of the problem as popularly portrayed and the massive scale of the suggested responses have their own appeal. The Working Group I report of the Intergovernmental Panel on Climate Change suggested, for example, that 60 percent reductions in CO_2 emissions might be needed. Such a reduction would call for measures that would be greater than those that have been devoted to war and defense. And just as defense has dealt with saving the nation, curbing global warming is identified with saving the whole planet! It may not be fortuitous that this issue is being promoted at just the moment in history when the Cold War is ending.

Major agencies in the United States, hitherto closely involved with traditional approaches to national security, have appropriated the issue of climate change to support existing efforts. Notable among these agencies are NASA, the Department of Defense, and the Department of Energy. The Cold War helped spawn a large body of policy experts and diplomats specializing in issues like disarmament and alliance negotiations. In addition, since the Yom Kippur War, energy has become a major component of national security with the concomitant creation of a large cadre of energy experts. Many of these individuals see in the global change issue an area in which to continue applying their skills. Many scientists also feel that national security concerns formed the foundation for the U.S. government's generous support of science. As the urgency of national security, traditionally defined, diminishes, there is a common feeling that a substitute foundation must be established. "Saving the Planet" has the right sort of sound to it. I have already mentioned the phenomenal growth of the environmental advocacy movement. It seems that fund-raising has become central to their activities, and the message underlying some of their fund-raising seems to be, "Pay us or you'll fry."

Clearly, global warming is a tempting issue for many important groups to exploit. Equally clearly, though far less frequently discussed, there are profound dangers in exploiting this issue. There are good reasons why there has been so little discussion of the downside of responding to global warming.

Let me begin with a parochial issue, namely, the danger to the science of climatology. As far as I can tell, there has actually been reduced funding for existing climate research. This may seem paradoxical, but at least in the U.S. the vastly increased number of scientists and others involving themselves in climate, as well as the gigantic programs attaching themselves to climate, have substantially outstripped the increases in funding. Perhaps more important are the pressures being brought to bear on scientists to get the "right" results. Such pressures are inevitable, given how far out on a limb much of the scientific community has gone. The situation is compounded by the fact that some of the strongest proponents of global warming in Congress and the White House are also among the major supporters of science (Vice President Gore is notable among these). Finally, given the momentum that has been building among so many interest groups to "fight global warming," it becomes downright embarrassing to support basic climate research. After all, we would hate to admit that we had mobilized so many resources without the basic science being in place. Nevertheless, given the large increase in the number of people associating themselves with climatology, and the dependence of much of this community on the perceived threat of warming, it seems unlikely that the scientific community will offer much resistance. It should be added that as ever greater numbers of individuals attach themselves to this problem, the pressures against solving the problem grow proportionally—too many individuals and groups depend on the problem remaining.

In addition to climatologists, are other groups at risk? Here, you might expect that industry could be vulnerable and, indeed, it may be. However, at least in the U.S., industries seem to be primarily concerned with improving their public image. One way they attempt to do this is by supporting environmental activists. Moreover, some industries have become successful at profiting from environmental regulation. The most obvious example is the waste management industry. However, even electric utility companies have been able to use environmental measures to increase the base on which their regulated profits are calculated. It is worth noting that about $1.7 trillion have been spent on the environment over the past decade. The environment, itself, qualifies as one of our major industries.

If Wildavsky's scenario is correct, the major losers will be ordinary people. Wealth will be squandered that could have been used to raise living standards in much of the world. Living standards in the developed world will decrease. Regulatory apparatuses will restrict individual freedom on an unprecedented scale. We cannot expect much resistance to these proposed actions—at least not initially. Public perceptions, under the influence of extensive, deceptive and one-sided publicity, can become disconnected from reality.[6] For example, the state of Alabama has had a pronounced cooling trend since 1935. Nevertheless, a poll among professionals in Alabama found that about 95 percent of the participants believed it had been warming over the past 50 years and that the warming was due to the greenhouse effect. Public misconceptions coupled with a sincere desire to save the planet can force political action even when politicians are aware of the reality.

What the above amounts to is a societal instability. At a particular point in history, a relatively minor suggestion or event serves to mobilize massive interests. While the proposed measures may be detrimental, resistance is largely absent or coopted. In the case of climate change, the fact that the proposed actions will, for the most part, have little impact on climate regardless of the scenario chosen, appears to be of no consequence.

It goes almost without saying, that the dangers and the costs of these economic and social consequences may be far greater than the original environmental danger. This becomes especially true when the benefits of additional knowledge are rejected, and when it is forgotten that improved technology and increased societal wealth are what allow society to deal with environmental threats most effectively. The control of this societal instability may very well be the real challenge facing us.

Notes

1. It is nonetheless worth noting that the last 700,000 years have been characterized by lengthy periods of glaciation interspersed by relatively brief interglacials such as our present climate. Presumably, we will have another ice age in a few thousand years.

2. In a paper in *Science* in 1985, for example, Jim Hansen was already arguing that a "wait and see" attitude concerning warming was inappropriate because of the ocean delay. He suggested that because of ocean delay, we were already "committed" to substantial warming even though we might not see it for over a hundred years.

3. The recently released update to the IPCC report continues the tradition of sophistry. The updated summary begins "Findings of scientific research since 1990 do not affect our fundamental understanding of the science of the greenhouse effect and either confirm or do not justify alteration of the major conclusions of the first IPCC Scientific Assessment, in particular the following." There then follows a list of the more innocuous conclusions of the first report: "the size of the warming is *broadly* (emphasis added) consistent with predictions of climate models, but it is also of the same magnitude as natural climate variability," "there are many uncertainties in our predictions particularly with regard to the timing, magnitude, and regional patterns of climate change due to our incomplete understanding," followed by the change of a major earlier "certainty," the positive water vapor feedback, to a matter of uncertainty, and a number of other retractions as well.

4. The issue of deep clouds (cumulonimbus towers) and water vapor is, I have noted, rather technical. These towers are the main mechanism for surface air to communicate with the interior atmosphere. Moist air rises in these towers. As this air rises to levels of lower pressure, it expands and cools (as does refrigerator coolant). As air cools, its capacity to hold water vapor diminishes. The excess water vapor condenses into liquid water or ice (depending on the temperature). In the simplest models of cumulonimbus towers, all the condensed vapor falls out as rain. When the cloud reaches its top altitude (in this simple model), it merges into the atmosphere as saturated (100 percent relative humidity) air at the cloud top temperature. Our original point was that as the surface warmed, cloud air would be more buoyant, and would reach higher top levels where the air would be colder and thus hold less water vapor. Hence, the supply of water vapor to the interior atmosphere would be diminished in a warmer climate. However, since water vapor is the main greenhouse gas in the atmosphere, this reduction would act to restrain the warming—that is, provide a negative feedback.

   We then undertook two studies to check these ideas. In the first, we used some data from the last major glacial period (18,000 years ago) to see whether the colder atmosphere of those times had more water vapor. Our study showed that almost certainly it did, thus confirming the notion of a negative feedback. Our first study did not, however, tell us what mechanism was actually responsible for the negative feedback.

Our second study undertook to examine the atmosphere's water vapor budget in greater detail. Here we discovered that our original mechanism had a significant problem. Saturated air from cloud tops constituted too small a source to maintain present levels of humidity. The problem, it turned out, was our assumption that all condensed water vapor in the cloud fell out as rain. Significant amounts are, in fact, carried aloft in the cloud and thrown out into the atmosphere mainly as ice crystals (leading to extensive cirrus cloud cover). The main source of water vapor for the atmosphere proves to be falling droplets and ice crystals which reevaporate into the environment. What causes a cloud to loft more water substance is not totally well known, but it appears to be related (not surprisingly) to how fast cloud air is rising. Our first study did, in fact, show why cloud air would rise faster in a colder climate. The results of the first study appeared in the *Annales Geophysicae*. The results of the second study appeared in the *Journal of the Atmospheric Sciences*. Both papers were co-authored with a student, De-Zheng Sun.

5. In view of the previously mentioned Gallup poll, perhaps the agreement of scientists outside of the atmospheric sciences is needed. Unfortunately, a number of studies show that scientists outside a given discipline are (with respect to that discipline) more influenced by the media than by the scientific literature. This influence is particularly strong when the media proclaim that "all scientists" agree. There is a natural inclination to support our peers.

6. The flavor of much of the journalistic coverage of the environment is given by the following quote from Teya Ryan, senior producer of Turner television's "Network Earth" and vice president of the Society of Environmental Journalists: "I think the environment may be the one area where you can say advocacy journalism is appropriate, indeed vital. . . . At some point balanced journalism simply does not give them the answers, it gives them issues. . . . Now does seem to be the time for rethinking some of our journalistic canons. The 'balanced' report, in some cases, may no longer be the most effective, or even the most informative. Indeed, it can be debilitating. Can we afford to wait for our audience to come to its conclusions? I think not."

CHAPTER 7

With Respect to the Ozone Hole—Gore is Part of the Problem

Hugh W. Ellsaesser

Vice President Gore makes it clear that his book, *Earth in the Balance*, is a spiritual exercise based on faith as opposed to an intellectual investigation based on logic. To Mr. Gore, the roots of the global environmental crisis are spiritual—"what other word describes the collection of values and assumptions that determine our basic understanding of how we fit into the universe?" (p. 12) What does one make of this presumably honest outpouring of one's soul?

Following the admired example of Rachel Carson's epochal *Silent Spring*, Gore seeks to convert readers to his view by a sequence of vivid mental images—skilled visual rhetoric. The first vision, from the deck of a fishing boat stranded in the sands under what used to be the Aral Sea, is followed pell-mell by a litany culled from yesterday's headlines: "billowing clouds of smoke" from Amazonia "silencing thousands of [bird] songs we have never even heard . . . to create pasture for fast-food beef. . . . But one doesn't have to travel around the world to witness humankind's assault on the Earth" (p. 23).

In *Earth in the Balance* Gore has chosen the role of crisis engineer. With explosive and misleading language, he describes what he believes are definitive answers to very complex scientific questions. Gore has dismissed the need for continued scientific inquiry and based his work on faith. With faith like his, what need have we of knowledge? It is thus not

137

surprising that Gore says of the extra chlorine—in the form of chlorofluorocarbons (CFCs)—that we put in the world's air; "Like an acid, it burns a hole in the earth's protective ozone shield above Antarctica and depletes the ozone layer worldwide. . . . In Patagonia, hunters now report finding blind rabbits; fishermen catch blind salmon" (p. 85). Gore is quick to blame human behavior for the thinning of the ozone layer, while my 50 years of atmospheric and climate research lead me to believe additional forces are at work.

HISTORICAL REVIEW OF OZONE DEPLETION

The original Rowland and Molina (1975) theory of catalytic destruction of ozone predicted that chlorine would attack ozone primarily in a layer near 40 km. The theory predicted that the release of CFCs at a standard rate would put the system in equilibrium after 75 to 100 years. At equilibrium, the chlorine would cause a thinning of the ozone layer of "perhaps 5 percent sometime near the middle of the twenty-first century" (Solomon, 1990, p. 347). As the SAGE satellite and Umkehr surface observations in Figure 1 show, ozone has shown some decrease near 40 km, but only about half of that predicted by the models for the present time. While showing ozone decreases near 40 km, these data have generally shown at the same time *increases* in ozone above or below the level of the decreases. This behavior is more indicative of dynamic (circulation) changes than of a chemical attack on ozone near 40 km.

From the above theoretical prediction, the appearance of the ozone hole during spring over Antarctica (Farman et al., 1985) came as a complete surprise. The ozone hole resulted from an apparently drastic reduction in ozone in the layer between about 12 and 22 km, producing a thinning of the ozone layer within the Antarctic winter polar vortex by about 50 percent. The theory since developed to explain this phenomenon is as follows:

1. After the sun departs the Antarctic, the atmosphere cools
   by infrared radiation. The colder air over the pole
   contracts vertically. As air rushes in from the sides to fill
   the partial vacuum, the earth's rotation, or Coriolis force,
   causes a deflection to the left (in the southern hemisphere)
   and development of a cyclonic vortex. As winter
   progresses the cooling continues and the vortex
   strengthens. At temperatures below about -78° C, nitric
   acid and water vapors condense into solid nitric acid

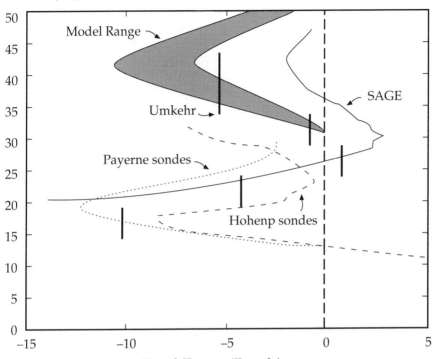

Altitude (km)

Trend (Percent/Decade)

FIGURE 1 Comparison of ozone profile trend estimates from several measurement systems, SAGE, Umkehr, and two ozonesonde stations. SAGE data is an average over the latitude ranges 20–50° N and 20–50° S. The Umkehr is the average over five northern mid-latitude stations. Shaded area shows the range of two model calculations at 50° N and 50° S. (Adapted from WMO, 1991).

trihydrate crystals forming polar stratospheric clouds (PSCs) type #1. At temperatures below about -81° C, water vapor alone condenses into ice crystals forming PSC type #2.

2. At these temperatures the crystal surfaces act as catalysts for heterogeneous chemical reactions, freeing chlorine from the inactive or reservoir compounds such as hydrochloric acid (HC1) and chlorine nitrate (C1ONO2). The reactions convert the odd nitrogen (nitrogen other than N2) into nitric acid and condense it onto the crystals so that they grow large enough to fall out of the

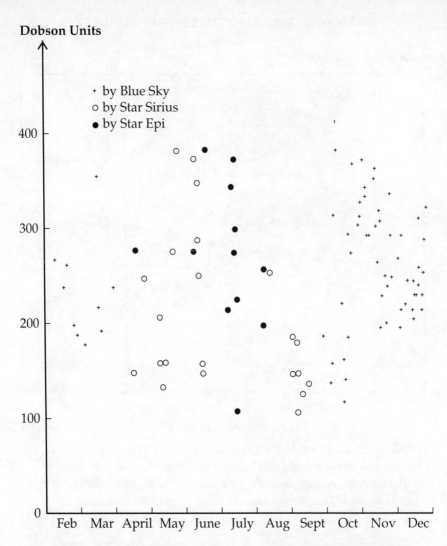

Dobson Units

FIGURE 2 Daily values of the total ozone column at Dumont d'Urville, Antarctica in 1958. (Adapted from Rigaud and Leroy, 1990).

stratosphere taking with them most of the odd nitrogen in the form of nitric acid.

The main confirmation of this theory has been the NASA flights that found a simultaneous decline in ozone and increase in ClO as they penetrated the south polar vortex into the Antarctic ozone hole in 1987. Within the vortex they found levels of the active form of chlorine (ClO) up to 1,000 times those at the same altitude outside the vortex.

3. When sunlight (ultra violet) returns in the spring, the chlorine becomes active and, since there is little if any odd nitrogen around, the chlorine attacks the ozone. In 1987 the ozone in the cold layer between 12 and 22 km was essentially completely destroyed—reduced to about 5 percent of normal, which was effectively zero considering the precision of the instruments.

While this theory appears reasonable, at least three major problems have arisen. First, the ozone observations taken by the French at their IGY Antarctic station Dumont d'Urville in 1958, recently republished by Rigaud and Leroy (1990), appear to show a spring dip in ozone in September and October of 1958 very similar to what we now call the ozone hole (see Figure 2). This suggests that the ozone hole is ephemeral as suggested by Fred Singer (1988).

Second, no current model can explain how we could have progressed from no hole in 1979 to what appears to be the maximum possible hole (ozone in the 12 to 22 km cold layer within the vortex reduced essentially to zero) in 1987, when the anthropogenic effect on total chlorine in the stratosphere over this period was at most a 40 percent increase. That is, the man-induced 40 percent increase in total chlorine pales into insignificance compared to the 1,000-fold increase in the active form of chlorine (C1O) found by NASA as it flew into the vortex.

And finally, currently available data indicate both that global mean total ozone has been increasing (see Figure 3) and that the intensity of the Antarctic ozone hole has itself, if anything, been weakening (see figures 4 and 5) since the sunspot minimum circa 1986/87. It is also true that the total chlorine in the stratosphere has continued to increase due to photolytic decomposition of continued releases of CFCs, halons, and so forth.

DISAPPEARANCE OF OZONE
FROM THE LOWER STRATOSPHERE

In contrast to the theories of ozone destruction cited above, essentially all of the decrease in stratospheric ozone observed since about 1979 has occurred in the lower stratosphere near 20 km (see Figure 6). As yet, no one has proposed a viable mechanism for such a reduction in ozone outside the Antarctic. The two explanations that have been proposed are strongly contradicted by currently available information.

One claim is that ozone-poor air over the poles is being mixed

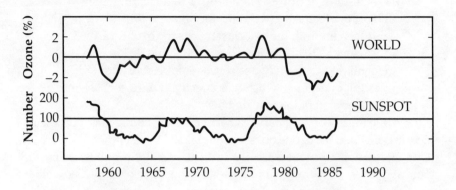

FIGURE 3 Comparison of seasonal values of sunspot number (lower curve) with the smooth variations in global total ozone, 1958 through August 1988. The seasonal values have been smoothed by a 1-2-1 weighting applied twice to seasonal deviations from the long-term mean. The time ticks mark northern summer. (Adapted from J. K. Angell, 1989.)

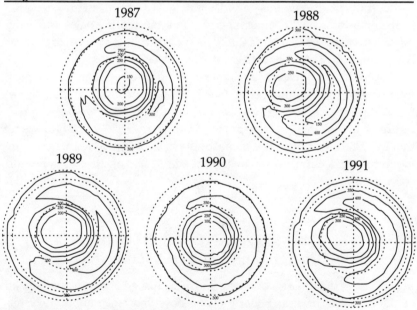

FIGURE 4 Polar orthographic projections of TOMS Southern Hemisphere maps of October mean total ozone for each of the last five years. The south pole is at the center; the equator, 30° S, and 60° S latitude circles are shown; and Greenwich is to the top. The contours are in Dobson units. (From WMO, 1991.)

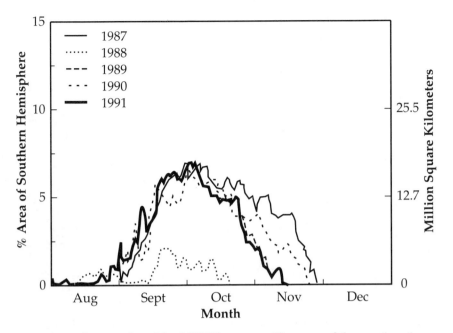

FIGURE 5 Area enclosed by 200DU contour. The area of the south polar region with total ozone amount less than 200 Dobson Units as measured by TOMS on a daily basis for each of the last five years. (From WMO, 1991.)

horizontally to lower latitudes. This argument is strongly contradicted by our present understanding of tropospheric/stratospheric exchange for which the major downward leg is at the winter pole at the time of the breakup of the winter polar vortex; that is, the major fraction of the cold, ozone-poor air within the vortex is somewhat abruptly dropped into the troposphere. Such an explanation is also inconsistent with Figure 7, which shows that outside the spring season the greatest declines in ozone in high southern latitudes have been in winter, the season preceding the ozone hole, rather than in summer, the season following the ozone hole. It would be expected that the greater declines in ozone would occur in summer if ozone-poor air were being mixed to lower latitudes after the polar vortex breaks up.

The second proposal is that the sulfate particles of the Junge layer near 20 km are serving the same catalytic role for heterogeneous chemistry as do the nitric acid trihydrate and ice crystals of the PSCs of the Antarctic winter polar vortex. There are three problems with this theory. First,

143

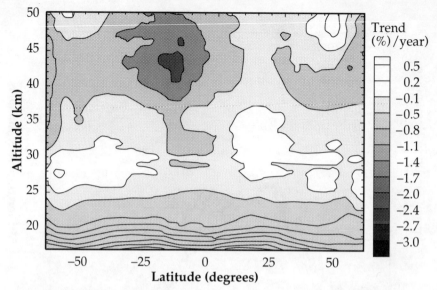

FIGURE 6 SAGE I/II Stratospheric Ozone Trends (1979–1990). Trends derived from the SAGE I and SAGE II measurements of the ozone profile in percent per decade as a function of latitude and altitude. (From WMO, 1991.)

laboratory experiments have failed to confirm sufficiently rapid heterogeneous chemical reactions on sulfuric acid particles at the temperatures of the Junge layer outside the polar regions. Second, we have no evidence that Junge layer particles grow large enough to precipitate and thus remove the odd nitrogen from the lower stratospheric layer. And third, as far as we know, the Junge layer has always been there. If it served the hypothesized role, we should have seen similar 20 km ozone destruction at least following the Agung eruption of 1963, the El Chichon eruption of 1982, and the Pinatubo eruption of June 1991. A decline in ozone in the lower stratosphere was observed following the El Chichon eruption (Angell et al., 1985) and one now appears to be under way following the Pinatubo eruption, but no one has yet proposed a viable mechanism for hemispheric or global decline in ozone in the lower stratosphere following a volcanic eruption. At the present time, there is no reason to relate such a decrease in ozone to chlorine from man-released CFCs.

A more plausible explanation—so far proposed by no one other than myself—that appears to explain both the decrease in lower stratospheric ozone and the thus far unexplained increase in tropospheric ozone in the northern hemisphere is that these changes are related to the global surface

144

% **per Decade**

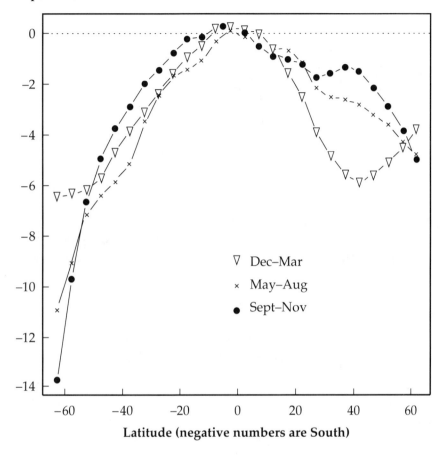

FIGURE 7 TOMS trends in zonal mean ozone versus latitude, by season. The data period is November 1978 through March 1991. (From WMO, 1991.)

warming of the past several decades that has been occurring primarily in the tropics. Such warming may accelerate the global Hadley circulation and thus speed the transport of ozone from the lower stratosphere to the troposphere. The ozone hole itself would explain why this mechanism appears to have had no effect on the level of tropospheric ozone in the southern hemisphere. Such an explanation is also consistent with the inverse correlations between tropical sea surface temperatures and thickness of the ozone column found by Komhyr et al., (1990).

145

SIGNIFICANCE OF NO DECLINE
IN OZONE OVER THE EQUATOR
AND CHEMICAL ATTACK

An even more serious argument against the theory that global ozone has been decreasing because it is under chemical attack is that every study has confirmed that there has been no decrease in total ozone over the equator (see figures 7 and 8). Since ozone is created where the solar UV is strongest, that is, over the tropics, and is then advected poleward and downward toward the poles—primarily toward the winter pole—building up deeper and thus thicker columns of ozone in higher latitudes, it is the depth of the ozone column over the equator that least ambiguously reflects the chemistry of the stratosphere. As you can see in Figure 6, the lower stratospheric decrease in total ozone also occurred over the equator. Thus, if there has been no decline in total ozone over the equator, there must have been a compensating increase in ozone at some higher levels in the stratosphere. This does not support the argument that stratospheric ozone is under chemical attack.

OTHER ARGUMENTS AGAINST
THE OZONE APOCALYPTICS

In addition to the discrepancies between the theory and the observations pointed out above, there are two even stronger reasons for questioning the program set in motion by the Montreal Protocol, an international treaty adopted in 1987 that phases in a series of quotas and bans on the use of refrigerants, halons, and soil fumigants.

First, on an annual basis, UV flux at the surface increases some 50-fold from the poles to the equator (Mo and Green, 1974). This can be thought of as a doubling every thousand miles or an increase of approximately 1 percent for each 10-mile displacement toward the equator. This means that the catastrophic increases in UV predicted for future ozone levels are already experienced by those living only 100 to 200 miles equator-ward of us. Actual statistics show that skin cancer incidence in the U.S. increases approximately 1 percent for each 6-mile displacement toward the equator. If these are the hazards they are pictured to be, why aren't all of us scrambling to move poleward?

And second, the Montreal Protocol was adopted with no considera-tion whatsoever of the benefits of UV exposure. For most land vertebrates including man, the only source of vitamin D—required for the metabolism

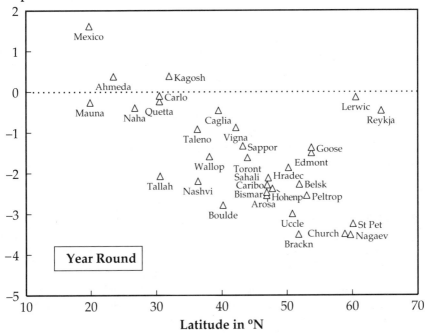

% per Decade

FIGURE 8 Individual station long-term annual mean trends for 39 Northern Hemisphere stations, versus station latitude. The estimates were derived from the standard seasonal model using data from 1958 through 1969 as a baseline, and monthly linear trends over the period 1970 through March 1991. (Adapted from WMO, 1991.)

of calcium into bone—is derived from the action of UV on the oils in the skin, fur, or feathers. (Furred and feathered creatures get their vitamin D by self-grooming). A shortage of vitamin D during the period of formation of the skeleton leads to rickets in the young and to osteoporosis in the old. Among the estimated 25 million people in the U.S. suffering osteoporosis today, there are approximately twice as many bone fractures per year, typically of the femur, as there are new cases of skin cancer. Theoretically, increased UV flux, as from decreases in the thickness of the ozone layer, would alleviate this condition in future generations. Research already done (Gorham et al., 1989) suggests that there are other diseases, such as cancer of the breast and colon, that would also be alleviated by increases in UV exposure.

147

THE APPEAL OF THE GORE APPROACH

Gore quotes Yogi Berra who said, "What gets us into trouble is not what we don't know. It's what we know for sure that just ain't so" (p. 41). But Gore fails to understand Berra's point. Rather than confront the endless conflicts and contradictions between our theories and the data and between costs and benefits, Vice President Gore applies blind faith to his conclusion that the problem is within ourselves, "I have therefore come to believe that the world's ecological balance depends on more than just our ability to restore a balance between civilization's ravenous appetite for resources and the fragile equilibrium of the earth's environment; it depends on more, even, than our ability to restore a balance between ourselves as individuals and the civilization we aspire to create and sustain. In the end, we must restore a balance within ourselves between who we are and what we are doing" (p. 12).

One point on which Gore cannot be faulted is his understanding of today's politics. He writes, "The way we make political choices has been dictated by the awesome power of the new tools and technologies now available for political persuasion. Thirty-second television commercials and sophisticated public opinion polling can now calibrate and target a political message with frightening speed and accuracy.... [T]he substance of politics ... hard choices ... are excluded wherever possible.... [S]killful 'visual rhetoric' has become as important as logic, knowledge, or experience" (p. 167–168). He continues, "Too many people now feel that they have no way to exercise any real influence over the important decisions by government that affect their lives, that large campaign contributors have access to the decision makers but the average citizen does not, that powerful special interests control the outcomes but a mere voter does not, that self-interested individuals and groups who can benefit from the decisions find a way to hot-wire the process while the broader public interest is ignored" (p. 180).

I cannot help but wonder why a person so familiar with the political process does not raise the question, "Do not our present major environmental organizations fit the above description of those most capable of access to and of control of the outcome from our decision makers?" Might not they, out of self-interest, have fabricated or exaggerated most of the very ecological crises of which Gore writes? And should we not ask, "Might not the seasoned politician—Al Gore himself—be a part of this same process?"

References

Angell, J. K. (1989). On the relation between atmospheric ozone and sunspot number, *Journal of Climate 2*, 1404–1416.

Angell, J. K., Korshover, J., and Planet, W. G. (1985). Ground-based and satellite evidence for a pronounced total-ozone minimum in early 1983 and responsible atmospheric layers, *Monthly Weather Review 113*, 641–646.

Farman, J.C., Gardiner, B. G., and Shanklin, J.D. (1985). Large losses of total ozone in Antarctica reveal seasonal ClOx/NOx interaction, *Nature 315*, 207–210.

Gorham, E.D., Garland, C. F., and Garland, F.C. (1989). Acid haze air pollution and breast and colon cancer mortality in 20 Canadian cities, *Canadian Journal of Public Health 80*, 97–100.

Komhyr, W.D., Oltmans, S. J., Grass, R. D., and Leonard, R. K. (1991). Possible influence of long-term sea surface temperature anomalies in the tropical Pacific on global ozone, *Canadian Journal of Physics 69*, 1093–1102.

Mo, T. and Green, A. E. S. (1974). A climatology of solar erythema dose, *Photochemistry and Photobiology 20*, 483–496.

Rigaud, P. and Leroy, B. (1990). Presumptive evidence for a low value of the total ozone content above Antarctica in September 1959, *Annales Geophysicae 8* (11), 791–794.

Rowland, F.S. and Molina, J. M. (1975). Chlorofluoromethanes in the environment, *Reviews of Geophysics 13*, 1–35.

Singer, S.F. (1988). Does the Antarctic ozone hole have a future? *EOS 69* (47), 1588.

Solomon, Susan (1990). Progress towards a quantitative understanding of Antarctic ozone depletion, *Nature 347*, 347–354.

World Meteorological Organization (WMO) (1991). *Scientific Assessment of Ozone Depletion: 1991, Global Ozone Research and Monitoring Project—Report No. 25*, WMO, Geneva 20, CH 1211 Switzerland.

PART III

RESOURCE ISSUES

CHAPTER 8

Tropical Rain Forests Myths and Facts

Evaristo E. de Miranda

To build a constructive response to Vice President Al Gore's treatment of the science and ecology of tropical rain forests in his book, *Earth in the Balance*, it is important to outline some of the unique and complex characteristics of tropical rain forests. Tropical rain forests represent some of the world's most diverse, rich, and uncharted ecosystems. In the following pages, I will describe a number of the basic characteristics of rain forests and examine the Brazilian Amazon in depth.

Because of growing public concern over the condition and management of tropical rain forests around the globe, it is imperative that researchers, government officials, environmentalists, indigenous populations, the media, and concerned citizens work together to create the best rain forest management policies possible.

The controversy over rain forest management stems in part from misinformation. The international media has contributed to the general public fervor over the present and future condition of the Brazilian Amazon, and *Earth in the Balance* perpetuates some of the tropical rain forest myths.

I agree with Vice President Gore on a number of basic points, including: (1) human activities have decreased the size and number of tropical rain forests; (2) the threat of species extinction is real, in fact, deforestation causes species extinction; and (3) it is important to protect

153

rain forest biodiversity. But we disagree on some major issues, including: (1) the rate at which deforestation is taking place in the Brazilian Amazon; (2) the fact that humans have induced only negative impacts on the forest ecosystem (studies indicate that humans may have contributed to the level of biodiversity); (3) the kinds and degree of human-ecological interaction that take place in tropical rain forests; and (4) the potential for ecological restoration.

TROPICAL RAIN FOREST FACTS

Rain forests are among the most complex, sensitive, endangered, and unknown ecosystems on earth. Today, only about half of the earth's original rain forests remain. These remaining forests exist in large blocks throughout 37 countries in Latin America, Africa, Asia, and Australia. Rain forests once covered some 16 million square kilometers (km^2), but human activities, such as farming, logging, cattle ranching, large-scale development projects, and mining, have reduced the world's rain forest area to less than 9 million km^2. About 7 percent of the world's landmass is still covered with this unique ecosystem (Corson, 1990).

Almost all the remaining rain forests are located in the so-called intertropical or tropical zone of the globe, an area generally characterized by its main climatic aspect: high temperatures (Tricart, 1974; Demangeot, 1976). In this zone, daily thermal amplitude is exceptionally high, four or five degrees over the day; whereas, annual thermal amplitude is exceptionally low, two or three degrees over the year. The mean temperature is around 25°C (Lemps, 1970). Some other important characteristics of rain forests are their high humidity levels and their plentiful rainfall—regularly more than 1,500 mm/year (Hallé et al., 1978). In this kind of climate—uniform temperature, water conditions, and light throughout the year—without seasonal fluctuations, the optimum conditions exist for an evergreen, broad-leaved, vegetation to flourish.

Tropical rain forests have three main characteristics. First, lush vegetation. They are dense, closed forests with high canopies that allow little light to reach the ground. Second, they have rich flora and several endemic species. These characteristics are a result of both the climatic conditions, which are favorable mainly to the trees, and the climatic history. The climatic changes over time are never as severe as those in temperate latitudes, thus leading to intense competition and granting various tropical rain forest species the opportunity to adapt themselves to the environment and to diversify. The third main characteristic of tropical

154

rain forests is stratification: ground plants, shrubs, vines, lianas, epiphytes and tress form a complex system of layers ranging from a few centimeters to over 60 meters high. Alexander von Humboldt described the stratification as "a forest above a forest" (Lemps, 1970). Von Humboldt's observation highlights how rain forest ecosystems differ from temperate forests not only in tree arrangement but also in tree architecture. In the rain forests, trees tend to be bigger and taller. Rain forest trees also contain a major part of their biomass as stems and leaves, and they have superficial roots (Demangeot, 1976; Hallé et al., 1978).

Despite the lush vegetation, tropical rain forests often thrive on poor and highly weathered soils. Seventy-five percent of the nutrients found in tropical rain forests is located in the plants, 17 percent is located in the decomposing matter, and only 8 percent is located in the soil itself (Meirelles Filho, 1986). Therefore, these forests have evolved as "closed" nutrient cycles. The anatomical, physiological, biochemical, and ecological mechanisms at work in a tropical rain forest ecosystem guarantee little loss, little uptake from the sources and, thus, conservation of nutrients (Golley, 1983).

These "closed" nutrient cycles scientifically deny the popular characterization of the rain forests as the planet's "lungs." Rain forests are mature forests; they operate at their climax. They have been recycling the same amount of carbon for centuries. The oxygen they produce is totally consumed by the vegetation breathing. The balance between oxygen production and consumption is zero.

Controlled numerical experiments with complex models of the atmosphere have shown that tropical rain forests, as well as their destruction, may play a role in determining local and regional climates (Cutrim, 1990; Shukla et al., 1990). Biosphere-atmosphere interactions are significant within these areas. For instance, the incidence of sunlight is higher in tropical zones than in any other place on earth. The lush vegetation contributes to the sunlight's dissipation, because as water vapor forms it acts as a regulator of temperature and supplier of moisture, working much like an air conditioner.

Tropical rain forests are home to a vast biological array of living organisms. These forests support more plant and animal species per unit area, as well as overall, than any other ecosystem on earth. Current estimates of the total number of living species on the planet range from five to 30 million or more, of which only 1.4 million have been described by scientists (Wilson, 1988; Corson, 1990). More than two-thirds of these species come from tropical rain forests, basically because the forests are

155

home to the most species-rich groups in the world—arthropods and flowering plants (Wilson, 1989).

Peru, for instance, is home to around 30,000 species of plants (Itlis, 1988); Colombia, a country as big as New Mexico and Texas combined, has more than 1,550 bird species (twice the number found in North America) (Schauensee, 1964); a single river in Brazil harbors more species of fish than all the rivers in the United States, and ten one-hectare plots in Borneo, Indonesia contain 700 species of tree (Corson, 1990); the Amazon Forest is home to perhaps 80,000 plant species (including 600 kinds of palm alone) and millions of animal species, most of them insects (Colinvaux, 1989). A world record was established in 1988 by Alwyn H. Gentry, who identified about 300 tree species in each of two one-hectare plots in Iquitos, Peru (Wilson, 1989).

Such great richness constitutes a constraint for the commercial exploitation of the forest. In one hectare there are usually no more than two or three trees of the same species (Lemps, 1970). Besides sheltering native populations and providing habitat for millions of plant and animal species—which constitute an important genetic bank—tropical rain forests are also important because they supply a great variety of commercial and noncommercial products: timber (some highly prized woods such as teak, mahogany and rosewood); fuel wood; fruits, vegetables, nuts and spices; medicines (a quarter of all medically active substances come from tropical plants, and according to Caufield (1984) around 70 percent of the 3,000 plants identified by the U.S. National Cancer Institute as having anti-cancer properties are tropical rain forest species); and various industrial products such as oils, waxes, gums, resins, latexes, fibers, rubber, dyes, tanning agents, turpentine, lubricants, rattan and bamboo (Corson, 1990).

This richness and diversity has been threatened by man in three different ways: (1) by destroying species individually; (2) by destroying resources important to survival (such as habitat or food supply); and (3) by introducing exotic species that kill or compete with the native species (Emmons, 1990). In the case of tropical rain forests, the destruction and the fragmentation of habitats due to deforestation are the main causes of losses in biodiversity (Lovejoy et al., 1984). Deforestation reduces the area covered with forest and thus the number of habitats available in this ecosystem. This leads to a reduction in the number of species.

Deforestation is caused by three main factors: (1) agricultural and livestock expansion (human population growth leads to expanded needs for crop and grazing lands); (2) increased demand for commercial forest products (national economic development and international trade stimulate mainly timber harvesting); and (3) increased demand for noncommercial forest products (fuel wood, fodder, and others) (Gregersen et al., 1989). The causes vary from region to region. In Asia, for example, although timber harvesting plays a large role, the major culprits are population growth and extensive agriculture; in America, beyond the above factors, poorly designed governmental policies during recent years plays a significant role; in Africa, the main causes are uncontrolled population growth and nomadic agriculture practices (Siqueira, 1989). The rain forests have been globally destroyed not because of ignorance or stupidity but largely because of poverty and greed (Robinson, 1988).

THE BRAZILIAN TROPICAL RAIN FORESTS—A CASE STUDY

Around 57 percent of the world's tropical rain forests are in Latin America, 30 percent of which are located within Brazilian borders. Brazil has two domains of tropical rain forest; the Atlantic Forest and the Amazon Forest (The World Resources Institute, 1990).

The Atlantic Forest, designated as one of the three top priority areas for conservation in the world, is the most deforested. It originally covered some 450,000 km^2 (5 percent of Brazil's national territory) along the Atlantic coast, from the state of Rio Grande do Norte in the northeast to the prairies of Rio Grande do Sul in the south. But, since the year 1500 when the first Europeans reached these coasts, the forest has been constantly and indiscriminately altered and cleared. The early Portuguese pioneers chopped down the Brazil wood to extract dye; subsequent settlers cleared the forest to open the way for sugarcane and coffee plantations and for settlements; and in the last 50 years, industrial activities, urbanization, and road construction have reduced the forest to just 30,000 km^2, of which only 15,000 km^2 is considered primary forest (Fundacao SOS Mata Atlantica, 1988).

Today, 80 million people and a great part of Brazil's heavy industry are crowded in the area originally covered by the Atlantic Forest. Only a few remnants of forest can be found in scattered patches throughout the southeast. In the northeast, practically nothing remains. The current demand for raw materials and space and the current rate of deforestation (around 4,000 km^2 year) could cause the total eradication of this forest by the year 2000 (Vieira & Meirelles Filho, 1989). Despite the deforestation, the Atlantic Forest did keep a great diversity and even now shelters around 200,000 different species, many of them endemic (53 percent of the known trees, 40 percent of mammals, and 80 percent of the nonhuman

157

primates cannot be found anywhere else) (Fundacao SOS Mata Atlantica, 1988).

Extinction is, however, a constant threat—30 percent of the species are in danger of extinction. The primates, golden lion tamarin (*Leontopithecus rosalia*), golden rumped tamarin (*Leontopithecus crysopygus*), and muriqui (*Brachyteles arachnoides*); the trees, jacaranda (*Dalbergia nigra*) and Brazil wood (*Caesalpinia echinata*); the birds, red-tailed parrot (*Amazona brasiliensis*) and tinamou (*Tinamous solitarius*) are just a few examples (Fundacao SOS Mata Atlantica, 1988).

The Amazon Forest, on the other hand, is still almost intact and therefore attracts the attention of conservation groups that fear the threat of an uncontrolled and predatory human occupation. The term "Amazonia" refers to an area that comprises 50 percent of Latin America (nine countries) and contains the largest continuous tropical rain forest in the world—the 6.5 million km^2 Amazon Forest. More than 50 percent of it (3.5 million km^2) is in Brazil alone.

For planning purposes, the Brazilian government created "Legal Amazonia," an area of 4,906,784 km^2 (57 percent of Brazil's total territory). Legal Amazonia includes areas of nine states and is defined and based on geographic, physiographic, social, and political criteria. To understand its size, the entire European continent could fit in Legal Amazonia. Seventy percent of it is tropical rain forest (78 percent of the Brazilian forests), and the remainder is savanna and other vegetal formations (Siqueira, 1989).

The Amazon has been studied for a long time, in fact, as early as colonization in the sixteenth century. But it was not until the 1970s that the first systematic and homogenous study was made—the governmental project RADAM/BRASIL. The whole Amazon, along with the rest of the country, was surveyed by radar, and the final result included 34 reports on natural resources (20 about the Amazon region) and several cartographic products based on radar images (geology, geomorphology, pedology, vegetation, potential land use, agricultural suitability, subsidies for regional planning, hydric resources, and relief evaluation maps). The material collected revealed some of the region's great diversity: different substrata, altitudes, soil types, climates and, consequently, forests. Today, satellite images (from the American satellite LANDSAT or the European SPOT) confirm this diversity (John, 1989).

Formed 50 million years ago between two Pre-Cambrian shields, probably with the arrival of exogenous nutrients through trade winds, Amazonia is a vast sedimentary plain covered by a forest that is not at all homogeneous. From zero to over 3,000 meters altitude, you can find several different kinds of forest. The equatorial climate is permanently hot and humid, but annual precipitation ranges from 1,200 to 3,000 mm, with a brief dry season.

The forest functions in a complex way and plays a significant role in determining local and global environmental conditions (Molion, 1988; Shukla et al., 1990; Setzer and Pereira, 1991). It is a source of biogenic gases and aerosols that, because of the region's intense convective activity, can be rapidly mixed to higher altitudes where they impact global tropospheric chemistry and thus may affect global climate (Harriss et al., 1988). Twenty percent of the world's fresh water cycles through the Amazon basin, which acts as supplier of heat and water vapor to the rest of the country and other parts of the globe. Numerical models have shown that the removal of the forest could cause a reduction in precipitation and evapotranspiration and an increase in surface temperature (Cutrim, 1990). Biomass burning and deforestation in the Amazon generates gases such as CO_2, CH_4, and other pollutants (CO and oxides of nitrogen) that may accelerate the greenhouse effect (Harriss et al., 1988).

The Amazon has great potential for all kinds of exploitation:

⊃ *Vegetal products:* latex from *Hevea brasiliensis* (rubber), wax from *Copernica cerifera* (Portuguese, carnauba), oils from *Orbignya martiana* (Port., babacu) and *Astrocaryum aculeatum* (Port., tucuma), foods from *Euterpes oleifera* (Port., acai), *Bertholletia excelsa* (Brazil nut), *Bactris gasipaes* (Port., pupunha) (Balick, 1985), are only some examples of useful forest products, besides the valuable hardwood trees that may be worth as much as US$ 4,000 each.

⊃ *Animal products:* fishing (more than 2,000 species of fish) and hunting.

⊃ *Minerals:* some of the world's richest ore bodies are found in the Amazon (iron, manganese, cassiterite, bauxite, gold, copper and nickel are some of the commercially exploited) (Berbert, 1989).

⊃ *Hydroelectric resources:* about 45 percent of Brazil's hydroelectric potential is in the Amazon basin (Secretaria de Assessoramento da Defesa Nacional, 1989).

⊃ *Agricultural occupation:* although the soils, as in other tropical rain forests, are poor, shallow, and fragile—except in some wetlands along the Amazon, Solimoes. and Madeira rivers—the area is seen as the frontier for expansion of agriculture and cattle ranching (Miranda & Mattos, 1992).

This forest is the world's largest genetic bank and for the last few years has been the target of very controversial discussions about deforestation, biomass burning, global climate changes, and biodiversity loss (Setzer & Pereira, 1991). A lot has been said, but very little attention has been given to the process that has brought us to the present situation. Deforestation has it origin in local social relations and in the country's model for economic development. In the last few decades, the region's population has grown to almost 20 million, large industrial and hydro-electric complexes have been constructed, agricultural projects have been implemented, and nothing indicates that this process will stop or even slow down in the future.

Before we condemn or try to justify human occupation in the Amazon, it is necessary to understand the whole process. Also, it should be remembered that the human presence in the *past, present,* and *future* plays an important role in determining the region's biodiversity. Man has been the cause but could also be the solution to the Amazon's problems. Some aspects of this occupation will be presented next.

BRAZILIAN AMAZONIA: MYTHS AND FACTS

Many myths have been spread by the international media regarding the Brazilian Amazon. Vice President Gore's comments on deforestation in tropical countries seem to incorporate some of these myths. This has led to some damaging misinformation. According to Gore:

⊃ More than 20 percent of the Brazilian Amazon was deforested recently.

⊃ The deforestation is increasing at annual rates of more than 80,000 km^2/year.

⊃ Deforestation sterilizes the soil.

⊃ The entire region should be left untouched for humanity's sake.

I will address these issues in the hope that if the myths are separated from the facts, a more accurate understanding will lead to better policy decisions for the rain forest regions of the world.

Extent of Gross Deforestation in the Brazilian Amazon

The extent and the rate of deforestation in Brazilian Amazonia has interested many researchers in the last decade. The National Institute for Space Research (Instituto de Pesquisas Espaciais or INPE) has conducted full surveys of Legal Amazonia, based on LANDSAT satellite images, for the years 1978, 1988, 1989, 1990, and 1991, to map the extent of gross deforestation (that is, not accounting for forest regeneration or plantations), for a

TABLE 1 Extent (km^2) of Gross Deforestation in the Brazilian Amazonia

Year	Extent Deforestation (km^2)
1978	152,200
1988	377,600
1989	401,400
1990	415,200
1991	426,400

Source: Instituto de Pesquisas Espaciais (1992).

TABLE 2 Annual Rate of Gross Deforestation (km^2/year) in the Brazilian Amazonia

Period (years)	Rate of Deforestation km^2/year	%/year
1978–1988	21,130	.54
1988–1989	17,860	.48
1989–1990	13,810	.37
1990–1991	11,130	.30

Source: Instituto de Pesquisas Espaciais (1992).

total surface area between 3.9 and 4 million km^2 (see Table 1). Each survey uses 230 LANDSAT images at the 1:250.000 scale.

The increment of the extent of gross deforestation in the sequence of LANDSAT satellite surveys was used to estimate the annual rate of gross deforestation in Brazilian Amazonia in the periods between consecutive surveys. Partial surveys of the extent of gross deforestation for parts of Legal Amazonia during the 1980s indicate that the mean rate of 21,130 km^2 per year was the result of a non-uniform rate in the period 1978–88, which is likely to have reached a peak in the second half of the 1980s and then tapered off. The height and timing of the peak will be better determined after completion of an ongoing survey for the intermediate year of 1985. Nevertheless, these partial data indicate that the peak cannot possibly have reached 80,000 km^2 per year as previously thought. In Table 2, the columns with the annual rates of gross deforestation expressed in terms of square kilometers per year are followed by the values expressed in terms of percentage of the remaining forest removed per year.

The present results are not estimations, nor projections, nor extrapolations. They are exhaustive measurements of the whole Amazon region. These results indicate that the present deforestation of the Brazilian Amazonia (426,400 km^2, including 97,600 km^2 of old deforested areas) corresponds to *less than 10 percent* of the total Amazon (the total Amazon region has 4,906,784 km^2). The deforestation rates have never reached the supposed 80,000 km^2 per year. In Brazil, the rate tendency is clearly decreasing, contrary of what Gore's analysis of tropical deforestation stipulates.

Biodiversity in the Brazilian Amazon

The human presence in the Amazon has simultaneously played a role in increasing, decreasing, and maintaining the region's biological diversity. Biodiversity, or biological diversity, is a global resource made up of the great variety of living forms on earth, both wild and domesticated. It can be understood in many different ways, for instance, genetic diversity (differences in genetic constitution among individual organisms), ecosystem diversity (distinctive assemblages of organisms that occur in different physical settings), and the most common measure, species diversity. It should never be forgotten, though, that man is part of the problem concerning biodiversity. This is a very complex matter, and any generalization is dangerous.

Very distinct situations coexist today in the Brazilian Amazon. In the case of the indigenous populations, several studies have shown how certain tribes have contributed, in a permanent way, to the partition and to the cultivation of vegetal species of their own interest, to the maintenance of a high polymorphism in their plantations, and to the management of several forest ecosystems (Posey, 1985; Taylor, 1988). Other studies indicate that this millenary influence has expanded to vast areas like the savannas, and could be the origin of some vegetation types considered natural until today (Ballée, 1988, 1989; Ballée & Campbell, 1990). Thus, the transformation of the Amazon Forest by man was probably much greater than what was assumed to be the case until recently (Mantovani et al., 1991). This fact raises the first question about the lack of knowledge and research on man-forest interactions in this region and their consequences.

Similar results, in terms of increasing biodiversity, have been observed in riverside populations and in some Caboclo communities (mestizo populations descended from Indians, blacks, and whites). In the state of Maranhao, along the eastern limits of the Amazon Forest, communities have practiced itinerant agriculture in small areas on very poor soils for

162

more than a century. Hunting, fishing, and the exploitation of forest products have also contributed to their success. The inhabitants of Maranhao employ the traditional methods of shifting cultivation: after deforestation the area is cultivated for a brief period (the soil tolerates the maximum of two years of cultivation) followed by a long fallow period. The non-eradication of the vegetation assures its reconstitution, and the agriculturists take 15 years or more to come back to the same place. This agricultural practice generates a mosaic of forests that differ in terms of phytodynamics and vegetal chronosequence, each one with its own characteristics in terms of fauna and floral communities. This spatial heterogeneity can be detected and monitored through satellite images. The diversity indices of these areas are greater than those for original forests. It appears that man—like wild and domesticated animals—can simultaneously exploit the forest and contribute to the growth of its primary productivity, cynegetic and energetic resources (Miranda, 1985).

There are some cases in the Amazon where creation of reserve areas—in an effort to protect rain forest—is leading to a simplification of the ecological systems and to a loss of biological diversity. The consequent expulsion of the agriculturists and the return of relative homogeneity of natural vegetation has not enhanced biodiversity. Several communities of Caboclos in the wetlands of the Amazon River have an extremely elaborate idea of the spatial and temporal partition of the natural resource supply. They practice complex systems of exploitation and production, which guarantee the perpetuity of the ecosystems they use (Frechione et al., 1989). This illustrates one of the complications inherent in creating national parks and reserves, an option many conservationists consider essential to preservation of rain forest ecological systems. It is necessary to apply new instruments and parameters to the research and monitoring of biodiversity in these areas of traditional occupation, many of them places with endemic species that need protection.

As the density of populations living in the forest increases and mobility decreases, the systems of production and exploitation tend to be simplified and seem to have an effect on certain aspects of the rain forest ecological system. The rubber tappers in the western state of Acre are a case in point. The increase in population density and the intensification of land use has been feasible and compatible with maintenance of the vegetal resources of the forest. On the other hand, animal communities, particularly vertebrates, have been subject to systematic, indiscriminate, and quotidian hunting that has lead to local extinction of species, and still does, despite the consequent and dramatic reduction of the remaining populations (Nunes et al., 1990). How is it possible to maintain the biodiversity

163

of these traditional intensified agro-forestry systems in the middle and long term?

The migration of thousands of families of small agriculturists from the South, Southeast and Northeast Brazil to the Amazon has caused changes in the forest ecosystems. The emergence of agro-ecosystems with a great spatial-temporal dynamism has created complex environmental consequences. In the states of Rondonia and Mato Grosso, this colonization process had led, on the one hand, to the loss of biological diversity, stemming mainly from deforestation, eradication of habitats and disruption of traditional Indian, Caboclo, and rubber tapper production systems.

On the other hand, it has caused an expansion of the total number of species, the emergence of interesting cases of sustainable land use for a high density resident population, and the diversification of certain animal communities. Because it is a recent process, diachronic comparisons are only now beginning to emerge, showing a more subtle picture than the one given in several articles that completely disapprove of the agricultural occupation of that region. Even the announced failure of the agriculturists, who after some years of cultivation sell their lands to exploit a new area, has proven to be, in many cases, part of a capitalization strategy (Lena, 1988).

What is one to do with this reality? Even if the immigration of agriculturists into the agricultural frontier is reduced to zero, the thousands who are already there give us reason enough to look for new research alternatives for sustainable agro-forestry systems that could be adapted to the existing settlers' socio-economic conditions.

Finally, in the Amazon there are hundreds of thousands of hectares that are completely deforested, a result of an old agricultural occupation in the region of Belem (Para state). Along highway Belem-Brasilia and in the state of Mato Grosso, extensive cattle ranching in large land holdings has caused extensive deforestation. Very little is said about these areas where deforestation is no longer carried out (since the forest has been eradicated), to which nobody migrates any longer (since all the land is owned and concentrated in the hands of a very few people), and where extensive productive systems have left little space for new industrial projects. The conditions are a result of an old fiscal incentive policy. Agrarian speculation dominates these rural landscapes in Tocantins, Mato Grosso, and Para (Instituto de Desenvolvimento Economico-Social do Para, 1987; Reydon and Herbers, 1989). They represent the largest loss of biodiversity in the Amazon, but it is not yet a permanent loss. Recent research indicates that some areas could have their biodiversity restored (Uhl, 1988; Uhl & Kauffman, 1990).

164

CONCLUSION

In Amazonia it is necessary to acknowledge that some of the remnant areas are more important to preserve than the vast areas of intact forest. The ecological restoration of these regions, especially the degraded pastures and some old mining areas, is essential for the preservation of the rest of the Amazon Forest. Second, and more important, these degraded areas need a new agricultural transformation to recover their biological and production potentials. It represents the possibility of reducing the pressure on the untouched forest, generating a kind of buffer zone in the southern section of the Amazon River. Ecological studies, in this case more than in any other, should be inserted in the region's social and economic contexts. Finally, it is also in this region that some scarce remaining areas of humid forest are still found, making preservation all the more urgent and important.

Within the last few years, the tropical rain forest preservation debate has been thrust into the international environmental policy arena. The danger of causing more harm than good is high. It is imperative that decision makers and researchers collaborate to ensure that the best available data are examined and utilized. For the debate to be rational, it is necessary to acknowledge that there are trade-offs involved. It is important that we set priorities and make economically sound decisions.

Cultural and developmental issues must be taken into consideration in creating rain forest conservation policy. We must also realize that the policies for one region may not meet the needs of another. It is crucial that we include a role for the human population of the rain forest by creating policies that guarantee their stake in the forest and make preservation in their best interest.

References

Balick, M.J. (1985). Useful plants of Amazon: A resource of global importance. In G.T. Prance and T.E. Lovejoy (Eds.), *Amazon* (pp. 339–368). Pergamon Press: Oxford.

Ballée, W. (1988). Indigenous adaptation to Amazon palm forests. *Principles*, 32(2): 47–54.

Ballée, W. (1989). Cultura na vegetacão da Amazonia Brasileira. In W.A. Neves, (Organizer), *Biologia e Ecologia Humana na Amazônia: avaliacão e perspectiveas*. Museu Paraense Emilio Goeldi, Belém, PA, Brazil, pp. 59–76.

Ballée, W., & Campbell, D. G. (1990). Evidence for the successional status of liana forest (Xingu River Basin, Amazon - Brazil). *Biotropica*, 22(1) : 36–47.

Berbert, C.O. (1989). Mineral exploration in the Amazon. In *Anals of the Symposium Amazônia - Facts, Problems, and Solutions*, July 31–August 2, 1989, São Paulo, SP, Brazil, pp. 1–21.

Caufield, C. (1984). *In the rain forest*. Chicago: University of Chicago Press.

Colinvaux, P.A. (1989, May). The past and future Amazon. *Scientific American*, pp. 68–74.

Corson, W.H. (ed.) (1990). *The global ecology handbook. What you can do about the environmental crisis*. Boston: The Global Tomorrow Coalition, Beacon Press.

Cutrim, E.M.C. (1990). Amazon, a dynamic habitat: Past, present, and future dynamic Amazon weather. Unpublished paper for AAAS meeting, February 15–29.

Demangeot, J. (1976). *Les espaces naturels tropicaux*. Paris: Masson.

Emmons, L.H. (1990). *Neotropical rainforest mammals: A field guide*. Chicago: University of Chicago Press.

Frechione, J., Posey, D.A., & Silva, L.F. da (1989). The perception of ecological zones and natural resources in the Brazilian Amazon: An ethnoecology of Lake Coari. In D.A. Posey and W. Ballée (Eds.), *Resource management in Amazon: Indigenous and folk strategies*. New York: New York Botanical Garden.

Golley, F.B. (1983). Nutrient cycling and nutrient conservation. In F.B. Golley (Ed.), *Tropical rain forest ecosystems: Structure and function*. Amsterdam: Elsevier Scientific Publishing Company.

Gregersen, H., Draper, S., & Elz, D. (1989). *People and trees: The role of social forestry in sustainable development.* Washington, DC: The World Bank.

Hallé, F., Oldeman, R.A.A., & Tomlinson, P.B. (1978). *Tropical trees and forests: An architectural analysis.* New York: Spring-Verlag.

Harriss, R.C., Wofsy, S.C., Garstand, M., Brwell, E.V., Molion. L.C.B., McNeal, R.J., Hoell, J.M., Jr., Bendura, R.J., Beck, S.M., Navarro, R.L., Riley, J.T., & Snell, R.L. (1988). The Amazon Boundary Layer Experiment (ABLE 2A): dry season 1985. *Journal of Geophysical Research,* 93(D2) : 1351–1360.

Instituto do Desenvolvimento Econômico-Social do Pará (IDESP), 1987: Conflitos Agrários: semestre sangrento no meio rural. *Pará Agrário,* (3): 25–37.

Instituto de Pesquisas Espaciais (INPE) (1989). *Diretoria de Sensoriamento Remoto. Avaliacão da alteracão da cobertura florestal na Amazônia legal utilizando sensoriamento remoto orbital.* INPE, São José dos Gampos, SP, Brazil.

Instituto de Pesquisas Espaciais (INPE) (1992). *Extent of Gross Deforestation in the Brazilian Amazonia/Annual Rate of Gross Deforestation in the Brazilian Amazonia.* São José dos Gampos, SP, Brazil: INPE.

Itlis, H. (1988). Serendipity in the exploration of biodiversity. In E.D. Wilson(Ed.), *Biodiversity.* Washington, DC: National Academy Press.

John, L. (1989). *Amazônia - olhos de satélite.* Editoracão Publicacões e Comunicacões, São Paulo, SP, Brazil, p. 143.

Lemps, A.H., de (1970). *La végétation de la terre.* Paris: Masson.

Lena, P. (ed.) (1988). "Amazônia: A fronteira agricola 20 anos depois." *Seminar Proceedings.* Museu Paraense Emilio Goeldi, ORSTOM, Belem, PA. Brazil.

Lovejoy, T.E., Rankin, J.M., Bierregaard, R.O., Brown, K.S., Jr., Emmons, L.H., & Van der Voortm, M.E. (1984). Ecosystem decay of Amazon Forest remnants. In *II Congresso Latin-Americano de Ecologia,* December, 1992, Caxambu, MG, Brazil. Resumos, pp. 179–180.

Mantovani, L.E., Mattos, C.O., Scaramuzza, C.A. de M. (1992). *Reflexões sobre a gênese das paisagens tropicais Sul Americanas.* Paper presented at the 11th Latin-American Congress of Ecology, Caxambu, MG, Brazil, Rio Claro, SP, Brazil.

167

PART III: RESOURCE ISSUES

Meirelles Filho, J. (1986). *Amazônia: o que fazer por ela?* Editora Nacional, São Paulo, SP, Brazil.

Miranda, E.E. (1985). *Consequências agroecológias da instatlacão da base de lancamento de foguetes no Municipio de Alcântra (MA).* EMBRAPA/CNPDA, Jaguariuna, SP, Brazil.

Miranda, E.E., & Mattos, C. (1992). Brazilian rain forest colonization and biodiversity. *Agriculture Ecosystems and Environment, 40*: 275–296.

Molion, L.C.B. (1988). A Amazônia e o clima da terra. *Ciência Hoje, 8*(48): 42–47.

Nunes, V.S., Miranda, J.R., & Souza, M.F.B. (1990). Utilization of cynegetic resources by rubber tappers of Tejo River Basin, Acre State. EMBRAPA/NMA, Campinas, SP, Brazil (unpublished).

Posey, D.A. (1985). Indigenous management of tropical forest ecosystems: The case of the Kayapo Indians of the Brazilian Amazon. *Agroforestry Systems, 3*: 139–158.

Reydon, B.P., & Herbers, R.G. (1989). Politica governamental para a agropecuária na Amazônia e degradaão do meio ambiente. *Reforma Agrária, 1*: 42–51.

Robinson, M. (1988). Beyond destruction success. In J. Gradwohl and R. Greenberg, *Saving the tropical forests* (p. 11), London: Earthscan.

Secretaria de Assessoramento da Defesa Nacional (SADEN) (1989). *Programa Nossa Natureza: relatório da comissão executiva instituida pelo decreto*, No. 96,944/88. SADEN, Brasilia, DF, Brazil, p. 81.

Schauensee, R.M., de (1964). *The birds of Colombia.* Narberth, PA: Livingston Publishing Company,

Setzer, A.W., & Pereira, M.C. (1991). Amazonia biomass burning in 1987 and an estimate of their tropospheric emissions. *Ambio, 20*(1): 19–22.

Siqueira, J.D.P. (1989). Manejo florestal sustentado na Amazônia: necessidade versus pesquisas. In *Anals of the Symposium Amazônia - Facts, Problems and Solutions, July 31-August 2, 1989*, São Paulo, SP, Brazil, pp. 109–132.

Shulka, J., Nobre, C., and Sellers, P. (1990). Amazon deforestation and climate change. *Science, 247* (4948): 1322–1325.

Taylor, K.I. (1988). Deforestation and Indians in Brazilian Amazon. In E.O. Wilson (Ed.), *Biodiversity* (pp. 138–144). Washington, DC: National Academy Press.

Tricart, J. (1974). *Le modelé des régions chaudes: forêts et savanes.* Paris: Société d'édition d'Enseignement Supérieur.

Uhl, C. (1988). Restoration of degraded lands in the Amazon basin. In E.O. Wilson (Ed.), *Biodiversity* (pp. 326–332). Washington, DC: National Academy Press.

Uhl, C., & Kauffman, J.B. (1990). Deforestation, fire susceptibility, and potential tree response to fire in the eastern Amazon. *Ecology, 71* (2) : 437–449.

Vieira, M.L., & Meirelles Filho, J. (1989). Salve a Mata Atlântica Fundacão SOS Mata Atlântica, São Paulo, SP, Brazil.

Wilson, E.O. (1988). The current state of biological diveristy. In E.O. Wilson (Ed.), *Biodiversity* (pp. 3–18). Washington, DC: National Academy Press.

Wilson, E.O. (1989). Threats to biodiversity. *Scientific American*, Special Issue, 261 (3): 60–66.

The World Resources Institute (WRI) (1990). *World Resources 1990-91.* New York: Oxford University Press.

CHAPTER 9

Waste Not, Want Not

Lynn Scarlett

"We are the enemy," writes Vice President Albert Gore in *Earth in the Balance* (Houghton Mifflin, 1992). In the struggle to save the planet, we are "at war with ourselves." Gore sees a "frenzied destruction of the natural world," a world of excessive consumption. Nowhere is this presumed excess more colorfully evoked than through images of our garbage—what we discard every day, year after year. Gore warns that "the underlying problem remains that we are simply generating too much garbage and waste of all kinds" (p. 158).

Gore's overarching vision of civilization as imperiling itself underlies his interpretation of our "waste" problem and guides his agenda for overcoming that perceived problem. It is a vision that rests on a static worldview—one that takes a "freeze-frame" picture of current conditions and projects them into the future with drastic consequences. Only fundamental changes in behavior will bring us a reprieve.

As it relates to waste, Gore's interpretation of the human condition has five principle components.

- ⊃ We are running out of resources because of our current patterns of "conspicuous consumption."
- ⊃ We are a "throwaway" society that holds a "cavalier attitude" toward our waste.
- ⊃ We are "running out of places to put [our waste]."
- ⊃ Waste disposal methods are unsafe.

⊃ We must emphasize waste reduction, reuse, and recycling over disposal efforts as part of a new "conserving" society.

These are the particulars of Gore's interpretation of human consumption and its waste by-products.

Yet there is an alternative vision—one that emphasizes dynamic adjustments in the face of ever-changing prices and priorities. This vision evokes a different understanding of our "waste" problem. It sustains a different interpretation of observable phenomena. And it suggests different remedies to problems of resource consumption and waste handling.

This vision focuses on the impact of decision-making processes, "feedback loops," and institutional incentives on human action. Under this vision, market institutions—especially prices—give information about the relative scarcities of different resources, fostering a constant set of adjustments and readjustments in consumption.

That information system is imperfect either because there are "unpriced" resources like air or because of government action that subsidizes some kinds of consumption. These subsidies interrupt and distort information about resource use. This is, in fact, one of the central problems of "garbage" in the United States. Waste disposal has been offered as a "free" or subsidized service.

What is the result of this failure to charge fully for garbage collection and disposal? We ignore waste when we purchase goods. If waste is offered as a free service, we don't think about the waste we might be generating when we buy, say, deodorant in a boxed rather than unboxed package. This, in turn, means manufacturers have had little incentive to include waste considerations among the many other attributes they strive to incorporate in their packaging. In the absence of prices for resources and services, the "information loop" about resource scarcities is incomplete.

This is a broadbrush diagnosis of our fundamental waste problem. But what about the details of Gore's specific claims?

THE THROWAWAY SOCIETY

No doubt about it, Americans throw away a lot of stuff. Annually we produce an estimated 200 million tons of municipal solid waste, which includes household, commercial, and some light industrial waste. But are we profligate in our waste generation? Are we "cavalier," as Gore worries, toward our waste?

Terms like "profligacy" and "cavalier" are inherently loaded. They have no reference point. They are not terms with intrinsic meaning. Instead, one needs to ask, "Are we profligate relative to other industrial societies?"or "Are we increasingly wasteful compared to the recent past?"

How do we compare to others and to our own past? Several reports comparing U.S. per capita waste production with that of other affluent nations show the United States leading the pack. For example, *Waste Age* magazine reported that Japan produces only 76 percent of the amount of garbage generated per person in the United States. France and Germany are reported to produce only 60 percent and 40 percent, respectively, of the amount of waste that U.S. households produce.

These figures are, however, misleading. We are comparing apples and oranges when we contrast American per capita waste with that of Europe and Japan. The Office of Technology Assessment underscores this problem in its report, *Facing America's Trash*: "In the United States, post-consumer materials that are recycled are generally included in the definition of municipal solid waste (MSW). In contrast, Japan and many European countries . . . define MSW as including only those materials sent to waste treatment or disposal facilities."[1] Using this measurement standard, U.S. households produce about 3.2 pounds of waste per day compared to Japan's 3 pounds per day.

Even these figures obscure important differences between the two nations. More Americans live in single-family homes surrounded by lawn and trees and shrubs. Some 20 percent of our municipal waste is yardwaste. Most Japanese, by contrast, live in multi-family apartment complexes, which results in less yardwaste. Does this mean the Japanese are better environmental citizens?

What about our waste habits over time? Have we become increasingly wasteful? The EPA would have us believe so. We see figures indicating that each of us produced 2.5 to 3 pounds of waste 20 years ago. Today, they say, we produce 4 pounds per person daily.

Empirical evidence to support this contention is mixed. On the one hand, waste expert Harvey Alter of the U.S. Chamber of Commerce notes that *"per capita* generation from 1970 through 1984 was statistically constant" in the few cases in which we have actual weight information about waste.[2] On the other hand, data put out by waste consultants, Franklin Associates, suggest that total waste generated grew by some 34 percent over a similar time period (1972–1987).[3] While much of this growth simply resulted from population increases, even on a per capita basis, waste discards, according to Franklin Associates, grew by 16 percent.

This would seem to confirm Gore's picture of an evermore wasteful society. However, in its 1992 report on trends in waste generation, Franklin Associates explains these increases: Broad societal changes rather than a "throw-away ethic" account for much of the increased per capita waste generation.[4] Two changes have contributed especially to the increases, changes in demographics and changes in the workplace.

WHITE COLLARS, WORKING MOMS, AND WASTE: PATTERNS OF CHANGE

Between 1972 and 1987 the United States experienced a 34 percent increase in the total number of households. That number jumped at twice the rate of population growth. Why? An escalating divorce rate, delayed marriages, more single elderly people—all these trends boosted the number of people living alone. In fact, the number of people living alone surged some 72 percent over this time period.

What's all this have to do with waste generation? First, more households often mean more yardwaste. In fact, yardwaste grew between 1972 and 1987 by 34 percent—at about the same pace as the number of households. Second, more single-person households mean more consumption of single-serve food products. And finally, more households mean more appliances—where two married people might have shared a washing machine, those same two people, now divorced, will likely each have a washing machine. And they will each have a dishwasher and a refrigerator, as well as home furnishings.

In fact, discards of major appliances increased 74 percent from the early 1970s to the late 1980s.[5] Some of that increase might be characterized as a symbol of the "throwaway" society. For example, we appear, according to Franklin Associates, to redecorate more often than in the past, a sign of growing affluence. But, as the Franklin report points out, a lot of the increase simply resulted from other social and demographic trends that had nothing to do with a waste ethic.

What about changes in the workplace? Again, the Franklin report illustrates some dramatic shifts.[6] From 1972 to 1987 population grew by 16 percent. The work force, on the other hand, grew by 38 percent—more than twice the rate of population growth. And this work force shifted in composition, with the number of office workers increasing by 72 percent, over fourfold the rate of population growth. This growth in office workers, the Franklin report posits, resulted from a shift from a manufacturing to a service and information economy. Much of the work force increase was met by women, and that has meant more two-career families. In fact, while

174

the total work force grew by 38 percent, the number of women working climbed 60 percent.

This cluster of changes has had a big impact on municipal waste generation. More two-career families mean consumption of convenience food items such as prepackaged foods or mail catalogue purchases have increased. Is this emphasis on convenience "wasteful?" It's easy to condemn this trend, but anyone who has tried to work an 8- or 10-hour day and then has returned home to take care of a family may view the convenience of prepared foods or, say, disposable diapers as something close to a necessity.

The increase in office work relative to other forms of employment has also contributed to the growth of per capita municipal solid waste.[7] More office work typically has meant more paper discards, and, unlike manufacturing waste, these commercial discards are part of the municipal waste stream. According to Franklin Associates, discards of printing and writing paper increased 73 percent, office paper discards grew 123 percent, and copier paper discards rose 150 percent.

Can we do something about reducing this mountain of paper? Yes. But is this increase in paper discards, pure and simple, an emblem of sheer waste? No.

WHERE IS THE PACKAGING AVALANCHE?

Nowhere does the image of a "throwaway society" materialize more vividly than with packaging. We consume—and discard or recycle—some 90 billion cans of soda each year. We use over 1 million tons of corrugated cardboard each year. We discard almost 5 million washing machines annually.

We can, however, get carried away by these statistics and the images they evoke. A freeze-frame worldview like Vice President Gore's will zero in on this mountain of trash. By contrast, a longer time horizon allows us to identify trends and understand packaging in a broader context.

Before targeting packaging as the culprit, we need to ask a few questions.

➲ Do we have "excess" packaging?

➲ Is packaging waste on the upsurge?

➲ What are the options we face?

In the mid-1970s, the EPA examined packaging in the waste stream and determined that "excess" packaging—that is, containers developed

175

solely for the purpose of increasing product advertising or shelf space—contributed only insignificantly to the increase in packaging that emerged in the 1950s and 1960s. Two other factors played a far more important role: (1) increased affluence, which brought about increases in overall consumption and increased consumer emphasis on safety, sanitation, and convenience; and (2) population increases.

Consumption of packaged goods did increase in the several decades after World War II. However, most of this packaging represented a "solution" to some consumer problem—for example, a desire for low-cost, diverse foods, a push for greater safety, and so on.

Noted University of Arizona "garbologist" William Rathje and others have pointed to the role that packaging has played in reducing food waste and in "democratizing" food consumption.[8] In examining waste in Mexico and the United States, Rathje found that the average household in Mexico City "discards 40 percent *more* refuse each day than the average USA household." Rathje explains this phenomenon:

> This difference—1.6 pounds per household per day—is food debris, the skins, rinds, peels, tops, and other inedible parts discarded in food preparation. Because almost all packaging involves some processing, many unused food remains are disposed of in bulk by processing facilities (often as economically useful byproducts, such as fuel or animal feed) before they reach consumers.[9]

Rathje offers the example of orange juice consumption. In Mexico City, most consumers squeeze fresh oranges to make juice. The peels are then thrown away. U.S. households, by contrast, obtain juice from frozen concentrate containers. The result? The typical Mexican household tosses out 10.5 ounces of orange peel each week; the typical American household throws out 2 ounces of cardboard or aluminum from a frozen concentrate container. What about the peels discarded from the oranges to make the concentrate? They are used by industry for animal feed and other products.

Even this does not provide the full picture. To yield the same quantity of orange juice, a consumer requires 25 percent more oranges than does an industrial processor. This translates into less use of fertilizer, labor, water, fuel, and so on to produce a given quantity of juice.

This does not mean we should restrict the consumption of fresh foods. Such products offer many distinct benefits. But the orange juice example does help us to understand that the relationship of packaging with the environment is a complex one.

Moreover, we can begin to understand why environmental values

176

are part of a larger cluster of values, such as nutritional needs, safety, or even time savings. Take, for example, nutrition. Historian Daniel Boorstin has noted that increases over the last century in food processing, packaging, and food transportation have improved the American diet. Food packaging has "democratized" food consumption, helping to give all income groups access to a wide array of foods.

Why has this democratization occurred? William Rathje points out that it results partly from the role that "food processing and packaging play in reducing fluctuations in price, fluctuations in seasonal availability, and the shortages which can plague extremely large cities."[10]

While better food distribution was a challenge in the post-World War II setting, times have changed and so, too, have our priorities. Waste reduction is among those new priorities. Packaging is an obvious target.

Packaging does contribute significantly to our solid waste stream. Franklin Associates has shown that some 30 percent of the U.S. waste stream is composed of packaging—bottles, boxes, wrappers, cans, and so on.[11] But this snapshot picture is misleading. It gives us no sense of context and no notion of historical trends.

Contrary to prevailing popular perceptions, packaging as a portion of the waste stream is now declining. A 1988 Franklin Associates report revealed that containers and packaging made up 30.3 percent of the waste stream in 1986 compared to 33.5 percent in 1970.[12] This trend occurred despite population growth and increased consumption.

For some products the trend has been especially dramatic. Snack food *consumption* increased 43 percent from 1972 to 1987, but snack food *packaging* actually declined 9 percent. Beer and soft drink consumption climbed 52 percent during this same time; packaging by weight of these beverage containers decreased 28 percent.[13]

How could this be? Four packaging trends are largely responsible for these reductions:[14]

ᗡ replacement, or partial replacement, of rigid packaging with flexible packaging (for example, substituting a heavy corrugated cardboard box with shrink wrap);

ᗡ replacement of heavy packaging materials with lighter ones (for example, replacing glass with plastic or paper/plastic combinations);

ᗡ reduction in the number of packets or weight of packaging through an increase in the average package size for many products (there are a few exceptions, such as increased consumption of single-serve meals, for example);

⊃ decreases in the weight of packaging through "lightweighting" of glass, metals, paper, and plastics.

Several examples illustrate these trends:

⊃ In the early 1960s, the 12-ounce soda can required 164 pounds of material per 1,000 units. Today, the 12-ounce can requires only 35 pounds of material. This was made possible by replacing steel with aluminum, changing the can design, and improving the production technologies.

⊃ A plastic milk jug weighed 95 grams in the early 1970s; today that jug weighs 60 grams.

⊃ In 1976, plastic grocery bags were 2.3 mils thick; by 1989 they were just .7 mils thick.

RETHINKING THE WASTE PROBLEM

The decline in packaging as a portion of the waste stream by weight has resulted largely from competitive market processes in which industries, seeking cost reductions and introducing new technologies, have actually reduced packaging per unit of output. Most of this industry effort, however, has been on the input side of packaging, not on reducing waste volume. Lightweighting and shifts to flexible packaging have often meant reductions in materials usage for a given package. And these innovations have also often meant energy savings. Manufacturers have had an incentive to think about these matters, because reductions in energy or materials mean reductions in costs. Lower costs mean enhanced competitiveness. These costs—of material and energy—have been part of the business information loop about resources.

Waste volume is another matter. Less waste volume associated with their products does not necessarily save money for the manufacturer. And, without charges to the consumer for waste disposal service, less waste volume typically could not translate into savings to the consumer. Without charges for garbage service, consumers have, instead, had an incentive to purchase goods without any regard to how much waste was generated. Peter Menell, a policy analyst at University of California, puts the problem this way: "because disposal is free, consumers favor products with *more* packaging so as to reduce the risk of breakage (i.e., more insulation) or increase convenience (e.g., smaller size units). While reducing breakage and increasing convenience are worthwhile product design objectives, so is reducing disposal cost. But the traditional incentive structure ignores the costs of disposal."[15]

This, then, gives us one important perspective on the waste problem. We need to put garbage onto the consumer's agenda by charging for garbage service.

Historically, refuse collection has often been funded out of local general funds, financed largely through property taxes. A 1990 survey of 246 cities with populations ranging from 5,000 to 1.75 million showed that 39 percent of the cities did not charge any user fees for garbage collection.[16] Of those that did have fees, about half charged flat rates regardless of garbage volume or weight collected. Thus, over two-thirds of the cities surveyed had no pricing mechanism by which to convey to individual households the marginal costs of each unit of garbage they produced.

Introducing prices to charge for waste collection and disposal service, thus, is an important link in addressing our waste problems. Manufacturers have made big improvements in packaging, improvements that have reduced energy and materials usage. And, as concern about waste has increased, they have begun to redesign packaging and products to yield less waste. This effort, however, needs reinforcement. Charges for solid waste service, especially fees that vary depending on how much stuff we set out for disposal, introduce a missing information link and keep "waste" permanently on our agenda as we think about product choices.

Even if we change our buying patterns and reduce the amount of waste we generate, some waste will still remain. What can we do with this "stuff?"

ARE WE RUNNING OUT OF LANDFILLS?

Resource conservation concerns prompted some of the early efforts by environmental organizations to promote recycling. During the late 1980s, however, much of the push for mandatory recycling legislation resulted from the perception that we are "running out of landfill space." Vice President Gore repeats this sentiment in *Earth in the Balance*. "The volume of garbage," he writes, "is now so high that we are running out of places to put it" (p. 151). He asserts that we have assumed "there would always be a hole wide enough and deep enough to take care of all our trash" (p. 151). This assumption, he says, "like so many other assumptions about the earth's infinite capacity to absorb the impact of human civilization" (p. 151) is wrong.

Again, Gore's snapshot focus on a moment in time reinforces this kind of perspective. It encourages us to assume a fixed number of landfills, with no opportunities for expanding disposal capacity. We remember images of the peripatetic garbage barge from Islip, New York, coming to us over the network news as it roamed the high seas looking for a place to offload its infamous cargo. The prospect, understandably, filled citizens and legislators alike with dread.

Is this gloomy picture accurate? It is true, as Gore himself points out, that the number of municipal waste landfills has declined over the past decade rather dramatically. The United States had over 18,000 landfills in the late 1970s; by 1993 there remained between 5,000 and 7,000 municipal landfills.

This drop in number of landfills does not mean, however, that actual capacity has declined so precipitously. Though landfill closures have contributed to current solid waste disposal problems, their impact should not be overstated. The number of closures does not accurately convey the net loss in landfill space, since most new landfills are much larger than the older ones they have replaced. The EPA noted in 1986, for example, that the average size of landfills closed was 9.1 acres, while the average size of new landfills was 32.5 acres, with a capacity to hold on average four times the volume of waste handled in the now-closing landfills.

Nonetheless, net capacity is likely declining, particularly in some areas of the nation. One study reported that the United States was losing about 9 million tons of landfill capacity each year in the 1980s, while new landfills were providing only about 4 million tons of additional capacity.[17] By 1993, however, this trend had begun to change as the percentage of waste going to landfills declined and some large, new landfills were sited.

Even where capacity shortfalls exist, they are largely a product of politics, not physical shortages of land suitable for waste disposal. Economist A. Clark Wiseman calculated that in the United States, "*all* municipal solid waste for the next thousand years would require [a landfill 120 feet deep in] a square area having 44-mile length sides."[18] This comes to about 0.1 percent of the land space of the continental United States.

Yet citizens in many communities resist siting landfills. The proverbial not-in-my-backyard (NIMBY) syndrome has slowed, or even prevented, the siting of new waste facilities in many areas. In part, this opposition results from public perceptions that such facilities pose hazards to human health and the environment. Gore himself embraces this view that disposal facilities—landfills and incinerators—pose unacceptable risks to communities.

WHAT ABOUT SAFETY?

According to Gore, at least two problems justify dramatic changes in our waste generating activities. First, Gore argues that waste disposal practices are unsafe: "Basically, the technology for disposing of waste hasn't caught up with the technology of producing it" (p. 148). This verdict applies to both landfills and incinerators (facilities that burn waste, usually to turn it back into an energy source). In fact, Gore says of incinerators that they only masquerade as a rational and responsible disposal alternative. Instead, he says "major health and environmental concerns have never been adequately answered" regarding incinerators (p. 156).

Second, because Gore has already predefined our waste problem as that of "overgeneration" of waste, focusing on improving or expanding disposal capacity is, for Gore, counterproductive. Expanding waste disposal capacity through building incinerators, for example, "doesn't require a new way of thinking about waste" (p. 158). He underscores that, "the underlying problem remains that we are simply generating too much garbage and waste of all kinds. As long as we continue this habit, we will be under growing pressure to use even unsafe disposal methods" (p. 158).

Safety, like beauty, is in the eye of the beholder. What constitutes acceptable risk for one individual may not be acceptable for another. Still, it is possible to put risks associated with disposal facilities into some perspective. For both landfills and incinerators, potential adverse impacts can be significantly mitigated through state-of-the-art facility design, monitoring, and operation. Under these conditions, they pose relatively little risk.

In a report for the Center for the Study of American Business at Washington University, Ken Chilton and Jennifer Chilton conclude that "60 percent of the fills pose less than a one in ten billion risk of harm, which the EPA considers zero risk."[19] They note that an additional 29 percent of U.S. MSW landfills pose between a one in 100,000 and one in a million risk of harm. Using EPA's own (sometimes varying) definition of acceptable risk, this means that 95 percent of landfills analyzed by EPA pose (at least arguably) acceptable risks.

Landfill critics point to the number of MSW facilities on the National Priorities List (NPL) for clean-up under Superfund. While 42 landfills did appear in 1988 on the NPL list, these comprised only 0.5 percent of all MSW landfills.[20] Some of these actually were co-disposal sites—that is, they accepted hazardous as well as municipal waste. Almost all of the offending landfills were built long before implementation of current EPA landfill regulations.

New landfills increasingly incorporate a variety of design and operational controls to reduce potential health or environmental impacts. These include provisions for monitoring landfills long after they have closed.

The U.S. Office of Technology Assessment, evaluating modern land-fills, notes that a landfill with appropriate methods of mitigating leachate and gas-generation "should not be a major source of contamination of groundwater, surface water, or the air."[21] Additional measures to remove from the waste stream materials that could pose hazards further reduce risks associated with landfills.

Like landfills, incinerators can also pose environmental and health risks. However, these hazards, primarily from air emissions and ash residues remaining after the waste has been incinerated, can generally be mitigated through use of modern construction, operation, and control technologies and practices. In a 1989 report on incineration, the U.S. Conference of Mayors concluded that "the technology exists to carry out, monitor, and control the processes of incineration of municipal solid waste (inclusive of ash residue management) in such a way as to confidently ensure that potentially harmful constituents are not expected to pose risks to humans and/or the environment which would normally be of regulatory concern."[22]

Use of pollution-control devices can eliminate some 95 percent of particulates and trace gases from incinerator air emissions. Dioxin and furans, considered carcinogens, can also be significantly reduced from air emissions through combustion-temperature controls. The World Health Organization, reviewing MSW incinerators, has concluded that the natural "background" presence of dioxins and furans in the atmosphere exceeds concentrations in incinerator emissions from state-of-the-art facilities.[23]

Ash residues can also be safely managed or even recycled into building and construction materials. EPA has chosen not to characterize ash residue as hazardous waste, though this issue continued to receive scrutiny by regulators, the courts, and legislators under the Bush and then Clinton administrations. The U.S. Conference of Mayors' 1989 report found that "ash residue can be presently managed in a manner which is safe from the point of view of the protection of human health and/or the environment."[24]

Meeting basic safety requirements is the first conceptual hurdle that waste disposal facilities must overcome to gain acceptance as part of a waste management strategy. Not all facilities actually meet state-of-the-art safety standards. Gore is right that safety is a challenge, but it is a challenge that can be met.

WASTE DISPOSAL—UNPOPULAR BUT NECESSARY

Prompted partly by safety concerns and partly by the expectation that we can recycle our way out of the waste problem, many local communities have risen up in opposition to proposed new waste disposal facilities. The proverbial NIMBY syndrome—sometimes with exaggeration called the NOPE (not-on-planet-earth) syndrome—is a challenge to waste management authorities charged with ensuring waste disposal capacity.

We too often forget that waste disposal—whether through landfilling or incineration—is a socially valuable activity. That sounds perverse, but we need to remember that solid waste is simply the residual that results from our consumption of goods and services. These goods and services are sometimes basic necessities. Often, we buy goods and services because we perceive that they enhance our quality of life. This means consumption must be seen as a benefit to us. But an inevitable result of consumption will be the generation of some waste. And that means we need disposal facilities.

While recycling and waste-diversion efforts likely will reduce the percentage of waste handled by disposal techniques, disposal will remain an important part of waste management for two main reasons. First, for many materials and in many locations, disposal is still the lowest-cost option. Second, even aggressive recycling and composting efforts will likely divert not more than 40 percent of the municipal waste stream. Since the United States generates some 200 million tons of municipal waste annually, 40 percent diversion would still leave 120 million tons requiring disposal. At 3 cubic yards of waste per ton, that's about 12 million truckloads of trash—all needing someplace to go.

Consider first the question of costs. Costs are always a moving target, since improved technologies, new regulations, and changing land values can alter the relative costs of recycling, landfilling, and incineration. However, with the prevailing costs of the early 1990s, landfilling remained the cheapest waste-handling option in most communities. The average nationwide landfill tipping fee—the amount charged to offload waste at disposal facilities—hovered around $35 per ton.[25] Trash collection costs ranged from $40 to $70 per ton. Combined together, this meant typical 1993 waste collection and disposal costs came to somewhere between $75 and just over $100 per ton. Some areas, mainly in the northeast, had disposal costs higher than the average. There, waste-management costs sometimes exceeded $150 per ton. But these high-cost communities were the exception, not the rule.

Residential recycling costs in the early 1990s, by contrast, usually exceeded $100 per ton, and often climbed higher than $140 or $150 per ton.[26] This meant that many communities found their waste management costs increasing after they introduced curbside residential recycling programs. This, in turn, meant local governments had to take a close look at just how much recycling they were going to promote.

But there is another major reason why disposal will remain an important waste-management tool. Many trash experts say there are limits to just how much we can recycle and compost. Costs, practicality, and marketing issues all constrain recycling opportunities.

Estimates of the amount of the solid waste stream that could be diverted through recycling vary from less than 25 percent to as much as 80 or 90 percent. However, the lower range of 25 to 40 percent is likely to be most realistic, at least over the next decade or so. A 1990 Franklin Associates report suggested that "based on current trends and information, EPA projects that 20 to 28 percent of MSW will be recovered annually by 1995. Exceeding this projected range will require fundamental changes in government programs, technology, and corporate and consumer behavior."[27]

YES IN MY BACKYARD, FOR A PRICE

Economist Clark Wiseman put his finger on the central disposal problem we face: "The solid waste problem is not one of space, or even cost. The problem is a political one—that of siting new landfills."[28]

Disposal facilities do have some adverse impacts, particularly to those living near them. They can be noisy and sometimes smelly. They generate heavy truck traffic going to and from facilities. And, even with state-of-the-art technologies, they pose some, albeit small, risks to human health and the environment.

Past landfill (or incinerator) siting has been a top-down affair, with government officials simply picking a spot and siting a waste-disposal facility. Community members were left out of the equation. While this method brought benefits in the form of adequate disposal capacity, it did so at the expense of those dwelling near these disposal sites. In the absence of any compensation to these people, they are essentially shouldering many of the negative consequences of the facility without receiving any counterbalancing benefits.[29]

There is a way out of this inequity—host-community benefit packages. Through a negotiated process, these packages offer a series of monetary and other benefits to citizens in a "host" community that agrees to site a waste facility. They get guaranteed protection against any loss in property values, for example. The local community gets a portion of the revenues that come from others in the region using the waste facility. They

184

may get special protections above and beyond existing environmental regulations. Sometimes they may negotiate the siting of parks or other desirable community assets to be paid for by the owner of the waste facility. These packages do not compromise environmental standards. All state-of-the-art environmental mitigation measures are incorporated into the agreed upon package, and host-benefit packages often supplement these measures with additional environmental and monetary benefits.

This is not "greenmail" nor "environmental discrimination" nor "garbage imperialism" (Gore's term). Many—but not all—areas that have agreed to host-benefit packages are poorer communities. These benefit packages "introduce market-like decision-making processes that allow local citizens to make choices about whether, where, and how a disposal facility is sited."[30] In contrast to legislative proposals that would prohibit siting of disposal facilities in "poor communities," such benefit packages allow citizens to make their own choices—to weigh the benefits accompanying such a facility against potential risks.

WHAT IS THE PATH TO CONSERVATION?

For many environmental organizations, "saving" landfill space is only a secondary justification for requiring recycling. The larger issue, they argue, is to conserve resources and reduce overall environmental impacts from human consumption. Solid waste analyst John Schall, author of a provocative article, "Does the Solid Waste Management Hierarchy Make Sense?", attempts to persuade us that we face a resource and environmental crisis and that mandated recycling will help mitigate that crisis.[31]

Recycling, however, ought not to be viewed as an end in itself. It is a means to an end—the more appropriate end being efficient use of resources, including labor, capital, raw materials, and energy. Because recycling requires collection, processing, transportation, and remanufacturing activities, the net effect on resource use will depend on where and how recycling collection and processing occurs.

For example, a November 1991 report on wastepaper recycling in Europe attempted to compare through a "life-cycle" analysis the resource and environmental impacts under three different scenarios: (1) incineration of all wastepaper, with no recycling; (2) maximum feasible recycling (65 to 70 percent of all wastepaper); and (3) selective recycling.[32]

The report examined overall energy requirements under the three scenarios, as well as comparative air and water emissions and solid waste generation. The study found that overall nonrenewable fuel consumption, when taking into account replacement of wood residue fuel used to make virgin paper, as well as the energy captured through incineration, increased by 72 percent under the maximum recycling scenario. Some air emissions increased—sulfur dioxide, nitrogen oxide, and methane—under the maximum recycling scenario. Others decreased—for example, carbon dioxide and carbon monoxide. Similar results were found for water emissions, with total suspended solids and biological oxygen demand increasing under the maximum recycling situation and other water emissions decreasing.

Recycling did reduce municipal solid wastes, but total industrial wastes increased twofold in the European wastepaper scenario, since wood fuel (used to make virgin paper) is largely replaced under recycling processes with coal fuel, thus significantly increasing mining wastes.

All recycling efforts reduce consumption of some "virgin" materials. However, this single-resource focus ignores the cluster of other inputs—like energy, water, and labor, for example—that go into making products. And this single-resource focus ignores the trade-offs and complexities that result from substituting one material for another. The composition of air and water emissions or total waste will change with each substitution of virgin materials for recycled ones, or with each substitution of one material (for example, glass) for another (plastic).

The devil, as the saying goes, is in the details. A few examples show just how complicated questions of resource conservation can become.

While some paperboard with low-strength requirements can be readily made from 100 percent recycled content, some high-performance paperboard loses strength as recycled content exceeds 15 percent. Indeed, paperboard containers with 15 percent recycled content actually use 20 percent less total paper fiber than containers that contain 35 percent recycled content, because the latter requires addition of virgin fibers to attain necessary strength and humidity-resistance qualities.[33]

Or, consider coffee containers. The coffee brick pack is an innovation that uses an aluminum foil/plastic laminate. The brick pack, which is not now recyclable nor can it be made from recycled content, yields about 3 pounds of waste from 65 one-pound containers. By contrast, 65 one-pound metal cans, which are readily recyclable and can be made from recycled content, yield 20 pounds of waste. This means over 85 percent of the metal cans would need to be recycled just to achieve the same waste reduction of the nonrecyclable brick pack.[34]

All product choices involve trade-offs. Does a product deserve a "seal" of environmental approval if it conserves on landfill space but requires more water usage than available alternatives? The "great diaper debate" clearly illustrates this conundrum. In Canada, a green labeling program awarded reusable cloth diapers an environmental emblem. But reusable diapers consume—through their manufacture and use—six times more water than disposables.[35] Moreover, though reusables require one-eighth the amount of raw materials than disposables, the latter is composed primarily of renewable resource content. The nonrenewable resource content of the two products is almost the same. Reusables require over three times as much energy as disposables. On the other hand, disposables generate 100 times more solid waste.

So what is the verdict? Each product has environmental impacts. Which is more important—conservation of water or conservation of landfill space? Is the verdict the same in every location? There are no scientific answers to these questions because they relate to priorities that may vary by location and over time. Recycling has a role to play in the persistent drive for efficient use of resources. But it is markets, not mandates, that drive us toward this goal.

The history of aluminum recycling is instructive. When a U.S. aluminum company first introduced recycling in the late 1960s in Los Angeles, California, collection costs approached $0.75 per pound. By contrast, the recycled cans, competing with virgin aluminum ingot, could bring in only $0.25 per pound. Because the program was operated without subsidies, the aluminum company had a strong incentive to find ways of bringing collection costs down in the hopes of making the program cost-effective. Recycled aluminum did offer some benefits to the manufacturer, since energy costs to make new can "sheeting" from recycled aluminum were significantly lower than to make the end product from raw materials. But collection costs for recycled aluminum could not exceed projected savings on energy costs if the program were to be cost-effective overall.

After some experimentation, the company brought collection costs down to $0.35 per pound. At that cost, the company could just about break even when taking into account energy savings. After additional collection program changes, aluminum can recycling became highly cost-effective.

This brief tale of aluminum recycling illustrates three key ingredients for achieving sustainable recycling: (1) time to develop infrastructure; (2) flexibility to experiment with a variety options; and (3) a market context that provides incentives for entrepreneurs to seek ways of reducing costs so that recycled materials can compete with virgin materials.

WASTE NOT, WANT NOT:
MARKETS OR MARSHALL PLANS

Gore's own prescription for diminishing our waste problem goes well beyond an appeal for more recycling. He draws a contrast between human civilization and "nature." He sees nature as sustainable. Nature "actually avoids the creation of 'waste' at all, because the waste of one species becomes useful raw material for another" (p. 160). By contrast, human populations and their accompanying consumption have burgeoned such that our waste "far outstrips—in quantity and in toxic potential—the capacity of the natural environment to absorb or reuse it at anything approaching the rate at which it is generated" (p. 160).

Recycling, Gore says, is one part of the answer to this problem. However, he would prefer to reduce consumption altogether. "What's required," he writes, "is a new way of thinking about consumer goods, a challenge to the assumption that everything must inevitably wear out or break and be replaced with a new and improved model, itself destined quickly to wear out or break." This change, Gore adds, "will not be easy," since he sees our civilization built around the "constant consumption of new 'things'" (p. 160). He envisions a drastic reduction in the amount of waste we generate—and that means reduced consumption. It also means an environmental Marshall Plan of government action.

In his Marshall Plan, Gore sees some role for technology in meeting our environmental challenges. However, his laundry list of action items would put a yoke on market processes. His list would thrust governments into the forefront of picking technology "winners."

Ironically, while Gore is able to see the dynamic interactive processes of nature, he misses similar dynamics in self-organizing economic decision-making processes. In an introduction to an environmental economics course, Michael Edesses sums up an alternative to Gore's view. Edesses writes,

> Instead of being overdeveloped, perhaps the human economy is underdeveloped. Perhaps it still has many empty niches that should be occupied by agents passing materials and energy efficiently along to the next compartment in the cycle. Perhaps future development of the economy can continue to fill those niches. For example, when scientists introduce or stimulate bioorganisms that eat oil spills, they fill an important niche. They fill it with an agent that regards our . . . dispersal of oil into the ocean's sink as a resource for itself. In turn, this agent

will convert the resource into waste that will be food for another species.[36]

Edesses suggests that the economic process *is* the counterpart to the eons-old evolutionary ecological process that has filled nature's multiple niches. He challenges us, "dare we believe that, instead of bringing about its own and the planet's demise, humanity is building toward a rich, cycling economy, as sustainable as a rain forest?"[37]

For this evolutionary economic niche-filling to occur requires strengthening the information feedback loops of market economies rather than interrupting them with subsidies and legislative prescriptions. Formal rule-making—regulations—decrease the capacity for flexible responses to changing circumstances regarding resource cost, availability, and "niches" that need filling. The focus on prescribing ends diverts attention away from policies that will improve existing market processes such that externalities resulting from human production and consumption will be more fully incorporated into our decisions.

An English essayist once wrote that the world is divided into two kinds of people—those who focus on its imperfections and those who celebrate its working parts. It's time for us to refocus on those working parts—the competitive marketplace, which has prompted manufacturers, seeking ways of reducing costs, to reduce inputs (energy, raw materials, and so on) per unit of output. That same process, if price signals to consumers are introduced through direct user fees for service, will put "waste" on consumers' "radar screens" so that they will consider the costs of waste ·generation as they determine what to purchase and how to discard those purchases.

Notes

1. Office of Technology Assessment, *Facing America's Trash* (Washington, DC: U.S. Government Printing Office, October 1989), p. 102.
2. Harvey Alter, "The Future of Solid Waste Management in the United States," U.S. Chamber of Commerce, January 1990, p. 7.
3. Franklin Associates, *Analysis of Trends in Municipal Solid Waste Generation: 1972 to 1987* (Prairie Village, KS: Franklin Associates, January 1992), p. ES-1.
4. Ibid. This is the thesis of the entire Franklin Associates document.
5. Ibid. pp. 1–3.
6. Ibid., chapter 7.
7. Ibid.
8. William Rathje and Michael Reilly, *Household Garbage and the Role of Packaging* (Tucson, AZ: University of Arizona, July 1985), p. 48.
9. Ibid., p. x.
10. Ibid., p. xi.
11. Franklin Associates, *Characterization of Municipal Waste in the United States: 1992 Update* (Washington, DC: U.S. Environmental Protection Agency, 1992).
12. Franklin Associates, *Characterization of Municipal Waste in the United States: 1990 Update* (U.S. Environmental Protection Agency, June 1990).
13. Franklin Associates, *Analysis of Trends in Municipal Solid Waste Generation: 1972 to 1987* (Prairie Village, KS: Franklin Associates, 1992), chapters 5 and 6.
14. Gesellschaft fur Verpackungsmarktforschung (GVM), "Packaging Without Plastic" (Weisbaden, Germany, December 1987), p. 5.
15. Peter Menell, "An Incentive Approach to Regulating Municipal Solid Waste," John M. Olin Law and Economics Seminar, Washington, DC, Georgetown University Law Center, Feb. 22, 1990, p. 4.
16. "Survey of Solid Waste Charges," City of Worcester, Massachusetts, February 1990.
17. Jerry Taylor, "Municipal Solid Waste Management: An Integrated Approach," (Washington, DC: American Legislative Exchange Council, 1991), p. 3.
18. A. Clark Wiseman, "U.S. Wastepaper Recycling Policies: Issues and Effects" (Washington, DC: Resources for the Future, August 1990), p. 2.
19. Kenneth Chilton and Jennifer Chilton, *Municipal Landfill Risks: How Real Are They?* (St. Louis, Missouri: Center for Study of American Business, April 1991), p. 8.
20. Ibid.
21. Office of Technology Assessment, *Facing America's Trash*, chapter 7.
22. U.S. Conference of Mayors, *Incineration of Municipal Solid Waste: Scientific and Technical Evaluation of the State-of-the-Art*, Report of the Expert Panel (Washington, DC: U.S. Conference of Mayors, February 1, 1990), p. 8.

23. "The State of the Solid Waste Dilemma: Front-End vs. Integrated Waste Management," (Washington, DC: American Legislative Exchange Council, February 1990).
24. U.S. Conference of Mayors, p. 7.
25. "Solid Waste Price Index," *Landfill Price Digest*, May 1993.
26. Lynn Scarlett, "Recycling Costs:Clearing Away Some Smoke," in *Solid Waste & Power*, July/August 1993.
27. Franklin Associates, *Characterization of Municipal Solid Waste: 1990 Update*. Harvey Alter of the U.S. Chamber of Commerce suggests that the rate may even be much lower—nearer 16 percent—if experience regarding participation rates, even in areas with aggressive programs, is considered. See Alter, "The Future Course of Solid Waste Management."
28. A. Clark Wiseman, "U.S. Wastepaper Recycling Policies: Issues and Effects" (Washington, DC: Resources for the Future, August 1990).
29. See a discussion of this issue in Rod Fort and Lynn Scarlett, *Too Little, Too Late? Host-Community Benefits and Siting Solid Waste Facilities* (Los Angeles: Reason Foundation, April 1993).
30. Ibid., p. 1.
31. John Schall, "Does the Solid Waste Management Hierarchy Make Sense?" Yale University, School of Forestry and Environmental Studies, September 1992.
32. "Environmental Impacts of Waste Paper Recycling: A Feasibility Study," Draft Report, by Yrjo Virtanen, Laxenburg, Austria, November 1991.
33. Lynn Scarlett, "Sustainable Recycling: Markets or Mandates," speech presented at the Foundation for Research on Economics and the Environment, Integrated Waste Management Seminar, Big Sky, Montana, August 1992.
34. Tom Rattray, Procter & Gamble, Cincinnati, Ohio, 1992.
35. Franklin Associates, *Energy and Environmental Profile Analysis of Children's Single Use and Cloth Diapers*, revised report (Prairie Village, KS: Franklin Associates, May 1992). Other life-cycle analyses by Arthur D. Little and by C. Lehrburger, J. Mullen, and C.V. Jones show somewhat different results. The point here is not to assert a precise comparison of cloth versus disposable diapers but rather to illustrate the nature of potential trade-offs.
36. Michael Edesses, "Entropy, Economics, and the Environment," unpublished essay, January 15, 1993 (on file with the author).
37. Ibid.

CHAPTER 10

It Works Better
If You Plug It In

Dixy Lee Ray

Vice President Gore dedicated a great deal of time and energy to studying the nuclear arms race. In *Earth in the Balance,* he reveals that his study of the arms race "led [him] to think about other issues, especially the global environment, in a new, more productive way" (p. 7). Gore's general discussion of nuclear related issues is, however, limited in scope and substance. By just skimming the surface of the nuclear debate, Gore failed to address the importance and the potential of nuclear energy.

The position taken by Vice President Gore when he relates "global environmental destruction" to nuclear arms is, at best, strained. No one denies that the manufacture of nuclear warheads has resulted in the discharge of certain pollutants to the environment. But, this has happened in specific, discrete, and contained locations that are monitored. Cleanup operations are under way. Even the Japanese cities of Hiroshima and Nagasaki, which experienced the highly destructive, explosive force of an "atom bomb," are now both well-populated modern metropolises. They present no environmental threat to residents or to visitors. None of this equates to "global environmental destruction."

The Vice President is clearly against war, however his paranoia does not jibe with the facts. If anything, it is based on a deep-seated fear of some unarticulated, possible future catastrophe. Vice President Gore never acknowledges that wars are a present reality. He ignores the fact that 40

193

of them are being fought around the world today. People, both the combatants and the innocent, are being injured, maimed, and killed by weapons of war—none of them nuclear. Among the millions of war dead since 1945, none has been killed by nuclear arms.

Gore is probably alluding, not to the real world, but to his perception of the "spiritual and moral challenge" posed by the problems of controlling the weapons of nonconventional warfare (chemical and biological as well as nuclear). But, however important nonproliferation is, it is not an environmental issue per se.

It is this kind of fuzzy thinking that Gore also uses to link nuclear arms to nuclear-generated electricity. In fact, the whole subject of the importance of energy in modern society is given short shrift. Not until page 325 (of 368) does Gore acknowledge, "Energy is, of course, the life blood of economic progress." He remonstrates that using energy produces carbon dioxide, and therefore, he promotes conservation, efficiency, and "sophisticated and environmentally benign substitutes" for fossil fuel. By "environmentally benign substitutes," he apparently means renewable energy sources such as solar and wind power, so let us consider these possibilities.

Of all the ways of producing energy, none has greater appeal than solar power. After all, there's the sun sending all that heat and light and radiation to the earth for free—so why not harness it? And it makes good sense. Solar heat is used in many places (including Florida and the southwestern United States) to heat water for domestic use, to heat swimming pools, and even to heat homes or augment heating in buildings. Taking advantage of the warmth of natural sunlight is one of the enlightened ways to conserve energy.

But solar water heaters require maintenance. Despite large tax subsidies for solar power and heating, it turns out that conventional appliances like gas-fueled water heaters, for example, are much cheaper to install, maintain, and operate dependably. As a result, solar water-heating has never caught on or penetrated the market on its own merits.

It is also possible to produce electricity by harnessing sunlight if, and here's the big "if," all you need is a few watts of electricity—not *kilowatts* or *megawatts*—and if you are willing to pay exorbitant prices for them. The space program is one example of an appropriate use of solar energy. Solar cells produce electricity in space for several orbiting satellites—although not for deep space probes that range far from the sun or for spacecraft like the shuttle that require large amounts of power. Solar cells have also found an application for powering sensors, repeaters, beacons, and recording devices in remote and inaccessible places. But to produce large amounts

194

of electricity—such as are needed to run a home with modern appliances (vacuum cleaners, dishwashers, irons, washing machines, dryers, stoves, toasters, coffee makers, food processors, electric blankets, modern lighting, and so on) or to run a city or a business or an industrial operation— solar generated electricity is currently not a practical alternative.

Why not? Because, to begin with, sunlight is diffuse. To use it as a source of electricity, solar radiation must first be collected and concentrated. At best—that is, at noon on a sunny day—sunlight strikes the earth with an energy of about one kilowatt per square meter. There is no way to make the sun shine hotter or to collect more energy from sunlight, except to capture the one kilowatt per square meter from a very large area.

Solar collectors, therefore, are necessary. They can be built using mirrors or lenses, but these must be installed with small motors so they can tilt and rotate and be kept in position with relation to the sun as the earth turns on its axis. They must also be programmed to follow the sun in its seasonal cycle.

Direct conversion of solar radiation into electricity can also be accomplished by using solar cells, photovoltaics. Whichever method is adopted, solar heat or photovoltaics, a large amount of land is needed, about 50 square miles for a 1,000 megawatt plant. (Compare this to 75 to 150 acres for a 1,000 megawatt nuclear or coal plant). Suppose the 8 million of New York City were to be served by photovoltaic solar power. To supply 7,000 megawatts of electricity, New York City would need at least 350 square miles of solar cells, an area larger than the city itself.

To construct a 1,000 megawatt solar plant, the following amounts of material are needed: 35,000 tons of aluminum, 2 million tons of concrete (500 times more than for a nuclear plant), 7,500 tons of copper, 600,000 tons of steel, 75,000 tons of glass, and 1,500 tons of chromium and titanium. Moreover, photovoltaic cells are truly high tech, and considerable energy is required for their manufacture; their construction also requires toxic materials from cadmium to hydrofluoric acid. This, together with the large maintenance considerations involved in keeping the collectors, mirrors, lenses, and solar cells free from dust, greasy films, and snow, combines to make generating solar powered electricity more fallible than many realize.

Like solar power, the energy generated by windmills ultimately comes from the sun, since that is what sets the atmosphere in motion. Also like solar power, windmills have legitimate and important applications in *some* places and for *some* purposes. Windmills have been used for many years to pump water, and when placed in persistently windy areas—such as the North Sea coast of the Netherlands or much of the American midwest—they work very well for this purpose. But producing electricity introduces significant problems.

Windmill maintenance problems have proved to be severe. Wind never blows steadily or evenly. It pulses, and that contributes to the unpleasant sound created by windmills and the stresses on the vanes. Also, significant numbers of birds, including eagles, are killed by flying into the whirling blades. Experimental windmill "farms" in North Carolina and Vermont have been closed down because of noise complaints from neighbors. In the Goodnoe Hills of the Columbia Gorge in Washington State, an ambitious windmill project failed because of too many breakdowns.

Despite discouraging experience, private industry has been quite successful in developing small (17 to 600 kilowatt) machines that are dependable and economic. There are about 17,000 such turbines in California. U.S. Windpower operates 3,400 windmills of 100 kilowatts each in the Altamont Pass.

If windmills prove to work as their designers intend and without expensive maintenance, how many would it take to make a major contribution to this nation's electricity supply? According to a study done at Lockheed, wind power could supply 19 percent of America's power with 63,000 windmills having towers over 300 feet high, blades 100 feet across, and a steady wind. No one has suggested where these machines might be installed.

Renewable energy sources such as wood waste, biomass, geothermal, wind, photovoltaic, and solar thermal power presently supply less than one percent of the nation's electricity. Their contribution may increase and it may even double or triple, but for the foreseeable future, it will not make much of a difference.

We are left, then, with the sober fact that 99 percent of the electricity in the United States is produced from only three sources, and one of these, hydropower (at 4 to 6 percent of the total), is not likely to expand. That leaves us with nuclear power at 20 percent, and fossil fuel burning for the remaining 75 percent. Of the latter, coal accounts for about 80 percent and oil and natural gas for about 20 percent. These proportions will not change easily or very soon.

Since nuclear and coal are the two most abundant fuels available for production of the large quantities of electricity needed in today's world, it is both instructive and important to compare the relative environmental consequences of their use.

First, comparing the effluents from a 1,000 megawatt electric (MWe) coal plant with a nuclear plant of similar size reveals that the coal plant

196

produces carbon dioxide at a rate of 500 pounds per second or 7 million tons per year; the nuclear plant produces none. The coal plant produces sulfur oxides at a rate of one ton every five minutes, 120,000 tons per year; the nuclear plant produces none. The coal plant produces nitrogen oxides equivalent of 200,000 automobiles, 20,000 tons per year; the nuclear plant produces none. The coal plant produces quantities of smoke whose large particles are generally filtered out, but the small, dangerous ones remain and are spread widely; the nuclear plant produces none. The coal plant produces more than 40 different organic compounds that are released without control to the atmosphere; the nuclear plant produces none. Finally, since all coal contains some uranium, radium, and thorium, coal plants release unmonitored amounts of radioactivity; the only radioactive element released to the atmosphere by nuclear power plants is Krypton-85, a harmless, noble gas, which is released in minute quantities under strict control.

Solid waste is produced in a coal-burning plant at a rate of 1,000 pounds per minute, or 750,000 tons per year; the annual amount of spent fuel from a nuclear power plant is about 50 tons. The hazardous ingredients in coal ash include arsenic, mercury, cadmium, and lead, all of which maintain the same degree of toxicity forever. This material is discharged to the environment *without controls*. The nuclear plants' spent fuel continuously loses radioactivity, eventually decaying to background levels. Disposal of nuclear waste is strictly controlled. The annual amount of fuel required for a 1,000 megawatt coal-burning plant amounts to 38,000 rail cars of coal, 3 million tons per year; for a nuclear plant of similar size, 6 truckloads, or about 50 tons of fuel per year (and that includes the heavy metal carrying casks), are all that are used.

The lack of environmental effect in using nuclear power relates to the fact that the process does not involve chemical combustion and operates on the principle of containing wastes, not dispersing them. But nuclear power is not acceptable to Vice President Gore, and many agree with him.

There is no denying that both the high operation and maintenance costs of existing nuclear plants along with public apprehension over the disposal of radioactive waste have played a role in preventing nuclear power from gaining a greater share of the electricity market. Gore comments, "Growing concern about our capacity to accept responsibility for the safety of storing nuclear waste products with extremely long lifetimes also adds to the resistance many feel to a dramatic increase in the use of nuclear power" (p. 328).

No other aspect of nuclear science has so dominated and influenced

197

the public's negative view of nuclear power as has nuclear waste.[1] And this is ironic, because in truth there is no real *technical* problem either in handling nuclear waste or in treating it. Has the problem of waste from burning coal been "solved" by allowing the effluents to pollute the air and the ashes to be dispersed without control?

Some of the widespread apprehension about nuclear waste relates to governmental indecision and temporizing, because now, more than 45 years after radioactive waste began to accumulate, the debate continues about what is best to do with it. What is widely interpreted as the inability to find a solution is actually a political inability to implement a solution.[2]

Another source of apprehension is that much of the waste originated in the nation's military program. In the context of producing nuclear weapons, for a long time waste management was given low priority. Higher priority was given to stockpiling weapons. As pressure to stockpile continued, the people responsible for operations continually came up with ingenious plans for proper long-term care of nuclear waste, but their proposals regularly became victims of higher priorities.

Progress in waste management regulation has been slow. The government, after collecting contributions from nuclear utilities for research and development of a long-term, high-level waste storage facility, has indicated that it cannot meet the guaranteed date of completion. Delays in decision making have crippled the nuclear power industry, causing serious concerns among nuclear experts that the future of the industry is uncertain. Although Vice President Gore advocates vigorous research and development of nuclear technologies, he states, "the proportion of world energy use that could practically be derived from nuclear power is fairly small and is likely to remain so" (p. 328), which lends little faith to the nuclear industry.

The really important question is this: How will we, in the United States, produce electricity reliably and economically in the amounts we continue to need? Remember that electricity is the cleanest, safest, cheapest and most flexible form of energy yet known—but it's not perfect, it's dangerous. Yet, it is so common and so useful that its ready availability at reasonable cost is considered a right, a basic human requirement.

Strange how accepted a part of modern life electricity has become. Who remembers now the fear, often bordering on hysteria, that accompanied its introduction? Who recalls that the world's most eminent body of scientists, the Royal Society of London, met in special session to oppose its use? Declaring that Edison's ideas to electrify cities "defied scientific principle" and "wouldn't work," the Royal Society made a last-ditch effort to prevent electrification by passing a resolution that electricity is "too

198

powerful to put into the hands of common men." And who now remembers the bitter feud between Thomas Edison and George Westinghouse as to whether alternating or direct current should be used?

Let me emphasize once again that knowledge of and use of electricity is the hallmark of our time. Electricity makes the technological age possible. Everything we identify as "high tech" is electricity-dependent. What Thomas Edison once said of the light globe is equally true of the computer—"It works better," he said, "if you plug it in." Electricity powers the computers and wordprocessors and business machines, financial transactions and robotics and advanced industrial processes, it powers telephones and television, the entire communications industry, commercial and domestic life. In the electricity-dependent, industrial, technological nations, people live longer and healthier lives, have greater relief from drudgery and hard manual labor, enjoy a greater choice of goods and services, have more mobility and more personal liberty than in any other society. Ours is not a perfect society—it is only better than all the others. Given an average life expectancy exceeding three quarters of a century, we must be doing something right.

And yet, with all his fulminating against industrialized society and against all our present technologies, Vice President Gore fails even to address the question of just exactly how to generate electricity in a "sophisticated and environmentally benign" manner as a "transition to an environmentally responsible pattern of life" (meaning?!) and how to do this in an intensely practical world.

Indeed, is "Earth in the Balance"? If so, somebody's thumb is on the scale.

Notes

1. By far the best, most up to date, complete, and accurate discussion of nuclear waste in all its ramifications is found in chapters 11 and 12 of Bernard L. Cohen's book (1990), *The Nuclear Option: The Alternative for the 1990s*, Plenum Publishing, New York.
2. "Waste Management Update," 1988, special section in *Nuclear News*, ANS publication, Vol. 31, No. 3, March 1988, pp. 42–85.

CHAPTER 11

International Cooperation: The Role of Free Trade in Conservation

Barrett P. Walker

A subject of profound significance to the global environment that received little attention in Vice President Al Gore's book, *Earth in the Balance*,[1] is world trade. Recent years have witnessed growing recognition of a link between international trade and the environment. The North American Free Trade Agreement (NAFTA) is the first trade agreement to contain provisions that specifically address the environment. A few years ago, such an agreement tying environmental policy to an international economic treaty would have been unthinkable.

Trade policy—like environmental policy—has evolved dramatically over the last decade. Expansion of international trade and increased access to global markets have had a significant impact on trade policies. In addition, the ease with which information flows has contributed to worldwide economic growth in ways not previously contemplated. As a result, the links between trade and environmental policy have also become more visible and hotly debated. In *Earth in the Balance*, Vice President Gore ignores the potential for freer trade to contribute to continued economic growth and increased standards of living around the globe. While Gore advocates policies like technology transfer to the developing world, he fails to appreciate how free trade policies in general can foster economic progress and prosperity. Gore's discussion completely ignores the fundamental correlation between economic well-being and demands for environmental quality. He does not seem to recognize that as nations become wealthier they demand higher environmental quality.

HISTORICAL REVIEW

U. S. / Canadian Trade

The history of international trade and environmental agreements dates back over half a century. Traditionally, Canada has maintained a tariff barrier to raise the price of imported manufactured goods, thereby giving domestic manufacturers a competitive price advantage. This policy is known as import substitution. As time passed, however, the tariff came to be viewed as a barrier to the intrusion of American culture. In the words of Canadian author Robert Fulford, "Many of us learned in school that— without this tariff on manufactured products—there would be no manufacturing in Canada at all and no reason to have a country." Yet he also states that looked at rationally it would have been "foolish indeed if we declined to sell [Americans] our products and buy theirs, but trade, even then, was so potent a symbol of nationhood that this obvious truth was buried beneath anti-American and pro-British propaganda." Instead, trade continued to grow, but trade negotiations were conducted in secret.[2]

In 1944, the United States hosted an international monetary conference in Bretton Woods, New Hampshire. At the conference, which saw the birth of the World Bank and the International Monetary Fund, the U.S. and British governments maintained that trade conflict was one of the root causes of World War II. To encourage and regulate world trade, the United States proposed an International Trade Organization with binding rules. For reasons of sovereignty, the U.S. Congress refused to accept this treaty, known as the Havana Charter.[3] In 1947, 25 countries met in Geneva to negotiate a General Agreement on Tariffs and Trade (GATT). Since this pact was a non-binding agreement, approval by Congress was not necessary.[4] The United States embraced GATT, promoting the benefits of liberalized trade and the free enterprise system. As co-signatories of the agreement, the United States and Canada agreed to reduce tariffs through multilateral negotiations. Provisions of the treaty also included a non-discrimination code known as the "Most Favored Nation" principle, which stated that, apart from regional agreements, any lowering of barriers to trade must apply to all members of GATT.[5] Following GATT, both countries enjoyed a prolonged period of prosperity in which they continued to participate in periodic rounds of negotiations that lowered tariffs further. During this period, increasing concerns for the conservation of natural resources led to at least 18 agreements with trade provisions covering the protection of whales, quarantine of plants, and other topics. The agreements rely on import restrictions and trade sanctions among the participating countries. Inclusion of provisions for environmental protection within GATT itself was opposed as blocking the economic benefits derived from trade.[6]

In 1985 Canadian Prime Minister Brian Mulroney and U.S. President Ronald Reagan initiated bilateral free trade negotiations, convinced that free trade would increase economic growth and stimulate progress on world trade talks.[7] Following successful bilateral negotiations, the U.S.-Canada Free Trade Agreement (FTA) went into effect in January 1989. The FTA eliminates all bilateral tariffs by 1998 and reduces some non-tariff barriers as well. Unlike the European Community—which was formed for economic as well as political integration—the FTA is not nearly as far-reaching.[8] Despite a possible erosion of national sovereignty, the countries agreed to submit trade disputes to a binational panel of trade experts.[9]

Shortly after the FTA went into effect, Canadian political pressure forced the United States back to the bargaining table. Canadians wanted a reduction in emissions from coal burning power plants in the northern U.S.; sulfur dioxide emissions were being "exported" across the border by prevailing winds and falling in Canada as acid rain. Leveraging on the goodwill extended during the trade negotiations, Prime Minister Mulroney persuaded a reluctant President Bush to begin talks that resulted in a separate agreement in March 1991 to limit air pollution that originates in one country and adversely affects the other. The two types of pollution addressed are acid rain and emissions that reduce visibility affecting parks and wilderness areas. Additional provisions commit both countries to notify each other of any future activities that might create transboundary air pollution and take steps to reduce it. Another important part of the accord deals with a means for adding other types of air pollution not covered via "annexes" to the original agreement.[10]

In a further softening on the national sovereignty issue, both countries agreed to settle disputes that could not be negotiated directly by referral to a Joint Commission or, failing that, to "another agreed form of dispute resolution."[11] Although not directly a part of the Free Trade Agreement, the U.S.-Canada Air Quality Agreement continued the goodwill necessary between the countries to fully implement the terms of free trade.[12] The continued cooperation and success made trade negotiators more receptive to including provisions on the environment when they soon began the NAFTA deliberations.

Trade with Mexico

Just as Canada once relied on a policy of import substitution, Mexico's internal development policy also aimed to foster domestic industry by pricing imports out of the market. Constitutionally based laws and government institutions bred numerous state-run enterprises. In 1938, foreign dominated oil companies were nationalized and combined to form the Mexican Petroleum Company (PEMEX). In addition, key industries, such as railroads and large employers that went bankrupt, were taken over. Government ownership of business peaked at over 1,000 enterprises when Mexican banks were nationalized in 1982. By 1982, the state had almost complete control over the economy. After 1982, the process began to reverse itself.

When the pace of industrialization slowed in the late 1960s, an upward spiral in oil prices set by OPEC in the early 1970s allowed Mexico to borrow heavily from foreign banks and governments. This borrowing permitted the government to spend heavily on infrastructure projects, education, and public health, but there was also a great deal of waste. Despite the rapid growth in industrial employment, it was not enough to provide jobs to the more rapidly expanding population, and many Mexicans emigrated to the United States. Growing public expenditures and increasing state intervention came to an abrupt halt with the financial crisis of 1982.

The crisis occurred because Mexico and foreign lenders had risked that rising oil prices and investment would enable Mexico to repay its huge foreign debt. The spending spree lasted until the government deficit grew to unmanageable levels. As oil prices fell, foreign lenders stopped lending, causing private investors to look elsewhere. Mexicans with savings transferred their money outside the country to avoid loss in purchasing power from a falling peso and rampant inflation. This flight of capital left the government in a desperate situation. The peak of the crisis is described by Nora Lustig; "In August 1982 the Mexican government had to declare an involuntary moratorium on its debt, triggering a debt crisis that soon acquired global proportions. Tensions between the private sector and the government peaked in September 1982, when the government announced the nationalization of the banking system. . . . For some six years the Mexican government focused economic policy on restoring stability, particularly on lowering the rate of inflation and keeping the loss

204

of international reserves in check. It finally succeeded in 1988.... However growth did not follow."[13]

During Mexico's period of economic turmoil, living standards fell and suffering was widespread. Those environmental laws that had been on the books were widely ignored; conservation was considered a concept Mexico could ill afford. The concept of free trade would also have faced harsh criticism as "bargaining with the imperial power to the North."[14] Despite these strong feelings, economic adversity led to a 180-degree shift in government policy and caused the issues of free trade and environmental protection to converge.

Mexico renegotiated payments on its debt and, in an effort to stimulate exports, joined GATT in 1986. However, the long period of import protection had made Mexican manufactured goods uncompetitive in the world market. With such a bleak outlook for growth and a history of extensive government intervention, foreign investors had long since turned elsewhere. Mexico responded with a vigorous program to make the country more attractive to foreign investors. Laws restricting foreign ownership were repealed, business was deregulated, government firms were privatized, and laws respecting intellectual property rights were enacted. The General Law for Ecological Equilibrium and Environmental Protection, Mexico's first environmental law, was passed in 1988.[15] In May 1990 President Salinas announced the reprivatization of the banks.

Enterprise for the Americas Initiative

In June 1990 President Bush announced the Enterprise for the Americas Initiative, calling for closer U.S.-Latin American ties. With the United States continuing to run a trade deficit with most Latin American countries, including Mexico, Washington developed a plan to stimulate economic growth. With revitalized economies, it was hoped the countries would be able to pay back their burdensome debt to U.S. banks.

The initiative was shaped by the U.S. view that what was needed most was not monetary foreign aid but thorough market reforms. Many Latin Americans were "grudgingly coming to the same view, or at least could offer no good alternatives." Due to a deep budget deficit of its own following the Cold War, parts of the plan dealing with a proposed debt relief and development fund were never acted upon. Instead, in announcing the initiative President Bush focused on free trade in the Americas as "our long term goal" that "may take years to reach." The plan proposed a Western Hemispheric Free Trade Area that was enthusiastically received in Latin America.[16]

Approval of NAFTA

The pace quickened when in August 1990 President Carlos Salinas de Gotari of Mexico made a formal request to President Bush to begin negotiations on a free trade agreement. Six months later, Canada joined the negotiations.[17] And under "fast track"[18] procedures approved by the U.S. Congress, the North American Free Trade Agreement was ceremoniously initialed in October 1992 by George Bush, Mexican President Salinas, and Canadian Prime Minister Brian Mulroney. Shortly after being elected president, Clinton phoned President Salinas to express his conditional support.[19]

For countries that had worked so long to keep out the influence of the United States, Canada and Mexico had undergone revolutionary change. In fact, the quickening pace of trade negotiations was a recognition of changes already apparent in the markets. Canada and Mexico are the United State's first and third largest trading partners (Japan is second). Under NAFTA the three countries would form the world's largest common market, exceeding the European Community by $1.3 trillion.[20] However, NAFTA would be dominated by a single country. In terms of standard of living and environmental protection, Canada and the U.S. are very similar. The real contrast is with Mexico, which is politically controlled by a single party, has industrial wages only about 10 percent that of its neighbors to the North,[21] and until 1988 had no laws for environmental protection.

The rapid change in the relationship between the two countries is explained by Robert Pastor:

> In the past the United States and Mexico had been almost impervious to each other's political complaints. A typically unpleasant encounter occurred during the Senate hearings conducted by Jesse Helms in 1985, when he accused the Mexican government of corruption and authoritarianism, and the Mexicans accused him of arrogance and ignorance. This unproductive pattern of interaction was repeated often in U.S.-Mexican relations. Neither side listened to the other, or rather both sides pretended not to listen. During the NAFTA negotiations, both countries began to show a responsiveness to the other and to a common agenda which had never occurred before.[22]

The improving relationships between the countries was a sign of stability to investors, and money began flowing back into Mexico. The recovery was under way.

FREE TRADE, GROWTH, AND SUSTAINABILITY

Conflict Between Growth and Sustainability
The issue of free trade has placed the environmental movement at a crossroads. One position, expressed by Edward Goldsmith, favors a retreat to a pre-commercial world. He fears that if the present course is continued, "then the entire world will effectively be transformed into a vast Free Trade Zone, within which human, social and environmental imperatives will be ruthlessly and systematically subordinated to the purely selfish, short-term financial interests of a few transnational corporations." He believes that the solution is "not to increase the freedom of commercial concerns but, on the contrary, to bring those concerns back under control—to limit the size of markets, rather than expand them; to give local people control of their resources." In short, Goldsmith represents the view that development is to be opposed. If development continues in the Third World, he believes that much of the planet will be "rendered unfit for human habitation."[23]

An alternate view considers that Third World countries—now too poor to afford environmental protection—will begin reducing pollution once incomes rise to a level sufficient to meet basic needs. Grossman and Krueger studied air pollution in urban areas of 42 countries and found "that concentrations increase with per capita Gross Domestic Product (GDP) at low levels of national income, but decrease with GDP growth at higher levels of income. The turning point comes at about $5,000." Since per capita GDP in Mexico is now at this level, Grossman and Krueger conclude that "we might expect that further growth in Mexico, as may result from a free trade agreement with the United States and Canada, will lead the country to intensify its efforts to alleviate its environmental problems."[24] In fact, the Mexican government has already taken numerous steps to reverse the decline in air quality including a reduction in the lead content of gasoline, fitting new cars with catalytic converters, banning drivers from using their cars in Mexico City one day per week, and closing down 980 industrial sites, 82 of them permanently. The permanent closings included a government refinery on the outskirts of Mexico City that employed 5,000.[25]

Recognizing the futility of returning the world to a pre-commercial era, a more optimistic view holds that free trade agreements provide a mechanism for funding conservation and promoting sustainable development. This is possible because the efficiencies of free trade create a bigger economic pie for all trading partners to share. Two main reasons account for this. One is due to the economies of scale resulting from expanded markets, and the second results from increased specialization in the production of those goods that a country can produce most efficiently.

Certainly, the environmental deterioration witnessed in the former Soviet Union and Eastern Europe do not argue for a centrally planned economy. As in the former communist countries, Mexico's environment continued to deteriorate under decades of government management. Many industries pollute because they are inefficient. Such industries are forced to become more efficient to compete in free market countries.[26] In addition, the democratic political process, an integral part of a free market economy, ensures public participation in environmental decision making. This is vital for the environmental concerns of an increasingly affluent Mexican society to be expressed in the political process. An increasing awareness that trade and the environment are not either-or issues but an interlinked part of an overall measure of economic well-being is supported by the Grossman and Krueger study.

Improving the International System of Accounts

Because the internationally agreed upon Standard System of National Accounts, established at the end of World War II, measures economic prosperity in terms of the production of goods, economic success is taken to equal an increase in the measured Gross Domestic Product of a country. Robert Repetto, vice president and senior economist for the World Resources Institute, describes the need to include natural resources in our accounting system. "Buildings, equipment and other manufactured assets are valued as income producing capital, and their depreciation is written off as a charge against the value of production. This practice recognizes that consumption cannot be maintained indefinitely simply by drawing down the stock of capital without replenishing it. Natural resource assets, however, are not so valued. Their loss, even though it may lead to a significant decrease in future production, entails no charge against current income. . . . A country can cut down its forests, erode its soils, pollute its aquifers and hunt its wildlife and fisheries to extinction, but its measured income is not affected as these assets disappear. Impoverishment is taken for progress."[27] Fortunately the United Nations, which maintains the Standard System of National Accounts, has begun work on establishing

208

an optional satellite account for natural resources.[28] If natural resource accounting provisions were adopted by the NAFTA countries, it would remove a major distortion from the present system and help to identify environmentally destructive subsidies. Resource accounting would cause producers to internalize the costs from harmful effects such as pollution as well as provide an incentive for more efficient production.

Vice President Gore is also an outspoken advocate of natural resource accounting. *Earth in the Balance* discusses the potential value and importance of incorporating natural resource accounting into our current system of economic measurement. However, the book does not address the value of advocating natural resource accounting in trade agreements such as NAFTA. Gore may be in a position to promote natural resource accounting principles in NAFTA or other similar trade negotiations, which could prove more beneficial than blocking trade agreements on environmental grounds.

PROMOTING SUSTAINABLE
DEVELOPMENT THROUGH TRADE

Rather than trying to stop growth, a majority of national environmental and conservation organizations have directed their influence to ensuring that the development created by free trade will be sustainable.[29] One environmental group that took an instrumental lead in supporting free trade negotiations was the National Wildlife Federation. In response to a promise from President Bush to take environmental concerns into account, the federation announced support of the then-contested, fast track authority from Congress.[30] Then, in testimony before Congress, the Environmental Defense Fund advocated "strategies that combine trade liberalization with measures that protect the environment," and the largest private conservation organization in the world, the World Wildlife Fund, offered provisional endorsement of the NAFTA text.[31] Environmentalists' support of the agreement was sought and was considered necessary to assure its success.[32] Negotiators worked through many difficult problems to reach a complex and eminently technical compilation of trading rules that exceeds 2,000 pages, but questions remain. Will NAFTA be environmentally friendly, or will it cause environmental harm?

ENVIRONMENTAL CONCERNS AND NAFTA

Three principal concerns have been raised by environmentalists.[33] These concerns relate specifically to NAFTA but also apply to trade agreements in general.

The first concern is the creation of a "pollution haven." This is the fear that businesses will move to Mexico to escape environmental regulation and that U.S. and Canadian producers will face competition from cheap Mexican goods manufactured without the costs of environmental protection.

The 100-kilometer-wide area on either side of the border is cited as an example of what could go wrong. This partial free trade zone established in 1965 is known as the "Border Area." There, assembly plants called *maquiladoras* have been encouraged to locate, primarily to take advantage of low labor rates. A tremendous growth surge now counts 2,000 maquiladoras employing half a million workers in an overpopulated desert area short of infrastructure.

The worst problems center around water. Sewage treatment is inadequate or nonexistent. Juarez, for example, has no sewage treatment at all. As wells go dry from overuse, people increasingly draw water from the Rio Grande River, which also doubles as a disposal for sewage and agricultural runoff contaminated with pesticides. Pathogens for polio, dysentery, cholera, typhoid, and hepatitis found in the water could lead to a public health disaster at any time, especially during low water. Another major concern is hazardous waste: U.S. companies are required to transport this waste back over the border for disposal but don't comply due to lax enforcement. Beyond the threat to the human population, these toxic substances along with water shortages and clearing of land are threatening the area's once rich wildlife.

If not corrected, these environmental problems will diminish the competitiveness of the region. As a result of preferential treatment and a lack of planning, the Border Area has overdeveloped at the expense of underdevelopment in the rest of Mexico. NAFTA would reduce environmental problems on the border by taking away the artificial incentive for companies to locate there. Studies cited by Pastor indicate that environmental considerations play a minor role in the decision-making process of U.S. corporations that invest abroad.[34] In February 1992 both countries agreed to a three-year plan to begin cleaning up the Border Area. This was partly in recognition of the seriousness of the situation but also as a precondition for successful NAFTA talks and a result of the growing environmental awareness in Mexico nurtured by trade discussions.[35] Future "pollution havens" are discouraged by language contained within NAFTA dealing with investments.[36]

Admittedly, Mexico has a long way to go to clean up its environment. Nonetheless, major strides have already been made since the comprehensive General Law for Ecological Equilibrium and Environmental Protection was passed there in 1988. Enforcement is increasing, and public awareness and support are growing along with the economic rebound. John Audley of the Sierra Club has expressed the concern that although trade can help alleviate poverty, NAFTA as now written will harmonize U.S. environmental standards downward. The reverse side of the equation is that the NAFTA negotiations seem to have already harmonized Mexican standards upward. To speed this process, Mexico has asked the U.S. and Canada to fund a regional North American Development Bank and Adjustment Fund for projects including clean up of the polluted Border Area.[37]

A tremendous need exists for incentive-based solutions to environmental problems. One such proposal deals with hazardous waste. Rather than focus on burdensome regulations requiring a cadre of inspectors to implement, a simple deposit refund system[38] could reward companies for proper disposal or recycling of waste. Under the system, companies would pay a large deposit when they purchase containerized hazardous chemicals. The deposit would be returned when the used chemicals are delivered to a licensed disposal center. Those companies able to recycle toxins would pay the deposit only once as they continue to reuse the same solvents, for example.

The second concern is the preemption of environmental standards. Questions remain about whether trade negotiations will weaken existing environmental standards.

Perhaps the best known example of the concern that trade agreements could preempt environmental standards is the recent tuna-dolphin dispute. Acting on the requirements of its 1988 Marine Mammal Protection Act, the United States prohibited the import of yellowfin tuna from Mexico because the incidental dolphin taking rate exceeded that of domestic vessels by more than the 1.25 times limit.[39] Mexico reacted by filing a complaint with the GATT court and won. To satisfy the court, the U.S. would have to weaken its law designed to prevent the unnecessary drowning of dolphins in fishing nets. Despite the ruling in its favor, Mexico decided to join the U.S. and eight other nations in negotiations through the Inter-American Tropical Tuna Commission. In April 1992 an agreement was reached to reduce the killing of dolphins by 80 percent this decade.[40]

The U.S. ban on tuna from Mexico violated GATT only because it was a unilateral attempt to apply domestic environmental standards extraterritorially.[41] The solution was a negotiated settlement involving the consent of both the U.S. and Mexico, as well as the other nations involved. GATT does not prevent multilateral agreements to protect the environment. Such an international environmental agreement would become an exception to GATT obligations for its signatories.[42]

CONCLUSION

NAFTA has brought together free trade advocates and environmentalists from very different backgrounds. From the perspective of the science of ecology; NAFTA provides a way for the United States, Mexico, and Canada to cooperate rather than compete economically, enabling them to adapt to working with their environment. This is the principle of mutualism.[43]

A positive outgrowth of successful implementation of NAFTA may be the inclusion of environmental provisions in GATT. Proposals emerging from the Enterprise for the Americas Initiative recognize that open trade policies promote economic growth and prosperity. Rather than taking a confrontational approach to dealing with armed strife in Central America or narcotics trade in South America, for instance, the Enterprise for Americas Initiative proposes providing less developed trading partners with economically and environmentally sound alternatives. These alternatives can be created through increased Western Hemispheric Free Trade. Given the opportunity and proper incentives, countries like Mexico and Chile will be eager to trade legal goods in the global free market. After Mexico, Chile is the country most likely to join an expanded free trade agreement.[44]

The development of NAFTA has provided valuable lessons for trade and environment policymakers alike. The NAFTA negotiations have demonstrated that the linkages between trade and environmental policy cannot be ignored but can be surmounted. It is important to recognize the value of the experience gained and realize that future agreements will improve upon the lessons learned from NAFTA. In the words of environmental economist Pete Emerson, "It has helped people . . . who come from two very different political cultures better understand each other's objectives. In my view, the NAFTA represents a step forward in the integration of the international trade system and environmental protection measures."[45] Through cooperation on free trade, North Americans may also achieve the common goals of economic prosperity and conserving their resources for future generations.

212

Notes

1. Al Gore, *Earth in the Balance: Ecology and the Human Spirit*, New York, Plume Edition, The Penguin Group, 1992.
2. Robert Fulford, "Myth of Independence," *Wall Street Journal*, September 24, 1992, p. R19.
3. Joan Edelman Spero, *The Politics of International Economic Relations*, New York, St. Martin's Press, 1990, p. 69.
4. Thomas A. Walthan, *A Guide to Trade and the Environment*, New York, Environmental Grantmakers Association Consultative Group on Biological Diversity, July 1992, pp. 21, 30.
5. General Agreement on Tariffs and Trade, in Jackson and Davey, Documents Supplement to *Legal Problems of International Economic Relations*, St. Paul, West Publishing Co., 1989, p. 3.
6. Walthan, pp. 67–69.
7. The following year, the latest round of GATT talks began in Uruguay.
8. G. Pierre Goad, "Freer, But Not Free," *Wall Street Journal*, September 24, 1992, p. R18.
9. Gordon R. Ritchie, "A Disgruntled Canadian," *Wall Street Journal*, September 24, 1992, p. R18.
10. "Summary of the Agreement Between Canada and The United States Of America on Air Quality," Canadian Embassy, Washington, DC.
11. "Agreement Between the Government of the United States of America and the Government of Canada on Air Quality."
12. In his prepared speech, "Integrating Environmental Protection and North American Free Trade," Peter Emerson of The Environmental Defense Fund in Austin, TX describes a free market solution to emission reduction resulting from the Clean Air Agreement. Based on binational emissions trading, utilities that generate clean electricity sell their emission rights to less efficient producers. Clean companies can profit as long as the overall target for emission reduction is met.
13. Nora Lustig, *Mexico*, Washington, DC: The Brookings Institution, 1992, pp. 2–4.
14. Ibid., p. 132.
15. Robert A. Pastor, "NAFTA as the Center of an Integration Process: The Nontrade Issues," in *North American Free Trade*, ed. Lustig, Bosworth, Lawrence, Washington, DC, The Brookings Institution, 1992, pp. 183, 184.
16. Peter Hakim, "The Enterprise for the Americas Initiative," *The Brookings Review*, Fall 1992, pp. 41–45.
17. Lustig, p. 132.
18. Fast track authority is granted to a president by Congress to speed the negotiating process. It permits a president to reach an agreement and then present it to Congress for approval or rejection without amendments.
19. Peter Emerson, Draft of "Keynote Address for The United North Ameri-

can Conference on Industry and the Environment," The Environmental Defense Fund, Austin, TX, November 6, 1992, p. 13.

20. In 1990 the combined GDP of the three countries was $6.3 trillion with a population of 363 million compared to a European Community GDP of $5 trillion and a population of 375 million. Lustig, pp. 4, 5.

21. Barry P. Bosworth et. al., "Introduction" in North American Free Trade, ed. Lustig, Bosworth, Lawrence, Washington, DC, The Brookings Institution, 1992, pp. 4, 5.

22. Pastor, p. 179.

23. Edward Goldsmith, "GATT and Gunboat Diplomacy," The Ecologist, vol. 20, no. 6, November/ December 1990, p. 204.

24. Gene M. Grossman and Alan B. Krueger, "Environmental Impacts of a North American Trade Agreement," Discussion Paper #158, Woodrow Wilson School, Princeton University, Princeton, NJ; November, 1991, Abstract and pp. 19, 20.

25. Pastor, p. 184.

26. Wesley R. Smith, "Protecting the Environment in North America with Free Trade," Heritage Backgrounder, No. 889, Washington, DC, The Heritage Foundation, April 2, 1992, p. 2.

27. Robert Repetto, "Accounting for Environmental Assets," Scientific American, June 1992, pp. 94, 96.

28. Peter Bartelmus, lecture, "Accounting for Natural Resources," Meeting on Environmental Economic Policy, The Heritage Foundation, Washington, DC, December 9, 1992.

29. Telephone and meeting survey by the author. The following organizations were contacted: Center for Environmental Law, Environmental Defense Fund, International Institute of Ecological Economics, National Wildlife Federation, The Nature Conservancy, Sierra Club, Wilderness Society, World Resources Institute, World Wildlife Federation. Based on operations exclusively within the U.S., the Wilderness Society has taken a neutral position. Only the Sierra Club has opposed NAFTA.

30. Pastor, p. 205.

31. Kathryn S. Fuller, "Testimony Before Subcommittee on Internal Trade," World Wildlife Fund, U.S. Senate, September 16, 1992.

32. Commerce Department official Barbara Franklin in a speech at the Heritage Foundation, Washington, DC, December 8, 1992.

33. Peter Emerson, Outline, "The Environmental Side of North American Free Trade," Environmental Defense Fund, Austin, TX, November, 21, 1992. (For the sake of clarity, Dr. Emerson's concerns number one and three, which are very similar, have been combined.)

34. Pastor, p. 183.

35. Ibid., p. 186.

36. Emerson, Draft, p. 10.

37. Moffett and Solis, "Mexico Will Ask U.S., Canada for Aid to Smooth Its Entry to Free Trade Pact," Wall Street Journal, December 8, 1992.

38. Emerson, Draft, p. 14.

39. Peter Emerson, from a prepared speech, "Environmental Concerns and North American Free Trade," The Environmental Defense Fund, Austin, TX, April 10, 1992, p. 2.

40. James Brooke, "Ten Nations Reach Accord on Saving Dolphins," *New York Times*, May 12, 1992, p. B9.

41. Thomas J. Schoenbaum, "Agora: Trade and Environment," *American Journal of International Law*, vol. 86, 1992, pp. 703, 712.

42. Ibid., p. 719.

43. Eugene Odum, "Great Ideas in Ecology," *BioScience*, vol. 42, no. 7, July / August 1992, p. 543.

44. Hakim, p. 45.

45. Emerson, Draft, p. 11.

PART IV

TOWARD REAL REFORM

CHAPTER 12

Property Rights as a Central Organizing Principle

Nancie G. Marzulla

In *Earth in the Balance*, Vice President Al Gore asserts that our "modern industrial civilization" is "colliding violently with our planet's ecological system" (p. 269). According to Gore, this collision is the result of the use of our "vast technological power" in a way that dominates and exploits "our natural resources solely to achieve short term results" (p. 269). Gore offers only one solution to this catastrophe—that we make "the rescue of the environment the central organizing principle for civilization" (p. 269). Gore leaves no doubt that he is "playing for keeps" when he proposes that environmental protection become the world's new "central organizing principle." Gore suggests "embarking on an all-out effort to use every policy and program, every law and institution, every treaty and alliance, every tactic and strategy, every plan and course of action — to use, in short, every means to halt the destruction of the environment and to preserve and nurture our ecological system" (p. 274).

Gore also rewrites the Declaration of Independence, inserting "a commitment to healing the environment" as an "unalienable right" along with the rights to life, liberty, and the pursuit of happiness (p. 270), perhaps implying that in drafting the Declaration of Independence Jefferson merely neglected to include "environment" in his listing of rights.

Gore's use of a "central organizing principle" seems to suggest a government-imposed masterplan that ignores human rights, property

219

rights, and the free market. Moreover, Gore draws the wrong conclusions from the evidence he relies on, misreading history and the fundamental principles of human nature and economics.

FREEDOM AS A NECESSARY ELEMENT FOR ENVIRONMENTAL STEWARDSHIP

Gore first reports that under socialism the environment has suffered greater degradation and at a more rapid rate of decline than ever dreamed possible (p. 179). He points to the debacle in Eastern Europe as support for the notion that an essential element for saving the environment is the proliferation of democracy. As Gore explains, "Freedom is a necessary condition for an effective stewardship of the environment" (p. 179). He further adds: "This last point is critical: men and women who care must be potentially empowered to demand and help effect remedies to ecological problems wherever they live. . . . Indeed, almost wherever people . . . are deprived of a voice in the decisions that affect their lives, they and the environment suffer" (p. 179).

Gore is correct when he observes that socialism is a threat to the environment, but he seems oblivious as to why. The reason freedom is missing from socialist systems is because there are no private property rights. Property rights are a critical element of a free society; properly understood, these rights are more than simply land. Property rights are the rights to enjoy the fruits of one's labors. Many commentators have talked about the relationship between property rights and freedom. One of the most eloquent was Noah Webster, the famous American educator and linguist, who posited the following: "Let the people have property and they will have power—a power that will forever be exerted to prevent the restriction of the press, the abolition of trial by jury, or the abridgment of any other privilege."[1]

In the broadest sense then, property rights are human rights. Teddy Roosevelt, this nation's first and greatest conservation president, put it best when he said in 1910: "In every civilized society property rights must be carefully safeguarded; ordinarily and in the great majority of cases, human rights and property rights are fundamentally and in the long run, identical."[2] Even Karl Marx recognized the importance of private property rights as he explained in the *Communist Manifesto*: "You reproach us with planning to do away with your property. Precisely; that is just what we propose. . . . The theory of the Communists may be summed up in a single sentence: Abolition of private property."[3]

220

Fortunately for us Americans, the Founding Fathers also understood the relationship between freedom and property rights. To ensure that individual freedoms are secure, the framers of our Constitution envisioned vigorous protection of private property rights, realizing that "almost all other rights would become worthless if the government possessed an uncontrollable power over the private fortune of every citizen."[4]

Accordingly, Madison drafted and the states adopted a special guarantee for the protection of private property rights, the Fifth Amendment, which provides: "Nor shall private property be taken for public use, without just compensation." This amendment, along with the other amendments in the Bill of Rights, including those that protect freedom of speech and religion, due process of law, and the right to be free from unlawful searches in one's home, form the foundation for freedom in this country. But underpinning all of these rights is the protection afforded to private property.

A society in which individuals are free from the tyranny of oppression is one in which private property rights are vigorously protected. Indeed, there can be no true freedom for anyone if people are dependent on the state for their daily food, shelter, and other basic needs. That is, where the fruits of your labors are owned by the state and not you, nothing is safe from being taken by a majority or a tyrant. As a government dependent, the individual is ultimately powerless to oppose any infringement of his rights (much less degradations to the environment) because the government has total control over them. People's livelihoods, even possibly their lives, can be destroyed at the whim of the state. Had Gore understood the vital connection between freedom and property, he might have proposed "private property rights" as a central organizing principle instead of "environmental protection."

FREE MARKETS ARE A NECESSARY ELEMENT OF ENVIRONMENTAL PROTECTION

The other reason Gore might have selected private property rights as a "central organizing principle" is because he rightly recognized that "free markets" (albeit "modified free markets") play a significant role in ensuring environmental protection. Gore identifies "modified free markets" as a "preferred form of economic organization" (p. 298). According to Gore, the free market economies of the world, that is, the wealthiest and most technologically advanced countries, are the ones most willing and able in terms of resources and expertise to solve global environmental problems. Gore's idea of "modified free markets" would make sense if it meant assigning or clarifying property rights to environmental goods.

Instead of taking his language about markets seriously, Gore veered away and has concocted what he refers to as the "Global Marshall Plan," far more complicated than the original Marshall Plan, which "would combine large-scale, long-term, carefully targeted financial aid to developing nations, massive efforts to design and then transfer to poor nations the new technologies needed for sustained economic progress, a worldwide program to stabilize world population, and binding commitments by the industrial nations to accelerate their own transition to an environmentally responsible pattern of life" (p. 297).

Once again Gore misses the forest for the trees. The reason industrialized countries such as the United States have excess resources to devote to conservation is a tribute ultimately to private property rights, the foundation for the benefits provided by the free market system. There can be no free market if there are no private property rights. Simply put, if no one has anything to sell, trade, or barter, there can be no market. One need only look to the problems being experienced in the former communist states where people are trying to convert to a market system and yet everything is state owned.

Many economists have opined on the vital connection between healthy economies and private property rights. The Scottish economist John Ramsay McCullock (1787–1864) wrote that the right of private property "has powerfully contributed to make wealth."[5] Adam Smith described "property" as being one's "own labor" and as being the foundation of all other property. He further described property rights as "sacred and inviolable."[6] In 1991 the President of Poland, Lech Walesa spoke from personal experience when he wrote that "in our communist system, everything resembled one huge enterprise. It somehow did hold together in one piece, it did go on working, but now we know it didn't operate too well. . . . Now we know that private property. . . is the right solution, the right system."[7]

How does Gore conceive of a society in which people and markets are free if he does not recognize the importance of private property rights?

THE MOST INDUSTRIALIZED STATES
ALSO HAVE THE BEST ENVIRONMENTS

Where Gore does get it right is that the environment is better taken care of where there is freedom, both in the philosophical sense and in the economic sense. It is a fact that the most industrialized nations with the healthiest economies also have the best environments. Depletion of rain forests in South America, record deforestation in Bangladesh, deplorable air pollution in China, and wholesale slaughter of endangered species in Africa are partly the result of impoverishment.

But once again, Gore fails to apprehend a fundamental fact. Not only do democratic societies have the freedom and incentives to produce the surplus wealth and expertise to protect the environment but these societies, by protecting the right to own private property, naturally allow for the best form of environmental protection of all—private stewardship. The best steward of the environment is the owner of the property: "Give a man the secure possession of bleak rock, and he will turn it into a garden; give him nine years lease of a garden, and he will convert it to a desert. . . . The magic of property turns sand into gold."[8]

Time and time again the evidence clearly shows that privately owned natural resources are better conserved than are those resources for whom no one is the ultimate owner nor benefactor. Far from proving the best way to conserve natural resources, government ownership of land has proven to be disastrous in many cases. Witness the radioactive waste site in Chernobyl or the Superfund sites owned and controlled by the United States Department of Energy and the Department of Defense. Observe the vast environmental degradation, soil erosion, and general pollution in Eastern Europe and South Africa.

The notion that "when no one owns it, no one takes care of it" was well explained by Alexander Hamilton in *The Federalist Papers*: "It is a general principle of human nature, that a man will be interested in whatever he possesses, in proportion to the firmness or precariousness of the tenure by which he holds it; will be less attached to what he holds by a momentary or uncertain title, than to what he enjoys by a durable or certain title; and, of course, will be willing to risk more for the sake of the one, than for the sake of the other."[9]

HIDDEN AGENDA TO NEGLECT PRIVATE PROPERTY RIGHTS

Gore's omission of private property rights and his reliance on government control for global environmental protection is not really surprising. Al

223

Gore is, after all, a "home grown" environmentalist phenomenon, a product of the American environmental movement which hit its stride after the first Earth Day, April 22, 1970. That date can be viewed as the birthday of the most extensive and expensive government environmental protection program in the world.

Prior to 1970, the principal means of achieving environmental protection was through the common law theory of nuisance and the few conservation laws on the books such as the Rivers and Harbors Act of 1899. Today we have what can be fairly described as an explosion of government regulations designed to protect the environment. In just two decades, the United States has developed the most extensive government environmental protection program in the world. Environmental regulations have become an elaborate web of intricate laws and regulations covering every conceivable aspect of property use and indeed, human enterprise.

For example, we have federal programs dealing with endangered species, historic preservation, and landmark designations. We have federal programs dealing with occupational safety and health, Superfund, and clean water (including the wetlands program). Yet we do not have a single federal program dealing with the protection of private property rights. We have federal regulatory schemes dealing with marine protection, safe drinking water, and toxic substances control. We have federal regulations covering ocean dumping, global climate protection, clean air, and pesticides. But we do not yet have a single regulatory program dealing with the protection of private property rights.

We have over 800 pages of laws dealing with amendments to the Clean Air Act, yet not a single page devoted to the protection of private property rights. And, in the last ten years, the stakes for violating environmental laws have become significantly higher since every major environmental statute has been amended to enhance the civil penalties and to include felony criminal sanctions for violation.

And it is only going to get worse. Brock Evans, vice president of the Audubon Society, recently said, "After twelve years of dark night for the environmental movement, we see daylight. The big difference is that this administration will be a lot more receptive. Instead of getting maybe five percent of what we want, like under Reagan and Bush, we might get closer to seventy-five percent of what we want."[10]

If there is more environmental regulation, we can only assume that it will adversely affect private property rights.

224

CONCLUSION

Gore's fundamental misapprehension of freedom, economics, and private property not only lead him to the wrong conclusion when it comes to environmental protection but it also causes him to wholly misapprehend Thomas Jefferson. Gore, for example, states that what is required to solve the world's environmental problems is a "Jeffersonian approach to the environment" (p. 204). Jefferson, Gore notes, "aspired to a catholic understanding of the whole of knowledge, and when he and his colleagues in Philadelphia turned to the task of creating the world's first constitutional self-government, they combined an impressive understanding of human nature with a full command of jurisprudence, politics, history, philosophy, and Newtonian physics" (p. 204). Gore then admonishes that "we must be bold enough to use Jefferson's formula and seek to combine a catholic understanding of the nature of civilization with a comprehensive command of the way in which the environment functions" (p. 204).

Once again Gore misses the fundamental point. Thomas Jefferson was a vigorous proponent of private property rights, as many of his writings reveal. It was Jefferson, after all, who stated that a right to property "is founded in our natural wants, in the means with which we are endowed to satisfy these wants, and the right to what we acquire by those means without violating the similar rights of other sensible beings."[11]

It would behoove those of us who support the principles that Gore purports to advocate in his book—freedom, free markets, and environmental protection—to urge Gore to follow his own advice and to use Jefferson's formula, which also includes the protection of private property rights.

Notes

1. Noah Webster, [unable to locate original source].
2. Theodore Roosevelt, address at the Sorbonne, Paris, France, April 23, 1910. "Citizenship in a Republic," *The Strenuous Life* (vol. 13 of *The Works of Theodore Roosevelt*, national cd.), chapter 21, pp. 515–516 (1926).
3. Karl Marx and Friedrich Engels, *The Communist Manifesto*, 1848.
4. J. Story, *Commentary on the Constitution of the United States*, para. 1790 (1833).
5. John Ramsey McCullock, *Principles of Political Economy*, new edition, part I, chapter II, p. 87.
6. Adam Smith, *An Inquiry into the Nature and Causes of the Wealth of Nations*, (vol. 39 of *Great Books of the Western World*, R.M. Hutchins, ed., Chicago: Encyclopaedia Britannica, Inc., 1952), chapter X, part I, p. 52.
7. Lech Walesa, from a speech delivered shortly after his election, 1990.
8. Arthur Young, *Travels*, 2nd edition, vol. 1, pp. 51, 88 (1794, reprinted 1970). Journal entries from July 30 and November 7, 1787.
9. Alexander Hamilton, *The Federalist Papers*, (vol. 43 of *Great Books of the Western World*, R.M. Hutchins, ed., Chicago: Encyclopaedia Britannica, Inc., 1952), no. 71, p. 214.
10. Brock Evans, [unable to locate original source].
11. Thomas Jefferson, *The Writings of Thomas Jefferson*, edited by Albert Ellery Bergh, vol. 14: 1816 (Washington, DC: The Thomas Jefferson Memorial Association, 1907), p. 490.

CHAPTER 13

Sustainable Communities

Gus diZerega

Perhaps the best known argument for establishing a more sustainable society is presented in Al Gore's *Earth in the Balance*. The Vice President has produced a comprehensive and fascinating argument claiming that modern society is rapidly undermining the conditions necessary for its continued survival, concluding that "the environmental crisis is now so serious that I believe our civilization must be considered in some basic way dysfunctional."[1] In arriving at this conclusion, Gore consistently takes the most pessimistic projections of danger as being most likely, and he has justifiably been criticized for doing so.[2] I will not evaluate Gore's specific claims about environmental catastrophe. His concerns about ozone depletion and global warming seem to me to be overdrawn while his worry about genetic diversity and overpopulation seem more justified. But these are largely questions physical scientists are better equipped to answer than I. My analysis of *Earth in the Balance* does not depend on Gore being either mostly right or mostly wrong in his interpretation of the present environmental situation. Whether or not our position is fully as serious as Gore avers, there is ample evidence that we could and should substantially improve our society's relationship with the natural world.

HISTORICAL CASES

Based on history, concern with environmental sustainability is justified.

In remarking on his society's degradation of its environment, a noted philosopher once observed:

> What now remains of the formerly rich land is like the skeleton of a sick man, with all the fat and soft earth having wasted away and only the bare framework remaining. Formerly, many of the mountains were arable. The plains that were full of rich soil are now marshes. Hills that were once covered with forests and produced abundant pasture now produce only food for bees. Once the land was enriched by yearly rains, which were not lost, as they are now, by flowing from the bare land into the sea. The soil was deep, it absorbed and kept the water in the loamy soil, and the water that soaked into the hills fed springs and running streams everywhere. Now the abandoned shrines at spots where formerly there were springs attest that our description of the land is true.[3]

Plato was writing of his native Greece. Historian H. D. F. Kitto remarks that the degradation Plato described explained "the startling difference between the Homeric and the classical Greek diet; in the Greece of 850 BC, Homer's heroes eat an ox every two or three hundred verses, and to eat fish is a token of extreme destitution; in 5th Century BC classical times fish was a luxury, and meat almost unknown."[4]

The Greek experience was not unique, for this pattern has been repeated throughout the Mediterranean basin. From Israel and Lebanon to Tunisia and Eastern Spain, once-fertile farmlands were ruined, sometimes losing over three feet of topsoil. Displaced soil filled harbors, creating miasmic swamps. Soil scientist Daniel J. Hillel identifies the Romans as perhaps the chief European offenders, observing that "the very achievements which most impress so many observers to this day, and of which the Romans themselves were most proud (namely the grandeur and scale of their works) were the most destructive of the natural environment."[5] By the late empire the Bishop of Carthage wrote, "The world has grown old and has not retained its former vigor. It bears witness to its own decline. . . . The husbandman is failing in his field. . . . Springs which once flowed profusely now provide only a trickle."[6] Environmental destruction and not declining vigor was the problem.

The Mediterranean basin is not the only example where civilizations practiced unsustainable environmental policies that ultimately contributed to their demise. The Pueblo Indians of the American Southwest lowered the water table in their canyon homes by deforestation of valley floors. The resulting erosion contributed to the degradation of their environment and increased vulnerability to drought. Irrigation practices in both Mesopotamia and the Indus Valley destroyed much farmland by soil salinization, a disaster from which even today, many thousands of years later, the land has not recovered.

Clearly there is ample tragic precedent for concern with our society's long-term sustainable interaction with its environment. It may well be that the New World's abundant natural fertility, which so impressed European settlers, was due to its being only lightly exploited by its Native American population. The Old World, too, had once had such abundance, only no one could remember it anymore, for the only hints it had been so lay in ancient texts like Plato's *Critias*. It is beyond doubt that many earlier societies came to grief by undermining the environmental conditions necessary for their well-being. By virtue of its technological power, modern industrial society has a much more profound impact on the natural environment than did any of these earlier civilizations. It took Mesopotamia hundreds of years to ruin their soil through inappropriate irrigation. California's subsidized agribusiness is doing the same in certain regions within the span of a lifetime. Thousands of acres have already been rendered too salty even for weeds, and millions more are at risk.[7] Given the historical record of great civilizations undermining the bases for their own well-being through ecologically destructive practices, questions about modern industrial society's long-term environmental sustainability are well worth asking.

KNOWLEDGE AND INSTITUTIONS

Plato's observations should alert us to another problem. Knowledge alone will not result in wise action over a long time. Plato, Solon, Theophrastus, and presumably other Greeks, knew that Greek lands were being ruined by soil erosion.[8] Even so, their knowledge failed to reverse the degradation. Something more was called for. We need to look at the larger framework within which we apply our knowledge.

Knowledge is useful only when those possessing it have access to resources by which they can put their knowledge to work along with the incentives to do so. What is and is not a resource depends on the framework of social relationships within which we live. These frameworks, when maintained by custom and law, are termed *institutions*. The institutional framework within which we interact with our environment is of the greatest importance in determining how our knowledge will be used. It will be crucial in reinforcing or undermining environmentally sustainable practices.

When advocating solutions to environmental problems, we can take one of two basic approaches. First, we can say that we already have the knowledge needed to accomplish our goals, we need only organize people and resources in such a way as to attain those goals efficiently. Further, over time our environment will change either slowly or predictably. While our task may be complicated, little is problematic in knowing how to achieve it. The Apollo flight to the moon is a successful example of such an approach. This is an engineer's strategy. It works very well when our task is well defined and when we have the knowledge needed to achieve it.

The second approach is quite different. We may know the general outcome we want, but we are uncertain as to the best way of attaining it. If this outcome must be maintained over time, we cannot depend on the environment remaining constant. Continual adapting on the basis of new information will be necessary. Further, we may not know what will count as relevant information in the future, and those with access to this knowledge will be widely scattered and largely unknown. We must be continually prepared to search and discover new knowledge vital for accomplishing our goal. Our strategy must allow for unpredictable changes, discovery of new knowledge, and constant adjustment to changing conditions. Since we can neither predict nor control this process, we can only cultivate the conditions for it to succeed. If the first strategy was mechanical in essence, this strategy is agricultural, for to succeed we must cooperate and cultivate rather than command and control.

Gore's approach to environmental sustainability is an engineering one, but the problems he hopes to solve are more like those described as fitting our second strategy. This lack of fit between the knowledge he needs and the institutions he advocates will doom him to failure.

COMPLEXITY AND SIMPLICITY
IN PUBLIC POLICY

A primary consideration in evaluating the suitability of particular proposals for a community is whether the community is *simple* or *complex*. By "simple" I mean that the community is small enough that members can have a personal understanding of the whole. Within a simple community, relationships are largely based on personal knowledge of other members and on the conditions most immediately impinging upon them. These relationships require a great deal of attention by each person.

By identifying a community as "complex," I mean that it is too large and its overall circumstances too uncertain for its members to have any

230

but the smallest view of the whole over time. In such a community, our relationships are largely based on impersonal procedural rules and practices requiring no knowledge of others' personal qualities. Each relationship makes little demand on our time or knowledge. The concrete network of relationships essential to the community's well-being are too numerous and uncertain to be known consciously by the participants.

There is a paradoxical character in my terming these communities simple and complex. Seen from a participant's perspective, the concrete details of simple communities will be very detailed and complicated, for each relationship makes relatively great demands on all involved. By contrast, the concrete details of relationships within complex communities will be relatively straightforward and uninvolved. This paradox is fundamental to the distinction between simple and complex communities, for the less I need to know to enter into successful relationships, the more such relationships I can participate in. Simplicity in relationships leads to complexity in pattern.

Complex communities are necessarily based on impersonal and procedural rules because the communities to which they give rise are too complicated for any member to grasp. The order generated within such a community is a complex order, its specific details being unforseen and unforeseeable. Such a community's specific characteristics will be unpredictable even if its most general features are easily identifiable. Both modern society and natural ecosystems are complex communities.

THE CHARACTER OF SELF-ORGANIZATION

Complex communities are self-organizing. This is true of markets, science, and democracy. The coherence they exhibit is not the result of conscious planning by their members but rather arises from each person pursuing his or her goals within a framework of rules that channel individual actions so that a coherent order results. We know that order exists, even though its details are continually adapting, because people have a reasonably predictable environment within which to pursue their goals. So long as its members follow appropriate rules, a self-organizing order will arise regardless of the different projects each pursues.[9]

Usually when we say "organization" we refer to an *instrumental* organization, such as the Wyoming Farm Bureau Insurance Company, General Motors, the U. S. Navy, or the corner bakery. An instrumental organization exists to do something specific. Its overall purpose or plan determines the place of each member. When too big to be a committee, an instrumental organization is a hierarchy. From the organization's perspective, members are resources and derive their utility from their contribution to its goals. Because different people serve different roles within the organization, different rules will apply to different members. An instrumental organization exemplifies an engineering strategy to getting something accomplished.

Self-organizing orders do not pursue particular goals. Because they allow members to follow their own personally chosen ends, the same rules can apply equally to all. They are not hierarchies. Formal equality among members exists. For example, in the market all people are subject to the same rules of contract. In a democracy, freedom of speech and equality of the vote apply to all. In science, all are subject to the standards of the scientific community.

Rules generating self-organizing orders must promote cooperation. Because self-organization relies on each person benefiting from knowledge and actions of which they are unaware, the cooperation needed must be very complex. Consequently, all self-organizing orders harmonize self-interest with following basic rules common to all. If this were not so, our uncertainty about others' intentions would limit the variety of relationships into which we would enter. Cooperation would have to be based mostly on personal knowledge of one another's character, and society could scarcely become more complex than that of a small village.

As is the case in an instrumental organization, in self-organizing orders a perfect correspondence does not exist between successfully achieving a personal goal and being successful in terms of the criteria defined by the rules of a particular self-organizing system. Often, people go into business for themselves to gain independence from bosses and control over their time rather than to maximize monetary income. But the success of a project will also be success in terms of the values characteristic of a particular self-organizing system. Most successful business people acquire more money than those who are not successful. I will call success in terms of the *system's* values "systemic success." In a well-functioning self-organizing order, systemically successful outcomes will be reinforced and emulated whereas systemically unsuccessful ones will tend to be abandoned or remain idiosyncratic, no matter how personally desirable they may be.[10]

To maximize the opportunities for people to achieve both personal and systemic success, a self-organizing system's principles and rules must promote easy recognition of success or failure. In this way, many members unknown to one another and with no view of the whole can nevertheless act to promote both stability and adaptability. This stability and adaptability is an unintended consequence of people's behavior.

232

Oftentimes a self-organizing system, such as the market or an eco-system, is described as ideally operating at "equilibrium," or at a "climax" state. Strictly speaking, this claim is false. While islands of temporary stability may occur, a self-organizing order is in constant flux and adjustment. Each constituent part continually adjusts to its surrounding circumstances. For many decades, markets for both horseshoes and slide rules appeared stable. Today, one is a shadow of itself, the other nonexistent. From the standpoint of a human life, an old growth forest appears eternal, but we know that it is not. It was not that long ago that old growth forest covered the walls of the Grand Canyon while those of the Pacific Northwest were under thousands of feet of ice. Even a self-organizing system that appears unchanging in the whole can only maintain itself through a continual process of adjustment and adaptation by its members.

Grasping the self-organizing character of both a free society and an ecosystem provides us with several insights to bring these two communities into sustainable harmony. First, both are highly adaptive, and this flexibility is essential to their survival. Second, their power to adapt is decentralized to the basic constituent units of each community, be they individuals-as-consumers in the market or species-through-individuals in the natural community. Third, the rules and principles followed in the course of adapting to new circumstances must promote cooperation within the community. Cooperation is as important in nature as is competition, and the same is true in human society.[11] Social self-organizing orders are in these respects similar to ecosystems. Any attempt to harmonize modern society with nature must pay particular attention to this similarity. Unfortunately, despite his praise of the market and concern with the natural world, Gore's proposals do not respect these similarities.

THE GLOBAL MARSHALL PLAN

The Vice President advocates what he calls a "Global Marshall Plan" to rapidly move our economic, social, and political practices in a more sustainable direction. He argues for specific goals that would be incumbent upon all and that would be ranked in some order of priority and enforced by political authority. To accomplish this task requires "establishment of a single shared goal as the central organizing principle behind every institution in society."[12] Such a comprehensive approach is called for, he believes, because "Merely addressing one dimension or another or trying to implement solutions in only one region of the world or another

233

will, in the end, guarantee frustration, failure, and a weakening of the resolve needed to address the whole of the problem."[13]

In Gore's view, such a worldwide project is not authoritarian. He argues that free societies have pursued analogous goals in the past. During both world wars, for example, democratic societies united behind the common goal of defeating the enemy. In addition, Gore believes that the fall of communism came about because of "a conscious and shared decision by men and women in the nations of the 'free world' to make the defeat of communism the central organizing principle of not only their government's policies but of society itself."[14] Indeed, the original Marshall Plan reflected this commitment. He believes that the same can be done with regard to environmental sustainability.

Gore's strategic program emphasizes six basic goals. First, stabilize world population. Second, rapidly create and develop environmentally appropriate technologies. Third, comprehensively change the economic "rules of the road" used to measure our impact on the environment. Fourth, organize international cooperation to attain these ends. Fifth, comprehensively educate the world's citizens about the environment. Sixth, particularly in the developing world, establish institutions promoting "the social and political conditions most conducive to the emergence of sustainable societies."[15] His book discusses each goal in some depth.

Perhaps as befits a person who has been in politics all his life, at first glance Gore's own approach to developing sustainable policies appears purely technocratic and hierarchical. Looking more carefully, this judgment is only partially true—but to the degree that it is true, it undermines his program. To be sure, in many ways Gore appreciates both the strengths of markets and the weaknesses of bureaucracy and political planning.[16] Yet, as we shall see, he does not fully grasp what is most distinctive about both the market process and democratic societies. As a consequence, without really wanting to, and despite his praise of a Jeffersonian solution to the sustainability problem, at crucial stages Gore strengthens the very bureaucratic processes he distrusts.

We can begin to understand Gore's problem by carefully considering the following passage:

> Both democracy, as a political system, and capitalism, as an economic system, work on the same principle and have the same inherent "design advantage" because of the way they process information. Under capitalism, for example, people free to buy and sell products or services according to their individual calculations of the costs and benefits of each choice

are actually processing a relatively limited amount of information—but doing it quickly. And when millions process information simultaneously, the result is incredibly efficient decisions about supply and demand for the economy as a whole.

Similarly, representative democracy operates on the still revolutionary assumption that the best way for a nation to make political decisions about its future is to empower all of its citizens to process political information relevant to their lives and express their conclusions in free speech designed to persuade others and in votes—which are then combined with the votes of millions of others to produce aggregate guidance for the system as a whole. Other governments with centralized decision-making have failed in large part because they literally do not "know" what they or their citizens are doing.[17]

In the context of this passage, Gore is comparing markets and democracies with certain kinds of computers that handle massive amounts of data by computing them in a dispersed and decentralized way rather than through a central processing unit. While this passage contains some remarkable insights, Gore's comparison of markets and democracies with certain kinds of computers is seriously misleading.

First of all, in Gore's computer model the relevant data are given in advance. The questions of who collects the data and what counts as data are taken for granted. The task he describes is how to most efficiently interpret and use data. In the market and in democracy, the problem is somewhat different. There is no way to determine in advance what the relevant data may be. Data must be *discovered* as well as evaluated.

Second, most visibly in the market but also in democracies, it is misleading to say that data are simultaneously processed. It is more accurate to say that data are continually processed. We are speaking of an ongoing process of coordinated action within a context of continually shifting information rather than simply using decentralized means for solving a single enormously complex problem. In a democracy, for example, this process does not end with an election. No one, certainly not Al Gore, believes that after an election people simply sit back and let the leadership get on with their programs. The political process is continual, and potentially includes the input of all social institutions, not just those traditionally thought of as political.[18]

The coordination process in both markets and democracies (and in science as well) is always approaching but never arriving at a continually moving target of perfectly coordinated knowledge and plans. In part, this

235

is because the very act of approaching the target changes the data relevant to attaining it. This is why in retrospect we can always imagine a better way of doing something than had been the case in the market, democratic politics, or science. Whatever is done is done with less information than is available after the fact. It is also why this 20/20 hindsight is often utterly irrelevant to improving the effectiveness of our future action. Discovering what to do is qualitatively different from determining the most efficient way to achieve something that is not problematic. When participating in a self-organizing system, we never have access to all the data relevant to what we are striving to achieve because the simultaneous actions of others are constantly changing the environment within which we act.

Gore's failure to distinguish adequately between his computer analogy and his unusually perceptive comparison of democracy and the market lead to a consequent failure to distinguish the important differences between decentralized instrumental organizations and truly self-organizing processes. In a genuine self-organizing system, not only is information too vast to be comprehended at a single center, as I have emphasized, but it is also often unknown, and the specific uses to which it can be put are equally unknown. Such a system is truly a discovery process from beginning to end.[19] Thus, rather than approaching a particular goal ever more accurately over time, a self-organizing system is always at every point in time in the same kind of adaptation to ever changing conditions.

Large complex organizations are quite different. Increasingly, their leadership is discovering that self-organizing processes need to be integrated within the organization to preserve its adaptability in a changing environment. But unlike a pure self-organizing system, top directors are responsible for charting their organization's course, balancing creative innovation with the needs for managerial efficiency.[20] Unlike self-organizing systems, such organizations, no matter how innovative and adaptable, are directed toward specific ends and goals.

Complex instrumental organizations depend on being embedded within self-organizing systems. Because self-organizing systems economize on the information we need to act effectively within them, we are able to engage in far more intricate and complicated interactions than would be the case in the absence of such systems. Yet, within the organization, self-organizing processes must be kept subordinate to the director's goals even if the organization itself is subordinate to the larger self-organizing system.

A self-organizing order enables countless individual purposes to be pursued based on each participant's knowledge and desires and, in this
236

sense, has no hierarchy. All participants are equally subject to the procedural rules that, when followed, generate that order. Thus, in a self-organizing order, participants are identified by the same generic name: consumer, citizen, and scientist. If the rules are well developed, the overall tendency of multiple individual initiatives will be to maximize the likelihood that in pursuing our own plans we will help others unknown to us in pursuing theirs.

A complex organization utilizing self-organizing processes maximizes the opportunities for members to use their knowledge and creativity to further the organization's goals as determined by its directors. From the leadership's perspective, members are resources deriving their value from their capacity to help the organization achieve its goals. In any complex organization members will be formally unequal, for the rules that apply to each will be determined by the place he or she holds within the organization. These sets of relationships must be kept continually in mind to understand either complex organizations or self-organizing systems.

Unfortunately, Gore conflates these two different forms of association. For example, he writes: "Government, as a tool used to achieve social and political organization, may be considered a technology, and in that sense *self*-government is one of the most sophisticated technologies ever created. ... In a way, the Constitution is a blueprint for an ingenious machine that uses pressure valves and compensating forces to achieve a dynamic balance between the needs of the individual and the needs of the community."[21] Well, yes and no, and the "no" is as important as the "yes."

The Constitution's checks and balances do not exist primarily to balance individual and community interests because the Framers did not see that tension as particularly central to their enterprise. Rather, the Constitution was intended to balance different levels and branches of *government* so that those in power would not be able to substitute their interests, or the interests of a portion of the community, for the interests of all. Citizens were not the problem that needed balancing, government was. Particularly when the amending process is included, the Constitution provided a means by which citizens could peacefully pursue whatever policies they believed to be in the best interests of the community. It provides a way of deciding, but is largely mute as to what should be decided.

Madison's famous Federalist 10 argued that the size and complexity of the new nation would serve to prevent majority tyranny. But his argument was that tyrannical private interests would thereby be stymied—not the needs of the community. He did not see the community as being opposed to the individual. Rather, what was good for one was good

237

for the other. Both were threatened by corrupt private interests, including that of a temporary majority.

As usually used, the word *technology* implies the capacity to do specifiable and bounded things. In its usual sense, a technology is akin to an instrumental organization. Democratic government, by contrast, provides a set of procedures by which citizens may consider doing anything they have a mind to. Freedom of speech, press, and assembly are examples of such procedures. So long as democratic procedures are maintained (admittedly a complex issue), what comes out of such a government is democratic decision making, be it wise or foolish.

Only when citizens believe that their survival is at stake do they act as if they are part of an instrumental organization. Only under circumstances such as wartime and natural disaster is there likely to be anything approaching consensus over government priorities. Interestingly, it is also during such times that democracies act most undemocratically, for they have a sad tendency to abrogate democratic procedures under such circumstances. Commitment to a specific program believed essential for community survival leads all too easily to intolerance toward unconvinced or distrusted minorities who are easily perceived as disloyal. *Citizens have become resources*, valuable only insofar as they can further the common effort. Gore acknowledges this tendency, but seems unaware of its worrisome significance for his argument.[22]

So, we see that there is a fundamental difference between democracies' normal conditions of being self-organizing systems and their character under extreme circumstances, when they transform temporarily into instrumental organizations. Gore's confusion is to conflate these two states of democratic politics. He has plenty of company, but this confusion carries serious implications.

We can now begin evaluating his specific proposals. Gore's program raises two basic questions. First, is the environmental crisis such that we can reasonably seek to turn our polity into an instrumental organization devoted to maximizing sustainability? Second, if not, should we nevertheless rely on strategies favoring instrumental organization over self-organization in moving the world's societies towards a more sustainable relationship with the natural world? It is to the first of these questions that I now shall turn.

A MORAL EQUIVALENT TO WAR?

I believe Gore is mistaken in arguing that the present environmental crisis is such that a free society could unite around a quest for sustainability.

Even if we grant him his most pessimistic projections, in crucial respects this crisis is simply not analogous to being at war and is not conducive to effectively uniting society around a common purpose.

Issues in wartime are very simple and clear cut: Defeat the enemy. Standards for success and failure are also relatively unambiguous. Battles are fought and territory is gained or lost. Values such as efficiency, fairness, and even democratic liberties are ranked in terms of their ability to further the war effort. After Pearl Harbor, the United States approximated such a society because the attack had convinced Americans they needed to fight for their survival. Sinking the Arizona accomplished what no warnings by FDR and Winston Churchill had managed to do, uniting the American people against the Axis powers.

Gore argues that the Cold War was an analogous event. This is only partially true. The USSR was indeed a credible threat to the Western democracies. Even so, the political consensus opposing communism and Russian expansion was more tenuous than that prevailing against wartime enemies. Of course, no reasonable person favored communism, but reasonable people had many different ideas about how best to defeat or contain it. We should also remember that our 40-year policy of containment was practicable in part because much of the time it impinged relatively mildly upon the lives of most Americans.

The Vietnam debacle demonstrated what happens when a prolonged war affecting many people is conducted without solid popular support. Even though virtually no one favored the victory of communism, prolonged dissension over our involvement in Vietnam left deep wounds that even today are far from healed. Gore seriously overstates the matter when he emphasizes the enormous unity of purpose that supposedly prevailed during the Cold War. *There was unity in the abstract, but much less when specific issues and practices were addressed.* This distinction between agreement over abstract issues and specific measures is vital when evaluating Gore's overall strategic vision.

Three principles appear relevant in evaluating the capacity of a free society to pursue a common goal. First, the more complex and ill-defined the goal, the harder it becomes to build a political consensus around specific programs intended to achieve it. We can all agree that justice, truth, and sustainability are good things, while strongly disagreeing about what constitutes justice, what is the truth, and what is needed to ensure sustainability. Even a brief overview of the Vice President's proposal shows that the standards for success are enormously complex, far more so than was the case with the Marshall Plan.

Second, the greater the sacrifice called for, the more obvious the threat provoking it must become for the sacrifice to be acceptable. We are still far from a scientific or social consensus with regard to the immediacy of the threat of global warming. Without such a consensus, most people are unlikely to be convinced to take significant cuts in their material standard of living in the absence of an environmental Pearl Harbor.

Third, the longer the period of political mobilization, the harder it will be to maintain unity and the greater the likelihood that political and economic interests will capture the process, diverting it to furthering their own interests. Gore's program is completely open ended. There is no foreseeable time at which the problem of sustainability will finally be solved. It will exist as long as human societies have the capacity to undermine their environments.

Gore seriously underestimates the distorting impact organizational interests will have on his proposal. No social institution is simply a tool. The individuals who comprise institutions have interests of their own that need not be in harmony with those the organization was established to further. They also have a distressing capacity to interpret the organization's interests in terms of their personal interests. It is worth pondering long and hard that the World Wildlife Federation ignored the advice of its scientists and supported outlawing the ivory trade because its leadership thought such a "principled" stance would lead to bigger financial contributions, even as it also further endangered the African elephants they supposedly sought these funds to save! The history of the U.S. Forest Service and the Bureau of Land Management (BLM) suggest that government agencies are no better.

Gore himself seems aware that his proposal is too far reaching to be politically feasible at the present time.[23] He therefore urges that we take strong action now and prepare for a future when even stronger steps will be possible. But what kind of action should we take?

SELF-ORGANIZATION OR INSTRUMENTAL ORGANIZATION?

Many of Gore's specific proposals strike me as eminently reasonable. However, the institutional framework in which he embeds them is worrisome. Gore's frequent reference to the Apollo program and the defense industry as examples to emulate suggests that he increasingly sees our long-term sustainability *primarily* as an engineering problem. Gore seems confident that expert planners and technicians can lead the rest of us to an indefinitely sustainable future. But when the specific applications of knowledge are uncertain and local conditions vary enormously, technical skills, while certainly valuable, must be subordinated to self-organizing processes if they are to be utilized effectively. Much of the most environmentally relevant information is not available to experts and often must be discovered and rediscovered under constantly changing circumstances. Very often, overarching scientific visions fit poorly when applied in the field where local and unexpected variations continually trip up the most carefully considered plans.[24]

In addition, in the American system, any government program considered important will very quickly develop an intricate network of special interests bent on diverting it toward maximizing their own well-being. This has been as true in the space program and the defense industry he praises as it has been in the Forest Service, BLM, and Park Service. For example, NASA's space shuttle and later space station proposal were opposed by many scientists as diverting money best used for less spectacular but more scientifically productive ventures. Indeed, government programs appear to have a built-in bias toward bigness that argues against much sensitivity for the environmental values that Gore, and I, hold dear. We also have a long history of second-rate defense programs, from the TFX to the Bradley transport, that gained such momentum that enormous sums of money were wasted in their construction. Yet, as Gore would grant, designing environmentally sustainable practices will place an absolute premium on efficiency, adaptability, and close fit to local circumstances. These simply are not qualities that characterize government programs, particularly over time. We might legitimately wonder whether NASA could put a man on the moon again if it kept its present command structure but had to develop its technology from scratch.

An article in the *Oakland Tribune* perfectly illustrates some of the problems of attempting bureaucratic oversight of technical innovation. Two advanced tugboats were recently acquired to more safely move supertankers about San Francisco Bay. The law requires oil companies to use the best available technology in such cases, but the tugs are prevented by law from working on oil tankers because tugboat certification procedures have not caught up with changes in tugboat technology. To be certified, a tugboat must demonstrate that it can pull from both bow and stern with enough force to rescue a disabled oil tanker. Reporter Tracie Reynolds notes that "tractor tugs don't pull from the stern. Their eggbeater-style engines can push the tug in any direction, *making them impossible to test under the state's current regulations.*"[25] One can only shudder at the inhibitions extensive bureaucratic involvement in creating environmentally sustainable technological innovation would create.

That Gore ignores this problem seems all but inexplicable. I can only guess that he is very unclear on how self-organizing processes can address the issues that concern him and hopes that government, when adopting his ideas, will emulate its successes, such as Apollo, rather than its rather more common less-than-successes, like public education. Unfortunately, as we shall see, maintaining sustainable practices over time is more like providing quality education than it is like a one-shot Apollo program.

These considerations caution against seeking a primarily hierarchical strategy for solving environmental problems. At the same time, they point toward relying on self-organizing strategies to address these issues. For example, the market successfully solves problems that are open ended, complex, and require that success be unequally apportioned, which means that the less successful will often feel real misfortune. While Gore is quite correct in identifying some of the market's environmental blind spots, these shortcomings should not blind us to the very real strengths markets and other self-organizing processes have in responding to problems very similar in kind to those that would have to be addressed by a successful strategy for maximizing sustainability.

For example, growing and distributing food is enormously complex, requiring continual adaptation to changing harvests and tastes. Further, the task is never ending. Finally, there is sufficient uncertainty in farming that success is never guaranteed for anyone. For the most part, the market handles this vital process so effectively that we simply take it for granted.

To be sure, government is also involved in agriculture. But its measures generally lead to higher prices, overproduction, and environmentally unsustainable practices. No one argues that were this intervention to cease, Americans would cease having as great a variety of food available as they do today. The impact of government intervention in agriculture is usually subsidies for wealthy farmers and ranchers and increased environmental degradation. Gore himself admits that this is often true.[26]

Producing and distributing the nation's food is a type of task more akin to developing sustainable practices than is the Marshall Plan, the Apollo project, or the defense industry. Further, sustainable practices will have to be strengthened within agriculture if Gore's overall vision of a sustainable society is to have any chance of success. Similarly, public education requires maintaining an ongoing process with substantial sensitivity to local circumstances and great complexity in determining success and failure. I doubt whether the Vice President would point to American public education as evidence that government can adequately perform such a task.[27] In short, Gore's technocratic bias is unlikely to lead to as great an increase in sustainable practices as will reliance on utilizing self-organizing processes to harmonize human communities with the natural community.

A SELF-ORGANIZING
PERSPECTIVE ON SUSTAINABILITY

The market is a primary means for coordinating private plans within society. It must also be the primary means for coordinating environmentally sensitive actions. This does not mean that there is no role for government, far from it, but this role must be in keeping with primary reliance on self-organizing processes. As Gore emphasizes, the price system serves to signal to people what exchanges are advantageous and what exchanges are not. He correctly notes that "our economic system is partially blind. It 'sees' some things and not others."[28] Our problem is how to improve the market's vision.

The price system arises out of the exchange of property rights. When market economists emphasize the role of property rights in enabling a market system to work effectively, they are far more than half right. Having a property right is having the right to enter into a certain type of relationship with another. Having rights over which I exercise the power of contract and exchange generates a market order. The more contractual rights there are, the richer and more complex the resulting market economy.

When I say that I own "private property," what I in fact own are a *bundle* of property rights defining the types of relationships I may enter into with others with regard to this thing. Often I can sell some rights from this bundle while retaining others, as when a landlord lets out an apartment or a writer sells a book but retains the copyright. In Norway, landowners do not have the right to prevent people from passing over their land so long as these people do no harm. The roots of this limitation on the Norwegian bundle of property rights lie in her early history when freedom of access was vital in a country where so much land was impassable. Norwegians own "land" but their bundle of ownership rights is different from those prevailing in the U.S. Similarly, in Germany owners of old buildings will often be able to remodel their interiors extensively but are prevented from greatly altering the building's exterior. Yet Germany is no less a viable market society than is the U.S. These examples demonstrate that what we own in a market order is not property but *property rights*.

Just because something can be made a contractual property right
243

does not means that it should be. We once had property rights in other human beings, and an efficient market developed in slaves. The market *order* as a whole was not weakened when slavery was abolished, even if substantial adjustments in economic activity were subsequently required in the American South.

Today there is a slowly growing realization that to own property does not necessarily mean that one can rightfully exercise despotic power over what is owned. For example, I may not legally torture my pets. Further, if I mistreat them, they can be removed from my possession. I lose all my property rights over the animal because of doing what I had no right to do. This limitation on my bundle of property rights does not lessen the value of having pets. For the overwhelming majority of pet owners, even having the right to mistreat an animal would not lead to its being exercised. We are gradually learning that despotic power is not appropriate anywhere in our lives.

We live in communities that may make certain legitimate demands on us. They can legitimately limit our actions without necessarily themselves becoming despotic. This is particularly true when the actions thereby limited would otherwise destroy the basic relationships that perpetuate the community. Consequently, at least certain kinds of community demands are in keeping with the realm of private liberty.

Legitimate community demands have to do with preserving the well-being of the community itself. In politics this is termed the *public good*. Most of us willingly concede the legitimacy of such demands by our family, the neighborhood, and the larger society. Our property rights can be legitimately limited by our responsibility to support our children, abide by neighborhood noise ordinances, and support the courts and police, including serving on jury duty. We need to recognize a similar legitimacy attaching to requirements for preserving the natural community.

The most critical step for bringing modern society into sustainable relations with its environment is bringing its system of property rights into harmony with what is needed to preserve the natural community. There are at least three principles that, when followed, allow the natural community to sustain itself. They are: (1) that wastes for one member of the community are goods for another; (2) that renewable resources are used in ways that preserve their indefinite availability; and (3) that a diverse flora and fauna be preserved so that no right exists to cause extinction of a species that is not fundamentally harmful to human life.[29] Limiting property rights to those activities that can be performed in harmony with these three principles no more cripples the market process than does the limitation against slavery. In addition, these limitations do

244

not undermine the vitality and well-being of the other basic communities to which we belong: our families, neighborhoods, and the larger society.

Obviously enforcement of such relationships will call for changes in many of the ways economic activity takes place today. Wise public policy will seek to minimize the disruption in people's lives occasioned by such a transition. Outright and sudden prohibition of widely practiced activities would be extraordinarily disruptive and over the long run less likely to harmonize than exacerbate relations between the different communities. Customary changes in what constitutes appropriate behavior will be most important.

An ironic effect of greater prosperity and its resulting urbanization is that more and more Americans are becoming concerned about environmental well-being. This unexpected development is due, at least in part, to separating people's narrow self-interest from overly exploitative relationships with the natural community. Anthropologist Kris Hardin wrote that in the Sierra Leone community she studied people were careful with their environment more from necessity than from a sense of stewardship. "It was all too clear that as more efficient alternatives became available, the overwhelming attitude was one of exploitation."[30]

Rather like a judge, prosperous urbanites are not directly interested parties. They can take a more judicious view of the desirability of preserving the natural community from short-term interests. But as Ms Hardin also observes, the complexity of doing this through conscious sacrifice in daily decisions is overwhelming. We lack the information and the institutions to follow through effectively on our intentions. This is why self-organizing institutions are so necessary to provide an appropriate institutional framework within which to live our lives. Clear and reformed property rights and the signals of the price system help us make decisions that would otherwise overwhelm us with their complexity.

Traditional politics is a fairly crude way for people to act on their values, and it carries very real costs of its own. Where possible, alternatives to centralized politics need to be explored. Most important, there should be an expansion and reform of the realm of individual and small community property rights. Even where a resource is government-controlled, this principle can be implemented. For example, when grazing land allotments are bid for or a portion of a national forest is to be logged, environmental groups should be free to bid for the allotment along with extractive interests, and if they win have their wishes honored.

When an active political approach is necessary, it should be implemented in a way that harmonizes with self-organizing processes rather than trying to second guess them. Prescriptive regulation should be

245

avoided. Far better would be instituting the equivalent of a slowly increasing "sin-tax" on such activities to gradually increase the economic incentives to adopt more sustainable policies. Pollution permits that could be traded on the market would be another option.

The point, however, is to provide a predictable environment within which people can adapt their practices, and (equally important) to do nothing to predetermine *how* they will adapt. If mainstream environmentalism is guilty of one oversight, it is in underestimating the power of human creativity. Gore is in his own way similarly guilty, for it seems as if he has largely decided the technologies that will be needed to attain sustainability. In fact, we do not really know. We cannot foresee the creative discoveries that have not yet been made.

From this perspective, Gore's list of technologies he wants promoted is far too long. We should not promote specific technologies. Such a strategy will often retard, and even penalize, technological adaptations rather than promote them.[31] Instead, we should slowly *and predictably* increase the costs of using inappropriate technologies and acting in ways contrary to sustainability so as to encourage people to develop their own adaptations in more appropriate ways.

Sometimes more aggressive political action may be necessary, perhaps to prevent a looming extinction, but prescriptive intervention should be done with the greatest caution. Our bias should be against it. Too great a reliance on governmental direction will both undermine the self-organizing framework of an effective sustainable strategy and trigger the multiple pathologies that arise from subjecting complex phenomena to prolonged political direction.

More generally, a self-organizing strategy will *cultivate* the conditions for certain kinds of changes but will determine nothing about the specific forms that will arise on account of those circumstances. Fittingly, our guiding metaphor is rooted in agriculture, not technology. A self-organizing approach seeks to cultivate desirable change rather than plan, manage, or control change in the desired direction. It is respectful of the extraordinary and intricate diversity of the world within which we live and thus seeks to harmonize rather than dominate in its relationships. This principle of self-organization is how the scientific community, the market, liberal democracy, and nature itself works. Its wise use will maximize the likelihood that modern society will increase its compatibility with natural processes, ensuring sustainability for the seventh generation and seven times that.

Notes

I wish to thank John Baden for his helpful comments on earlier drafts of this paper.

1. Al Gore, *Earth in the Balance*, (Boston: Houghton Mifflin, 1992), p. 230.
2. A critique of views such as Gore's over ozone depletion and global warming can be found in Dixy Lee Ray and Lou Guzzo, *Trashing the Planet*, (New York: Harper, 1992). I know of no critiques of Gore's concern with the genetic impoverishment of important food plants.
3. Plato, *Critias*.
4. H. D. F. Kitto, *The Greeks* (Harmondsworth, England: Penguin, 1951) p. 34.
5. Daniel J. Hillel, *Out of the Earth: Civilization and the Life of the Soil* (New York: Free Press, 1991) p. 107.
6. Quoted by Hillel, Ibid., pp. 106–107.
7. See Marc Reisner, *Cadillac Desert: The American West and Its Disappearing Water*, (Penguin: New York, 1986), pp. 452–494.
8. Hillel, op. cit., p. 105.
9. There is a growing literature in many fields where the concept of self-organization, or spontaneous order, has proven vital. Perhaps the seminal work is Michael Polanyi, *The Logic of Liberty* (Chicago: University of Chicago Press, 1951). See also F. A. Hayek's three volume *Law, Legislation and Liberty*, (Chicago: University of Chicago Press, vol. I, 1973, II, 1976, and III, 1979); Ludwig M. Lachmann, *The Market as an Economic Process*, (Oxford: Basil Blackwell, 1986); John Ziman, *Public Knowledge*, (London: Cambridge University Press, 1968); and Gus diZerega, "Elites and Democratic Theory: Insights from the Self-organizing Model," *The Review of Politics*, vol. 52, no. 2, 1991, pp. 340–372.
10. Gus diZerega, "Social Ecology, Deep Ecology, and Liberalism," *Critical Review*, vol. 6, nos. 2–3, 1992.
11. On cooperation in nature, see Lynn Margulis, *Symbiosis in Cell Evolution* (W.H. Freeman, 1981). See also Margulis and Rene Fester, eds., *Symbiosis as a Source of Evolutionary Innovation: Speciation and Morphogenesis*, (Cambridge, MA: MIT Press, 1991). On the deeper similarities between markets and ecosystems see Donald Worster, *Nature's Economy*, (Cambridge: Cambridge University Press, 1977) and Michael Rothschild, *Bionomics: Economy as Ecosystem* (New York: Henry Holt, 1990). Interestingly, while Rothschild is well aware of the political implications of these similarities, Worster appears largely impervious to them.
12. Gore, op. cit., p. 270.
13. Ibid., p. 295.
14. Ibid., p. 271.
15. Ibid., pp. 305–307.
16. Ibid., on the market see pp. 183–184, 194–195, 277, 298; on government see pp. 247–248.
17. Ibid., p. 359.

18. Gus diZerega, "Democracy as a Spontaneous Order," *Critical Review*, vol. 3, no. 2, Spring, 1988.

19. F. A. Hayek, "Competition as a Discovery Procedure," *New Studies in Philosophy, Politics, Economics, and the History of Ideas*, (Chicago: University of Chicago Press, 1978).

20. See for example, David F. Hardwick and James E. Dimmick, "Administering the Clinical Laboratory: How Directors Relate to Their Laboratory Innovators and Managers," *Modern Pathology*, June, 1993; Richard N. Langlois, "The Capabilities of Industrial Capitalism," *Critical Review*, vol. 5, no. 4, Fall, 1991.

21. Gore, op. cit., p. 171.

22. Ibid., p. 272.

23. Ibid., p. 305.

24. Karl Hess, *Visions Upon the Land: Man and Nature on the Western Range*, (Washington, DC: Island Press, 1992) and Alston Chase, *Playing God in Yellowstone*, (New York: Harcourt, Brace, Jovanovich, 1987).

25. Tracie Reynolds, "Red Tape Ties High-Tech Tugs to Dock in the Bay," *The Oakland Tribune*, August 20, 1993, p. 1.

26. Gore, op. cit., pp. 339–341.

27. The best analysis of the institutional causes for progressive failure in public education is in John E. Chubb and Terry M. Moe, *Politics, Markets, and America's Schools*, (Washington, DC: Brookings Institution, 1990), pp. 26–68.

28. Ibid., pp. 182–183.

29. While extinction occurs in nature, the evidence suggests that it is not common. For periods of less than 100,000 years, extinction is simply not normally a threat. In paleontologist David Raup's words, "Species are at low risk of extinction most of the time." In Raup, *Extinction: Bad Genes or Bad Luck?*, (New York: W. W. Norton, 1991), p. 84.

30. Kris Hardin, "Symbols," in Michael Katakis, ed., *Sacred Trusts: Essays on Stewardship and Responsibility*, (San Francisco: Mercury House, 1993), p. 24.

31. Richard Stroup and John Baden, "Property Rights and Natural Resource Management," *Literature of Liberty*, vol. 2, no. 4, Sept.–Dec., 1979, pp. 5–44.

CHAPTER 14

Clear Thinking About the Earth

Lynn Scarlett

"Rashomon," a celebrated Japanese film, presents four witnesses observing a single crime. Each witness perceives the situation so differently that the audience experiences what appear to be four distinct events.

Current discourse on the environment raises a "Rashomon-like" specter of competing perceptions. The world presents us with a single reality; but expositors on the environment view that world and its workings through multiple and radically different lenses. Among this medley of lenses, two perspectives predominate.

On the one hand, we have what I will call the pessimists. They see a world in trouble. They focus on the moment, see despoliation, and predict doom. They believe we can evade doom, but only through sweeping changes wrought through single-minded pursuit of an environmental imperative.

On the other hand are the optimists. They view today as one moment on a long and largely progressive landscape of human achievement, a landscape in which human action propels us forward in a never-ending problem-solving quest.

Vice President Albert Gore fits squarely among the pessimistic visionaries. In *Earth in the Balance*,[1] he tells us that "our children will inherent a wasteland" unless we "dramatically change our civilization and our way of thinking about the relationship between humankind and the earth" (p. 163). This is Gore's overarching vision. What are the elements of that vision?

GORE'S WORLD VIEW

Gore's vision is of a (relatively) static world. He purports to look far into the future, but his view of the present is static—like a snapshot of a moment. He sees current patterns of resource use, projects those patterns into the future, and labels them "unsustainable."

This snapshot view also gives rise to a basic pessimism about technology and human action. Understandably, in a snapshot world view, technologies look like the problem rather an evolving sequence of solutions. In Gore's snapshot focus, past ills are forgotten, leaving us to dwell only on present woes, which, in turn, are easy to blame on present technologies. His snapshot view compels us to forget that those technologies were the answer to some earlier challenge. Indeed, for Gore, change and adaptation are themselves suspect: "Our willingness to adapt," he says, "is an important part of the underlying problem. . . . Believing that we can adapt to just about anything is ultimately a kind of laziness" (p. 240).

Gore's freeze-frame world view has three chief consequences. First, it underplays the omnipresence of trade-offs in human action. Gore tends to focus on a single problem (or set of problems) at a single point in time, which then prompts him to propose "solutions" to these problems outside of any historical context. This results in ignoring past problems whose redress may have given rise to present problems. It leads him to ignore (or at least greatly underplay) how his proposed "solutions" themselves may mitigate one problem, while giving rise to others. It results in what American Enterprise Institute economist Robert Hahn calls Gore's "kitchen sink" approach to problem-solving—throw every tool at the problem with no thought given to costs and adverse (including environmental) impacts.[2]

Second, with technologies identified as the culprit for current problems, Gore is easily led to the conclusion that the only remedies to the problems before us lie in fundamental changes in our thinking. Our effort, he writes in Earth in the Balance, "has to involve more than a search for mechanical solutions" (p. 161). He then adds that we need to "find a way to dramatically change our civilization and our way of thinking about the relationship between humankind and the earth" (p. 163).

Third, since technology springs primarily out of the world of industry, this view makes industry a leading offender standing in the way of a cleaner environment.

Resilience and adaptation are natural components of a dynamic world—a world in which human action is a constant process of confronting problems, adjusting, and readjusting. By contrast, in a freeze-frame world, problems take on a more cataclysmic cast. Problems are "out there," the product of accumulated human actions. And "solutions" take the form of some imagined "new" picture of the world, some set of endpoints like "clean air," "clean water," protected wetlands and forests, some future Eden.

With a set of endpoints in mind, reaching that future becomes a process of prescribing new "managed" technologies, new products, new lifestyles, new mandates for action. A freeze-frame view thus often gives rise to an emphasis on prescriptive regulations and pre-defined solutions.

This freeze-frame view also nourishes a sense that "we are running out of resources." At any point in time, the mix of resources that are "out there" appears to be finite and fixed. If we are running out of resources, then recycling and reduced consumption become compelling requirements for sustainable development.

This is a tough theme to refute. Intuitively, it would *seem* self-evident that most of the earth's resources are finite. There are, of course, exceptions. These include resources that reproduce—like plant matter. Or those that are recreated in never-ending cycles—like water. And they include resources that we take advantage of but do not deplete in the process—like the sun.

However, rocks and minerals, and plant matter like old-growth forests that took eons to come to their present majesty, and fragile environments that house critters in a delicate balance—all these resources surely are finite in some real sense.

In fact, this emphasis on scarcity highlights an important constraint on human activity. Economics is all about the decisions by which we marshal scarce resources to satisfy virtually infinite desires and needs. But this scarcity in an economic sense does not imply that we are "running out of resources" in the sense set forth by so many who share Gore's apocalyptic world view. How could this be?

ANOTHER WORLD VIEW

Looking at the environment through a different lens gives us a different interpretation of the world around us. A longer time horizon that stretches into the past and projects into the future helps nourish a more optimistic view of our resource base for several reasons.

For example, this longer time frame allows us to focus on the processes of change—how we moved from a Stone Age to a Bronze Age

251

to an Iron Age and eventually on into the present Information Age. This focus invites two observations.

First, this perspective underscores that it is the attributes of particular raw materials that we seek, not each stone, chemical, or organic product per se. We seek fuel, not necessarily oil; material that can be woven, not just cotton, wool, or nylon; materials that are malleable, strong, or conductive, not copper or iron or silica per se. This opens up vast possibilities for invention, exploration, substitution, and expansion of our resource base. It is human action that turns a sow's ear into silk—or, more realistically, sewage sludge into energy, oil into usable fuel, or old plastic scrap into tennis ball fuzz.

This is not mere speculation. In the 1970s, authors of a bestselling book, *Limits to Growth*, predicted that gold, silver, mercury, zinc, and lead would have been thoroughly depleted by the year 2000. Instead, as Harvard economist Robert Stavins points out in a 1993 article, "reserves have increased; demand has changed; substitution has occurred; and recycling has been stimulated."[3]

One dramatic example helps us to understand how, even in the face of population growth and increasing incomes, we do not appear to be "running out of resources." Consider our telecommunications system— the linchpin of the modern age. In the 1950s some doomsayers, eyeing the increasing consumption of copper to provide communications wire, presaged severe copper shortages and impending interruptions of our worldwide communications network.

What, instead, has come to pass? Today, copper wire is increasingly being replaced by fiber optic cable. We are moving away from the relatively high-value copper to abundant sand as our basic input into communications networks. The impact on resources is stunning. We consume 25 kilograms of sand to produce a cable that can carry 1,000 times the messages over its length as a cable made from one ton of copper.

This example does not settle the issue. Not all efforts at substitution yield such compelling results. Examples such as these, however, should at least cause us to ask: Under what conditions does this evolution occur; does it apply to all resources; and what are the implications for general concern about resource conservation? The historical world view prompts questions about process and change that the freeze-frame view unwittingly neglects.

There is another point that a longer time horizon and a focus on dynamic processes makes apparent. Changing circumstances give rise to changing priorities. When requirements for basic food and shelter absorbed the attention of most of humankind, it is not surprising that certain

252

environmental values were neglected. As those more fundamental needs have been met, we naturally have developed a revised hierarchy of values, one in which environmental amenities, conservation, and long-term health concerns become top priorities. This is, however, an evolutionary, not a revolutionary, process.

It is likewise not surprising that technological innovations of earlier decades and centuries turned more toward efforts to efficiently produce food, clothing, shelter, and other tangible consumption items than toward redressing environmental problems. As our hierarchy of values has changed, however, so, too, do our innovations evolve to satisfy new goals and overcome new problems.

The apocalyptic world view, with its shorter time frame, neither perceives nor appreciates this evolutionary and iterative process. Hence, again, problems appear cataclysmic, with their resolution depending on revolutionary alterations in human action.

None of the adjustment process described by optimists occurs by magic. This prompts us to ask under what conditions these evolutionary changes take place. One economic structure seems especially pivotal to this process of change, conservation, and resource stewardship: free market prices.

Free-market prices emerge through the dynamic transactions of buyers and sellers. They fluctuate, depending on supply and demand, giving us information about the *relative* scarcities of different resources, labor, and capital. They tell us—in a relative sense—which resources are becoming scarcer. They thus help us to conserve where it matters most at any point in time. And they provide a common denominator—a yardstick—with which we can compare and prioritize our multiple individual preferences, values, and needs. They tell us how much (in monetary terms) of a set of resources (including raw materials, energy, labor, capital, and, increasingly, environmental "goods") are required to satisfy our different needs.

This picture is imperfect. Not all "costs" associated with certain activities are incorporated into pricing systems. In fact, incomplete pricing is at the heart of many current resource problems—we don't "pay" for the air we use, or we don't pay the full costs for the water we drink, for example. Thus, the adjustment process only imperfectly encompasses our quest for enhancing environmental values.

There is another side issue here worth mentioning. Our "environment" is more than simply a set of "resources" ready and waiting for transformation into items useful for human consumption. For many, the concern about the environment goes beyond ensuring a steady supply of resources to meet tangible human needs. For example, historian Lynn

White has repudiated what he calls the "axiom that nature has no reason for existence save to serve man."[4] White called for the "spiritual autonomy of all parts of nature," a theme that Gore has repeated. Gore writes in *Earth in the Balance* that people have lost sight of the "intrinsic" value of nature. He states, "so many people now view the natural world merely as a collection of resources; indeed to some people nature is like a giant data bank that they can manipulate at will" (p. 203).

While it makes no philosophical sense to talk about flora or fauna or geological formations having "intrinsic" value, it is plausible to imagine that some of us value the earth and its living components for the aesthetic or spiritual nourishment they arouse.

"Intrinsic value" implies value outside the "valuer"—value beyond the presence of any moral consciousness. Spiritual values, however, do exist: They emerge from the moral choices and preferences of individuals. For these kinds of values, the economic dynamics of substitution offer little solace. As the oft-repeated poem puts it, "a rose is a rose is a rose." If that rose—or the grey whale or an Alpine lake—disappears, those who derive spiritual contentment from that rose will not find consolation in the prospect that other natural wonders still exist or that substitution processes will prevent our "running out" of those instrumental resources that we use for human consumption of tangible goods.

This leads us to the second economic structure important to the dynamic processes of change, conservation, and resource stewardship: property rights. In a pathbreaking 1968 article, Garret Hardin warned us of the perils of the "tragedy of the commons." Unfettered access to commonly owned resources, Hardin argued, leads us to despoliation of the environment. In a book Hardin edited in 1977 he wrote, "Individuals locked into the logic of the commons are free only to bring on universal ruin."[5]

Hardin identified a fundamental environmental problem, but many later commentors on his work did not draw the obvious conclusion from Hardin's observations about the commons. Instead of seeing the advantages of introducing property rights where they do not exist and sustaining them where they do, they saw regulations or *more* common ownership as the remedy.

Yet property rights, for all the negative emotional baggage and ambiguous issues they raise, establish conditions of responsibility. Property rights sustain responsibility because they directly link "actors" to the outcomes of their actions. It is (though with many caveats) the property owner that suffers from the consequences of poor stewardship. Hence, property rights promote stewardship. As Rob Stavins has pointed out,

254

"the reason why some resources—water, forests, fisheries, and some species of wildlife—are threatened while others—principally minerals and fossil fuels—are *not* is that the scarcity of the latter group (the nonrenewable resources) is well reflected in market prices, while this is much less the case for the former group, which, in fact, are characterized by being *open access* or *common property* resources."[6]

Property rights also establish boundaries for individual human action by restricting the spheres within which one can act autonomously. Beyond those spheres, where individuals bump shoulders with one another, autonomous actions are circumscribed at a minimum by a "do no harm to others" principle. But within those spheres, individuals can pursue self-defined values. This means instrumental values—for example, using land for grazing. And it means spiritual values—the "nature as cathedral" values that Gore worries about.

Without property institutions, the alternative remains the give-and-take of the political process, which means the processes of coerced compromise. Or one can, like Gore, press for a religious transformation, a sort of consciousness-raising whereby we all adopt a shared appreciation of "nature as cathedral" and environmental goals as the single organizing principle for our actions. One wonders where Gore can point to for a successful model of "consciousness-raising" of the scope he proposes. The most far-reaching attempts (revolutionary socialism) to create a "new human being" have been accompanied with massive coercive efforts. The legacy of such efforts has thus mostly been loss of freedom and only dubious accomplishments toward a better world.

THE LIMITS OF WORLD VISIONS

Competing world visions make dialogue about appropriate actions difficult, since different visions produce different interpretations even of what "the problem" is. And, by definition, different world visions produce different understandings of how the world works.

Sorting out the components of competing visions can help us explore where opportunities for better communications might lie. Yet this exploration will not dissolve differences. Gore blurs two very different aspects of human thought and sentiment. World visions are all about how we think the world works; they are not about what we "value." To some extent, world visions can be altered by honing our powers of observation and understanding—by taking a bird's eye view where we had previously looked only with feet planted on the ground.

255

Values, however, spring from a complex interplay of reasoned thought and human sentiment. Thus, at least part of the environmental policy debate is a tug-of-war between those who value, for example, "freedom of human action" not for any utilitarian results it might have but because it "feels good" to be free. The same can be said for those who embrace the "nature as cathedral" notion. They value nature because it "feels good" to walk in its beauty.

This is why so much talk of "market mechanisms" to address environmental problems misses the central questions. If markets are *only* about finding lower cost ways to achieve predefined goals, these mechanisms simply push aside values questions. And the embrace of these market mechanisms in terms of "problem-solving" puts these tools on a level with proposed new technologies or new regulations. All three are merely instruments to solve problems.

On the other hand, there is another way of looking at markets—a way that views markets as a set of decentralized institutions and decision processes through which individuals "reveal" their preferences and through which they undertake mutually agreeable transactions. This is another way of saying that, through their choices among competing options, individuals translate their values into sets of actions. And they do so through what amounts to a give-and-take process of negotiation. Markets, thus, are about individual freedom and voluntary transactions.[7]

A historical lens, with an emphasis on evolution and adjustment, permits us to see a dynamic world and to focus on process rather than particular "freeze-frame" outcomes. The focus on process moves us away from the "markets-as-tools" notion toward an appreciation of markets as a means by which individuals pursue their individual hierarchies of values. It is the feedback loops of decentralized market decision-making institutions that will allow individuals to pursue those values into the future. And it is those same feedback loops that will make environmental values rise higher and higher on the hierarchy as our other needs are met and as these tangible environmental and spiritual values loom larger.

Notes

1. Al Gore, *Earth in the Balance* (Boston, Houghton Mifflin, 1992).
2. See chapter 2 of this volume.
3. Robert Stavins, "Comments on 'Lethal Model 2: The Limits to Growth Revisited, by William Nordhaus," in *Brookings Papers on Economic Activity*, 1993.
4. Lynn White, cited in Robert James Bidinotto, "The Green Machine,"*IOS Journal*, May 1993.
5. Garret Hardin, ed., "The Tragedy of the Commons," *Managing the Commons*, (New York, W.H. Freeman, 1977), p. 29.
6. Stavins, op. cit.
7. This is a notion of freedom strongly at odds with that put forth by Gore. Gore claims that "freedom is a necessary condition for an effective stewardship of the environment" (p. 179). Yet he means by freedom the political empowerment to demand remedies to problems.

Gore and the Clintonistas versus Skiers for Nuclear Winter

John A. Baden

The truth is that most people lack the intellectual ability and courage to resist a popular movement, however pernicious and ill-conceived.[1]

Vice President Al Gore exemplifies the new elite. He is sensitive, especially about the environment, ambitious, and confident of his superior knowledge of how things should be. When he decided to run for the Democratic presidential nomination in the spring of 1987, he was ahead of the popular movement in focusing on global warming as a campaign issue. While *Earth in the Balance*[2] deals with several important environmental issues, global warming illustrates the process and problems of Gore's environmentalism.

Let's examine Gore's approach to these issues. The following questions seem especially fruitful: Why is Gore's book so attractive to the new elite? Why are they so strongly immune to arguments countering the dangers of global warming? And given the recurrent and predictable failures of bureaucratic, command-and-control environmental management, why does Gore discount or ignore an environmentalism based on property rights and the market process?

Members of the new elite specialize in manipulating symbols, not material things. They don't get dirty or do heavy lifting. Few of them conduct the daily reality checks so familiar to agro-Americans and employees who sign paychecks on the front. As Mickey Kaus noted in *The End of Equality*,[3] this new elite really is a meritocracy. This is Al Gore's peer and reference group. Defining characteristics include intelligence and a dedication to politics. They seem confident in their ability to know what is good for other people—and quite willing to employ state coercion to enforce its realization. Like the news staff of National Public Radio (NPR), they

> believe that government is the fundamental agent of change, that government can and should solve most problems. They believe most of those solutions involve spending large sums of money. They believe not only that taxes are an appropriate way of raising money, but an important social responsibility. They believe that, although individuals cannot always be trusted to make correct choices, bureaucrats usually can. . . . [And they] are the kinds of people who voted for Michael Dukakis and Bill Clinton, not as lesser evils, but enthusiastically, in the firm belief that what the world needs is better social engineering.[4]

In many ways they are Thomas Jefferson's nightmare of a governing class.

Despite their many successes, Gore and his people have a serious problem, for most of their inferiors don't take them seriously. This is a recurrent theme, a low whine, in *Earth in the Balance*. In the late 1980s, while the Gore crowd was warning of our impending doom due to nuclear winter and crying that they were not taken seriously, the beer drinking, politically indifferent fun hogs of Montana advertised their disdain, good humor, and creativity with the sign, "Skiers for Nuclear Winter Meet Here." Gore and his fellow political ecologists, analogues of Tom Wolfe's "Masters of the Universe," and their media groupies may have been disappointed with America's reaction to the specter of nuclear winter, but they should not have been surprised. Americans have a long tradition of ignoring the warnings of their "betters."

Independent of its scientific implausibility, the specter of nuclear winter lost its force with the crisis of Leninism, the decline of the left, and the revolutions of 1989.[5] The remaining communist regimes, Cuba and North Korea for instance, are brutal, unjust, hypocritical, and desperately poor, but for the most part they are pathetic. Unlike the Evil Empire Ronald Reagan addressed, their forces are puny. They seem incapable of creating an early frost, let alone a return of the Pleistocene glaciers.

Gore and his environmental colleagues suggest a model of crisis entrepreneurship, but a bit of economics exposes the logical fallacies of this approach. For example, *externalities* is a useful concept in environmental economics. Francis Bator, an economist at Gore's *alma mater*, Harvard, has done some important work (as have economists at every other school of note) using this concept to advance environmental reforms. But Gore's use of this term would produce a failing grade in Economics 101. Despite the dozens of books, hundreds of chapters, and thousands of articles that use the word in a consistent way, Gore creates a new and unique definition for *externalities*. He sees our environmental problems as coming from "our economic system's ability to conceal the ill effects of many choices by resorting to an intellectual device labeled 'externalities'" (p. 188). He defines the term *externalities* as "the bad things economists want to ignore" (p. 188).

Gore may have good reason to dismiss economists, for their rigor and logic get in the way of the conclusions he prefers. But failure to recognize the problems of externalities is surely not included in the list of economists' sins of omission. Quite the opposite is true. The great attention economists and policy analysts give to externalities indicates their abiding concern with the problems of environmental costs.

As economists use the term, externalities identifies the consequences of an action that are external to the calculations of those taking that action. Some, such as the view of a garden from the street, are positive externalities. Others, such as pesticides leaking from that garden, are negative externalities. Negative environmental externalities are often cited as examples of problems government should address. For example, if a manufacturer must pay the full costs of raw materials, labor, capital, and equipment, he or she will economize on their use. Concurrently, if waste disposal is free—pumping smoke into the air, dumping pulp liquor into streams—the manufacturer has no such incentive to economize on this waste despite adverse impacts on the quality of the water or air. No one owns the air and water.

These negative externalities are often used to justify government regulations. Global warming has become the mother of all negative externalities. If global warming looms as a distinct possibility, and if its net consequences are so vastly negative, then nearly any set of regulations that promises to prevent this calamity is justifiable. This is why Gore and others feel compelled to stifle debate and declare the issue decided.

Global warming is the kind of environmental issue that has a huge benefit to politicians, for it gives them license to constrain our liberty. The political calculus is straightforward. The probability of global warming occurring times the expected losses generated suggests how stringent the regulations should be. When it is claimed that the lifestyle of the Western world will lead to global warming, politicians find justification to force us to modify our behavior. The changes are necessary to reduce the likelihood or severity of global warming. This is why Gore takes such pains to dismiss those who challenge his view, for his argument assumes that operating as usual will lead to disaster.

Time unstuffs ballot boxes and exposes special interests. As time passes, previously unavailable data are analyzed. Environmental alarmists like Gore are often seen as crisis entrepreneurs who cook data to manipulate opinion to justify regulation. This book suggests that his license to regulate is fraudulent. It originally may have been motivated by good intentions, but the license was gained by connivance and is maintained by fraud.

This book argues that it is not clear that global warming is upon us. If it is, the consequences may be beneficial—the externalities may be positive rather than negative. The problems are complex and highly emotional. These are ingredients for error and acrimony. Good data and clear thinking are required to deal with them. As Gore says, "to exclude inconvenient facts from the calculation of what is good and what is bad is a form of dishonesty" (p. 188). I invite Vice President Gore to look at the facts.

Notes

1. Ludwig von Mises, *Socialism: In Economics and Sociological Analysis* (New Haven: Yale University Press, 1951), p. 590.
2. Albert Gore, Jr., *Earth in the Balance: Ecology and the Human Spirit* (New York: Plume Books, 1992).
3. Mickey Kaus, *The End of Equality* (New York: A New Republic Book, BasicBooks, 1993).
4. Glenn Garvin, "How Do I Hate NPR? Let Me Count The Ways," *Liberty*, vol. 6, no. 6, August 1993, p. 39.
5. Daniel Chirot, *The Crisis of Leninism and the Decline of the Left: The Revolutions of 1989.* (Seattle: University of Washington Press, 1991).

INDEX